WITHDRAWN

Medieval Philosophy & Theology
VOLUME 2 (1992)

Medieval Philosophy & Theology

VOLUME 2 (1992)

EDITORIAL BOARD
Norman Kretzmann (chair)
Mark D. Jordan (managing editor)
Stephen F. Brown, David B. Burrell, Kent Emery, Jr., Eleonore Stump

EDITORIAL ADVISORS
Marilyn McCord Adams, Jan A. Aertsen, E. J. Ashworth, Thérèse-Anne Druart, Stephen Dumont, Sten Ebbesen, Alfred J. Freddoso, Charles H. Lohr, Scott MacDonald, Aryeh L. Motzkin, Luca Obertello, Edith Sylla, Avital Wohlman

EDITORIAL ASSISTANT
John William Houghton

Editorial correspondence and manuscripts should be addressed to Mark D. Jordan, Medieval Institute, University of Notre Dame, 715 Hesburgh Library, Notre Dame, IN 46556. Authors should send two copies of their manuscripts, which should conform to the *Chicago Manual of Style*, 13th edition, and which should be suitable for anonymous reviewing. Prepaid orders (for individuals) and standing orders (for libraries) should be addressed to the University of Notre Dame Press, Notre Dame, IN 46556.

Medieval Philosophy & Theology

VOLUME 2 (1992)

University of Notre Dame Press
Notre Dame & London

Copyright © 1992
University of Notre Dame Press
Notre Dame, IN 46556
All rights reserved
Manufactured in the United States of America

ISSN 1057-0608
ISBN 0-268-01400-0

Medieval Philosophy & Theology
VOLUME 2 (1992)

Abbreviations	vii
Richard Rufus of Cornwall on Creation: The Reception of Aristotelian Physics in the West REGA WOOD	1
St. Albert on the Subject of Metaphysics and Demonstrating the Existence of God TIMOTHY B. NOONE	31
Towards a Narrative Understanding of Thomistic Natural Law PAMELA M. HALL	53
St. Thomas Aquinas on Satisfaction, Indulgences, and Crusades ROMANUS CESSARIO, O.P.	74
On the Purpose of 'Merit' in the Theology of Thomas Aquinas JOSEPH WAWRYKOW	97
Another Look at St. Thomas and the Plurality of the Literal Sense of Scripture MARK F. JOHNSON	117
Duns Scotus on Autonomous Freedom and Divine Co-Causality WILLIAM A. FRANK	142
Pico, Plato, and Albert the Great: The Testimony and Evaluation of Agostino Nifo EDWARD P. MAHONEY	165

Abbreviations

AHDLMA	*Archives d'histoire doctrinale et littéraire du moyen âge*
AL	Aristoteles Latinus
BFSMA	Bibliotheca Franciscana Scholastica Medii Aevi
BGP(T)M	Beiträge zur Geschichte der Philosophie (und Theologie) des Mittelalters
BT	Bibliothèque Thomiste
CCCM	Corpus Christianorum, Continuatio Mediaevalis
CCSL	Corpus Christianorum, Series Latina
CHLMP	*Cambridge History of Later Medieval Philosophy*, ed. Norman Kretzmann et al.
CIMAGL	Cahiers de l'Institut du moyen âge grec et latin
CPDMA	Corpus Philosophorum Danicorum Medii Aevi
CSB	Collegium Sancti Bonaventurae (Quaracchi, then Grottaferatta)
CSEL	Corpus Scriptorum Ecclesiasticorum Latinorum
CSIC	Consejo Superior de Investigaciones Cientificas (Madrid and elsewhere)
MGH	Monumenta Germaniae Historica
PG	*Patrologiae cursus completus . . . , Series Graeca*, ed. J.-P. Migne
PIMS	Pontifical Institute of Mediaeval Studies (Toronto)
PL	*Patrologiae cursus completus . . . , Series Latina*, ed. J.-P. Migne
PM	Philosophes Médiévaux
RTAM	*Recherches de théologie ancienne et médiévale*
SCC	*Sacrorum Conciliorum nova et amplissima collectio*, ed. J. D. Mansi

Richard Rufus of Cornwall on Creation: The Reception of Aristotelian Physics in the West

REGA WOOD

Richard Rufus was an English philosopher-theologian, the fifth Franciscan Master of Theology at Oxford.[1] Like Bonaventure, he was Master of Arts at Paris before joining the Franciscans in 1238, five years before Bonaventure's entry and two years after the celebrated theologian Alexander of Hales had joined the order, bringing with him what became the order's first chair of theology. Together, Alexander of Hales, Robert Grosseteste, Bonaventure, and Richard Rufus helped make the Franciscan order a major force in the intellectual life of the thirteenth and fourteenth centuries.[2]

---

1. Thomas of Eccleston *Tractatus de adventu fratrum minorum in Angliam*, ed. A. G. Little (Manchester: University Press, 1951), p.51.
2. This paper is dedicated to the late James Weisheipl and to the late Frank Kelley, an esteemed collaborator on the Ockham edition at the Franciscan Institute. Fr. Weisheipl supervised Kelley's doctoral work and encouraged him to broaden his interests to include Franciscan as well as Dominican contributions to the history of Western philosophy. Work on this paper began in 1983 in Erfurt, East Germany, and in West Berlin. It was supported in part by an Alexander von Humboldt Fellowship and a grant from the American Philosophical Society. A preliminary version of this paper was read at Kalamazoo, Michigan, at the 1989 Medieval Congress. It was included in the sessions dedicated to James Weisheipl.

Rufus's influence was chiefly felt in England during the thirteenth century. His work emphasized Aristotelianism and logic. Rufus's enemy, Roger Bacon,[3] testified to his influence. Bacon blamed Rufus's "insane" views for dangerous trends in logic and theology at Oxford:

> I knew the [author] of the worst and most foolish of these errors well: he was called Richard of Cornwall. No author was accounted more famous by the foolish multitude, but the wise considered him insane. He had been reproved at Paris for the errors he invented [and] promulgated when he solemnly lectured on the *Sentences* there, after he had lectured on the *Sentences* at Oxford from the year of our Lord 1250. From that time . . . to the present . . . for forty years and more, the multitude has remained in the errors of this master. And this boundless madness is gaining most strength in Oxford, just as it began there.[4]

Clearly, Rufus's views were controversial.[5] Indeed, they were censured at least once.[6] Equally obvious is their importance for scholastic theology. The author of the earliest surviving Franciscan *Sentences*-commentary written at Oxford,[7] Richard Rufus anticipates John Duns Scotus's formidable argument for the existence of God.[8] Scotus seems to have had Rufus's *Sentences*-commentary before him when formulating his own important views on the sacrament of penance.

---

3. Roger Bacon lectured on Aristotle from 1237 to 1247, when he left his teaching position on the Arts faculty. Ten years later, in 1257, he joined the Franciscan order. Bacon's second *Physics*-commentary seems to have been influenced by the *Physics*-commentary attributed to Richard Rufus later in this paper. See the edition by F. Delorme and R. Steele, *Questiones supra libros octo Physicorum Aristotelis* 8.2–7, Opera Hactenus Inedita Rogeri Baconi 13 (Oxford: Clarendon Press, 1935), pp. 377–390.

4. Roger Bacon *Compendium of the Study of Theology*, ed. and trans. Thomas S. Maloney (Leiden: E. J. Brill, 1988), pp. 86–87. Though the translation is my own, it is indebted to Maloney's translation and is based on his edition.

5. He was occasionally eccentric. In the course of discussing arguments for the existence of God, he once addressed himself to the foot of a fly. Rufus *Quaestio disputa de exsistentia Dei*: "Dic mihi, pes muscae, numquid tu demonstras Deum esse?" See the edition in G. Gál, "Viae ad Existentiam Dei Probandam in Doctrina R. Rufi OFM," *Franziskanische Studien* 38 (1956): 177–202, at p. 201.

6. G. Gál, "Opiniones Richardi Rufi Cornubiensis a Censore Reprobatae," *Franciscan Studies* 35 (1975): 136–193.

7. D. A. Callus, "Two Early Oxford Masters on the Problem of Plurality of Forms: Adam of Buckfield—Richard Rufus of Cornwall," *Revue néoscolastique de philosophie* 42 (1939): 413.

8. Gál, "Viae ad Existentiam Dei," throughout.

Rufus seems also to have influenced Scotus's teaching on formal distinctions.[9]

Three indisputably authentic works by Richard Rufus of Cornwall have survived: the Paris *Sentences*-commentary (c. 1254), which is based on St. Bonaventure's lectures of 1250–1252;[10] disputed questions (dating from about 1250);[11] and a commentary on the *Metaphysics* written before Rufus became a friar in 1238.[12] In addition, the Oxford *Sentences*-commentary (c. 1252) is also almost certainly by Rufus, as Raedts has shown,[13] although its authenticity has been questioned by Noone. Rufus's *Metereologion* appears to be lost.[14] His *Physics*-commentary may also be lost, although, more likely, it is to be identified with the commentary (c. 1235) preserved in Erfurt, Amplonian MS Q.312. Finally, there is some reason to believe that Rufus wrote the very influential treatise on logic called the *Abstractiones*.[15]

My essay will consider the three early works attributed to Richard Rufus: the Oxford *Sentences*-commentary, the *Metaphysics*-commentary, and the Erfurt commentary on the *Physics*. Thus I shall be

---

9. Gál, "Opiniones Richardi Rufi," pp. 142–148.

10. Peter Raedts argues that these lectures were delivered in Oxford when Rufus "triumphantly" returned to lecture there in 1256. The argument is based on an added reference to Merlin and the deletion of a reference found in Bonaventure's commentary to the practices of the Gallican church. See Peter Raedts, *Richard Rufus of Cornwall and the Tradition of Oxford Theology* (Oxford: Clarendon Press, 1987), pp. 61–63. The suggestion that these lectures introduced Bonaventure's views to Oxford audiences is plausible but cannot be reconciled with Bacon's statement that Rufus lectured on the *Sentences* twice, first at Oxford and then "solemnly" at Paris. Also, it would be a bit odd if four Continental manuscripts and no English manuscript of an Oxford commentary survived. So, until more compelling evidence persuades us to disregard Bacon's statement, I have adopted the conventional view that these lectures were delivered in Paris.

11. Raedts, *Richard Rufus*, pp. 64–93.

12. See below, note 16 and related text.

13. Raedts, *Richard Rufus*, pp. 20–39.

14. W. Lampen, "De Fr. Richardo Rufo, Cornubiensi, OFM.," *Archivum Franciscanum Historicum* 31 (1928): 403–406.

15. The identity of the author of the *Abstractiones* is discussed in the introduction to the forthcoming edition of this work by Paul Streveler, Mary Sirridge, Katherine Tachau, and Calvin Normore. They consider the attribution to Richard Rufus the most plausible to date.

concerned chiefly with Richard Rufus's work as a Master of Arts at Paris. I shall discuss only one work written after Rufus became a Franciscan and a theologian, the *Sentences*-commentary preserved in Oxford, Balliol College MS 62. In his Oxford *Sentences*-commentary, Rufus refers frequently to the arguments he had made earlier while expounding the *Metaphysics*. His references have confused modern scholars: he refers to his own views as those of a secular master; he criticizes his own earlier opinions. Though misleading, the references are not incorrect, since the *Metaphysics*-commentary was written when Rufus was indeed a secular master. All doubt about Rufus's authorship of the commentary was removed when Leonard Boyle, using ultraviolet light, found an ascription to Rufus, in a contemporary hand, on the first page of the thirteenth-century Vatican manuscript copy of the work.[16] The commentary is preserved in slightly different forms in four manuscripts—Vatican, Vat. lat. MS 4538; Oxford, New College MS 285; Erfurt, Amplonian MS Q.290; and Prague, Metropolitan Chapter MS M.80.

The Erfurt commentary on the *Physics* is preserved only in Amplonian MS Q.312, an English codex written before 1250.[17] The work itself was written before 1235, when it was cited by Robert Grosseteste in his notes on the *Physics*, in the section from book 8 which also appears separately as *De finitate motus et temporis*.[18] Part of the set of early Aristotle commentaries in which a copy of Richard Rufus's *Metaphysics* commentary is found, the Erfurt *Physics*-commentary is an important help in understanding that other commentary. Robert

---

16. The ascription reads, "Hic incipit metaphysica magistri Richardi Rufi de Cornub" (fol. 1ra). See Timothy B. Noone, "An Edition and Study of the *Scriptum super Metaphysicam*, bk. 12, dist. 2: A Work Attributed to Richard Rufus of Cornwall" (Ph.D. dissertation, University of Toronto, 1987), pp. 46 and 150.

17. Letter from Richard Rouse to the author, 8 June 1985: "Your Erfurt books... would be on the early side of [the] middle of the century."

18. "1235" is the date indicated by Dales in his edition of the *Physics*-commentary (see below, note 19). Dales has since suggested a date as late as 1240 for Grosseteste's commentary on *Physics* 8 and *De finitate*, but that suggestion has not been adopted. R. W. Southern retains the 1235 date, suggesting that the commentary on book 8 was written between 1232 and 1235; see his *Robert Grosseteste: The Growth of an English Mind in Medieval Europe* (Oxford: Clarendon Press, 1986), p. 134. James McEvoy provides different dates for *De finitate* (c. 1237) and the *Physics*-commentary (1228–1232); see his *Philosophy of Robert Grosseteste* (Oxford: Clarendon Press, 1982), p. 514. Thus, while there is no general agreement, no one other than Dales has accepted thus far a date after 1235 for book 8 of the *Physics*-commentary.

Grosseteste cites it as the work of a "Master Richard."[19] Since Richard Rufus is known to have written a *Physics*-commentary at this time, it seems likely that he is the author of this work. Rufus's *Metaphysics*-commentary includes at least three references to his *Physics*-commentary.[20] There are corresponding passages in the Erfurt *Physics*-commentary, but none of the three references involves a verbatim quotation and so none permits verification of the reference. Hence the attribution of the Erfurt *Physics*-commentary must remain provisional. Nevertheless, I will here adopt the hypothesis that the Erfurt *Physics*-commentary is by Richard Rufus. Adopting this hypothesis will facilitate comparison between this commentary and Rufus's subsequent commentaries on the *Metaphysics* and the *Sentences*, a comparison of great interest for the history of the medieval reception of Aristotle.

THE DOCTRINE OF CREATION AND THE RECEPTION OF ARISTOTELIAN PHYSICS

The reception of Aristotle by thirteenth-century Christian philosophers provided an important stimulus to natural theology

---

19. The attribution is to "Magister Richardus de S. Victor." But the argument in question is not by Richard of St. Victor (d. 1173). Since Richard of St. Victor was not a university master, he would not be cited as "Magister Richardus." Dales recognized the citation as a reference to a contemporary author, but he accepted the mistaken reading "of St. Victor," commenting in a note that he could not find the argument in Richard of St. Victor's works. See Grosseteste *Commentarius in VIII libros Physicorum Aristotelis*, ed. Richard Dales (Boulder: University of Colorado Press, 1963), pp. xx, 154.

20. Richard Rufus cites his own *Physics*-commentary in the commentary on the *Metaphysics* 1.1 by saying, "Breviter autem intelligendum est, ordine supposito in omni genere causarum, quod sit primum et quod sit ultimum in illis. Et primo in causis formalibus quia definibiles, tactum est super secundum physicorum" (Vatican, Vat. lat. 4538, fol. 6vb; from an unpublished transcription by G. Gál, p. 55). Gál cites two other references to the *Physics*-commentary "Commentarius in *Metaphysicam* Aristotelis cod. Vat. lat. 4538, fons doctrinae Richardi Rufi," *Archivum Franciscanum Historicum* 43 (1952), p. 230. "Quid autem sit primum in causis efficientibus, finalibus et materialibus, dictum in secundo Physicorum, super capitulum de causis" (fol. 7ra). "Ad aliud quod causa materialis <*forsan pro*: multitudinis> potentiarum in materia est agens primum . . . et illud declaratum fuit diligentissime super primum Physicorum" (fol. 13va).

and also created difficulties in some areas. One problematic topic was the doctrine of creation. According to Scripture, "In the beginning, God created the heavens and the earth." Most medieval philosophers understood this text to mean that the world began at a certain moment of past time. By contrast, Aristotle argues that the world never began, that no absolutely first moment of time can exist, and hence that past time is necessarily infinite.[21] Christian philosophers in the thirteenth and fourteenth centuries dealt with this conflict in a variety of ways.

Some thirteenth- and fourteenth-century Christian philosophers maintained that creation in time can be known only by revelation. Latin followers of Averroës, the celebrated but heterodox Islamic commentator on Aristotle, held that according to natural reason past time must be beginningless and hence infinite. Others, such as St. Thomas Aquinas and William of Ockham, maintained that although the beginning of the world in time cannot be excluded by rational argument, neither can it be demonstrated by natural reason. Finally, some theologians undertook to refute Aristotle, maintaining that a temporal beginning of the world can be demonstrated by argument, without reference to the authority of revelation. Bonaventure is perhaps the most famous medieval Christian philosopher to argue directly against Aristotle on this point; Richard Rufus is an earlier Franciscan advocate of the same position.

I want to discuss Richard Rufus's arguments against the eternity of the world. The issues surrounding creation are subtle and complex. They concern the nature of time, causality, the continuum, and the concepts of change, beginning, and ceasing. Medieval treatments of these issues, moreover, are often extremely sophisticated. As Richard Rufus developed his views, his discussion became increasingly technical.

My discussion of Richard Rufus on creation will focus on four problems that confront all Christian philosophers: (1) How can an immutable God create the world without any change in God's nature?

---

21. But note that Aristotle himself may have held different views on this question at different times. In the *Topics*, he suggests that the question whether the world is eternal is so vast that it is difficult to argue (1.11.104b1–16). For a discussion of Aristotle's views and the question whether Aristotle entertained the view that there was creation in time, see Richard Sorabji, *Time, Creation, and the Continuum* (Ithaca: Cornell University Press, 1983), pp. 276–283.

(2) Can reason demonstrate that the world was created from nothing, *ex nihilo*? (3) Are there philosophically compelling arguments that show that the world had a beginning? Can arguments for the eternity or beginninglessness of the world be refuted? (4) Presuming that creation can be rationally demonstrated, what account should we give of the beginning of time and motion? In dealing with these topics, I shall take up Rufus's attitude toward Aristotle.

THE *PHYSICS*-COMMENTARY (C. 1235)

MUTABILITY AND CREATION

In the *Physics*-commentary, Rufus's approach to the problem of how an immutable God could create the world is quite traditional. His discussion is influenced by Boethius. Rufus states the problem as follows: A creator cannot be immutable; the creator's disposition must change. As a creator, God must have a disposition toward the world that God did not have before the world came into existence. In his resolution of this problem, Rufus affirms that God's will remains always unchanged. Since God is entirely simple, prior and posterior have no part in God's nature. God's creation of the world is not temporally prior to creatures; it owes its priority to the simplicity of God's nature.[22]

TIME AND ETERNITY

In what sense is God prior to creatures? Rufus describes God as an indivisible (*aliquod indivisibile*). Hence the world is like a

---

22. Rufus (?) *In Physic. Aristot.* 8.1–2: "Si ponamus mundum esse creatum, tunc videtur quod creator unde creans aliquam habuit dispositionem quam non habuit prius, cum non creavit. Et potest responderi quod non sequitur, 'quia ab aeterno voluit creare in *a c*, ab aeterno voluit creare in alio'. Et sic licet creavit <!> in *a c*, nulla facta est mutatio in eius voluntate, sed semper vult quod voluit et non vult quod noluit. Vel possumus dicere aliter quod haec ratio supponit falsum, cum ponat prius ante creationem mundi, prius dico duratione. Et hoc dicit Boethius quod creare non est prius creaturis temporis antiquitate sed simplicitate naturae, quia ipse [creator] cum sit simplicissimus, in eius esse non cadit prius et posterius" (Erfurt, Amplon. 312, fol. 11vb).

line flowing from an indivisible point.[23] The point remains, and the line flows. Within the point is neither before nor after, and yet the point itself is prior to the line and all of its parts. Before creation, the world exists with God; its (physical) nonexistence is its existence with God. The nonexistence of the world is not temporally prior to its existence. There is neither before nor after in its nonexistence, and no first moment of the world's existence.[24]

The concept of an eternal instant, called the 'now of eternity', plays a crucial role in Rufus's account of God's priority to the world. Rufus contrasts the now of eternity with temporal instants that measure mutable beings. Unlike temporal nows, the now of eternity is not the end of a past and the beginning of a future. The now of eternity does not limit the past and the future, and hence Aristotle was mistaken when he claimed that every now is a division between two periods of time.[25]

The now of eternity pertains to what is unchanging, to the first being and to being as such. There is no succession in immutable

---

23. Galfridus de Aspall espoused similar views in his *Metaphysics*-commentary: "Concluditur enim ibi [VIII Physic.] quod est unum primum movens, indivisibile etc." See G. Gál, "Robert Kilwardby's Questions on the *Metaphysics* and *Physics* of Aristotle," *Franciscan Studies* 14 (1954): 21; and Charles Lohr, "Medieval Latin Aristotle Commentaries," *Traditio* 24 (1968): 150–152. Compare William of Auvergne *De universo* 1.2.1: "ipse creator benedictus est simplex et impartibilis, et tamen est infinitus et immensus amplitudine sua" (ed. Paris, 1674), 1:683.

24. Rufus (?) *In Physic. Aristot.* 8.1–2: "Et potest responderi ita et dicere quod non-esse mundi fuit prius quam esse mundi uno modo, et tamen in ipso non-esse non cadebat prius et posterius. Et hoc sic possumus intelligere: non-esse creaturae non est nisi sola exsistentia eius apud Creatorem. Exitus ergo de non-esse in esse est fluxus eius a Creatore. Intelligamus ergo Creatorem ut aliquod indivisibile ut punctum quoad hoc, et esse creaturae tamquam lineam fluentem ex puncto. Et intelligamus punctum sicut manens et totam lineam sicut fluentem, adhuc erit dicere quod in ipso puncto non cadit prius neque posterius, et tamen ipse punctus est prius quam ipsa linea vel aliquod ipsius. Et hoc modo est dicere quod non-esse mundi est prius quam suum esse, et tamen in suo non-esse non cadit neque prius neque posterius. . . . /12ra/ [I]ntelligamus ens primum ut indivisibile et esse temporalium ut quidam fluxum ab ipso. Unde apparet quod ipse fluxus [est] ab alio, et tamen in ipso non est dicere primum. Sic est in creatione mundi vel motus, quod illud a quo est ille fluxus est sicut quoddam indivisibile, et in esse ipsorum non est dicere primum" (Erfurt, Amplon. 312, fols. 11vb, 12ra).

25. Rufus (?) *In Physic. Aristot.* 8.1–2: "Et possumus respondere sicut communiter respondetur <respondet E>, ut dicamus quod haec est falsa 'omne nunc est medium duorum temporum.' Sed contra illa supponimus ex quarto libro quod tota substantia temporis est unum nunc manens secundum substantiam. Et hoc nunc secundum quod

substances, no before and after. Like the beings it pertains to, the now of eternity is incorruptible and unfailing. Even mutable entities, insofar as they have being, belong to the now of eternity. For being mutable does not alter being itself, does not add a new nature. Being as such—the being that is common to both mutable and immutable beings—pertains to the now of eternity.[26]

It is the now of eternity that is (nontemporally) prior to creation. The now of eternity does not limit periods of time; it is (nontemporally) prior to time as a whole. The now of eternity measures created eternity, aeviternity. Aeviternal beings—such as angels or celestial bodies—are created by God in eternal and immutable existence. Unlike God, they have duration, but not the mutable duration measured by time. Since the nonbeing of the world pertains to the now of eternity, the nonbeing of the world has no temporal dimension.

CREATION DEMONSTRATED

Given this picture of time and creation, Rufus seeks to prove that the world began. He demonstrates creation by proving that time and the world cannot be beginningless or eternal. Six arguments

---

adhaeret toti transmutationi est tempus, et secundum quod adhaeret mutato quod est indivisibile in toto motu, sic est nunc temporis" (Erfurt, Amplon. 312, fol. 12ra).

26. Rufus (?) *In Physic. Aristot.* 4.10: "Ad intelligendum quomodo nunc manet idem in tempore, mihi videtur quod oportet incipere a nunc aeternitatis, ut ante intelligamus nunc aeternitatis intelligamus substantiam intransmutabilem sicut intelligentiam.... Et talis est duratio substantiae intransmutabilis sicut intelligentiae, quia eo quod intransmutabilis est, nihil in tali substantia succedit alteri.... Praeterea, nihil ibi prius et posterius.... Sic cum hoc intelligamus quod sicut ipsa intelligentia est incorruptibilis et indeficiens et similiter suum esse, quod similiter sua duratio sit indeficiens et incorruptibilis.// Et sic intelligimus nunc aeternitatis; et loquor de aeternitate creata. Sic enim intelligamus unam durationem indeficientem sine priori et posteriori....// Ulterius intelligendum quod esse mutabile non addit novam naturam super esse simpliciter.... Sicut ergo ipsum nunc aeternitatis debetur enti intransmutabili, similiter debetur omni enti in quantum esse habet. Sed in hoc est differentia, quod enti intransmutabili debetur indeficienter et ut aeternitas est. Enti tamen universaliter habenti esse debetur abstrahendo ab his differentiis 'deficientis,' 'indeficientis,' et sic habemus quod omni enti in quantum esse habet debetur ipsum nunc.... /8rb/ [Q]uaero de nunc corruptibili, utrum sit corruptibile in se vel in alio. Dicitur forte quod ipsum nunc consideratum in tali ratione in quantum adhaeret mobile hoc corruptibile est, sed illo eodem considerato secundum sui substantiam manet et incorruptibile est" (Erfurt, Amplon. 312, fol. 8ra, 8rb).

are advanced against beginningless time. The strongest is based on the nature of the past. Whatever has been traversed or completed cannot be infinite. But "having been traversed" pertains to the nature (*ratio*) of the past. Therefore, what is past cannot be infinite.[27]

In the later version of this argument presented in his Oxford *Sentences*-commentary, Rufus seeks to strengthen the controversial premise, "to have been traversed pertains to the nature of the past."[28] Rufus claims that "whatever is past was present," and concludes that "time past is finite." The text of this argument is garbled as it stands. But Rufus's intention is clear. He wants to demonstrate what he takes to be an unacceptable consequence of the view that past time is infinite. If past time is infinite, then some past time was never present. However far we go back in time, we can never go far enough that all of the past will have been present, since there is no all of the past. In what sense is time past, if it was never present? Later medieval Scholastics expounding the term 'past' might argue that the past 'was, but is not now, present'. The infinitist cannot employ this exposition. Instead he or she must accept the consequence, 'some past days are not now and never were present'.

In modern philosophy, the argument that past time must be finite is attributed to Kant, who advanced it as the First Antinomy of Pure Reason. This argument had earlier been advanced in late antiquity by the brilliant, but heterodox, Greek Christian philosopher, Philoponus.[29] Philoponus's argument was known to Arabic and

---

27. Rufus (?) *In Physic. Aristot.* 8.1–2: "Item, contra rationem infiniti est esse pertransitum, ut patet in capitulo de infinito. Sed de ratione praeteriti est esse pertransitum. Ergo contra rationem infiniti est esse praeteritum" (Erfurt, Amplon. 312, fol. 12ra). This argument is cited by Grosseteste as an argument by "Magister Richardus" in *Commentarius in Phys.*, ed. Dales, p.154. The manuscript mistakenly identifies this "master" as Richard of St. Victor. The Victorines were not university masters, and Richard of St. Victor did not make such an argument. Dales has since concluded that probably the reference is to Richard Rufus, though he doubts whether this portion of the work was really written by Grosseteste (letter from Dales to the author, 30 June 1989).

28. Quoted below, in the third section. See note 69 and related text.

29. Did Richard Rufus know Philoponus? Yes. Indeed, Rufus cites him as "Ioannes Grammaticus." But he knows only the arguments mentioned by Averroës. He quotes Philoponus approvingly and knows that Philoponus held that the world was corruptible since its power is finite. See Rufus *In Metaph. Aristot.* 12.7–8.1, ed. Noone,

Hebrew thinkers.³⁰ Whether and how it was transmitted to the Latin West is not clear.³¹ The argument first appeared among the Latins around 1223, in William of Auvergne's *De Trinitate*.³²

As presented by Richard Rufus, this argument differs somewhat from the one originally presented by Philoponus and repeated by authors like Maimonides. The original argument stresses the claim that successive synthesis cannot produce an infinite series; the infinite set discussed is the souls of the departed: if the world had existed from eternity, the number of the souls of the departed would constitute an actual and countable infinity, which is impossible. A further claim is

---

p. 234. But Averroës does not cite Philoponus's argument against the eternity of past time. This argument was stated in Philoponus's *Physics*-commentary, and repeated in his *Meteorology*-commentary. A more complete statement of this argument is from Philoponus's *De aeternitate mundi contra Proclum*, dated 529. His *Contra Aristotelem* also includes the argument. See Sorabji, *Time, Creation, and the Continuum*, p. 198. None of these works was available to Richard Rufus. Only Philoponus's *De anima* was translated into Latin before the Renaissance. Hence most medievalists agree with Anneliese Maier that Philoponus had no direct influence on Latin Scholasticism; see her *Zwei Grundprobleme der scholastischen Naturphilosophie*, 2nd ed. (Rome: Storia e letteratura, 1968), p. 127. Nonetheless, the similarities between Philoponus's views and some important developments in scholastic natural philosophy continue to raise questions. Fritz Zimmermann points to Philoponus's popularity among Arabic and Hebrew thinkers as evidence that indirect influence was possible; see his "Philoponus' Impetus Theory in the Arabic Tradition," in *Philoponus*, ed. Richard Sorabji (Ithaca: Cornell University Press, 1987), pp. 121, 128–129. For a discussion of Philoponus's views, see Sorabji, *Time, Creation, and the Continuum*, especially pp. 193–231.

30. H. Davidson, "John Philoponus as a Source of Medieval Islamic and Jewish Proofs of Creation," *Journal of the American Oriental Society* 89 (1969): 376–377.

31. No Arabic or Hebrew version of this argument appears to have been available in early thirteenth-century Paris. Maimonides' citations of Philoponus in the *Guide to the Perplexed* (available in Latin about 1225) make no reference to the claim that the past is by definition completed, traversed, or "exhausted" (to use Nazzam's term). Al-Ghazzali clearly knew the argument, but his work was first translated into Latin in 1328. For al-Ghazzali, see also below, the notes (38 and 39) on the following argument.

32. William of Auvergne *De Trinitate* 10, ed. B. Switalski (Toronto: PIMS, 1976), pp. 68–69. I owe this reference to Neil Lewis. William wrote not much before Rufus. *De Trinitate* is the first part of William's *Magisterium Divinale*, composed between 1220 and 1236. Some, if not all, of the *Magisterium* was written after 1228, when William became bishop of Paris. Kramp's claim that parts were written before 1228 is open to question. For example, Kramp reasons that a bishop would not have used examples in which someone suggests that an unworthy candidate had been elevated

based on the assumption that the infinitist is committed to the view that there was a first person. The argument correctly claims that if there were a first past person followed by an infinite series of people, the series would not reach the present generation.

By contrast, the argument presented by Richard Rufus, William of Auvergne, and some Arabic authors is based on the claim that being traversed or completed is intrinsic to the nature of the past. Some modern cosmologists—such as G.J. Whitrow—consider it the strongest argument against the beginninglessness of the world's existence.[33] Related arguments have been presented by William Lane Craig and Pamela Huby.[34]

The next argument that I shall present was also first advanced by the Greek Philoponus, was recovered for the Latin West by William of Auvergne,[35] and was widely known among Islamic and Jewish authors.[36] Rufus's version is based on our concept of priority. If the number of days before today is infinite, and the number of days before tomorrow is infinite, then the number of days before today

---

to the episcopacy. Hence it is possible, though exceedingly unlikely, that William formulated this argument at about the same time as the Erfurt *Physics*-commentary was written, and in similar circumstances. See I. Kramp, "Des Wilhelm von Auvergne 'Magisterium divinale,'" *Gregorianum* 2 (1921): 54–78. Other Latin versions of this argument—by Thomas of York, John Peckham, and Richard of Middleton—postdate the Erfurt *Physics*-commentary that I want to attribute to Richard Rufus. Dales has suggested in personal correspondence that Rufus may have been anticipated by an anonymous Latin author in Vat. lat. 185 (letter from Dales to the author, 11 August 1989; see also Dales, *Medieval Discussions of the Eternity of the World* ([Leiden: E. J. Brill, 1990], p. 80). The author of this two page gloss on Genesis 1:1, written in or before 1250, was a contemporary of Richard Rufus. Bonaventure's version of the argument against the infinity of the world, like Maimonides', makes no reference to the claim that past time is necessarily completed or traversed; see Bonaventure *In Sent.* 2.1.1.1.2, as in *Opera Omnia* 2 (Quaracchi: CSB, 1885), pp. 19–24.

33. G. J. Whitrow, "On the Impossibility of an Infinite Past," *British Journal for the Philosophy of Science* 29 (1978): 39–45; Norman Kretzmann, "Ockham and the Creation of the Beginningless World," *Franciscan Studies* 45 (1985): 14.

34. The arguments of modern advocates of this position are discussed by Sorabji in *Time, Creation, and the Continuum*, pp. 219–224, 445.

35. *Contra Aristotelem de aeternitate mundi*, as cited by Simplicius, *In Phys. Aristot.*, ed. H. Diels, Commentaria in Aristotelem Graecem 10 (Berlin, 1895), p. 1179; trans. C. Wildberg, *Against Aristotle* (Ithaca: Cornell University Press, 1987), pp. 145–146. William's argument is quoted below.

36. H. Davidson, "John Philoponus as a Source," pp. 376–377.

is not less than the number of days before tomorrow. Consequently, today does not arrive sooner than tomorrow, which is absurd. Rufus assumes here that unequal infinities are impossible. Since the end of the nineteenth century, philosophers and mathematicians, following Georg Cantor, have rejected this assumption, arguing that unequal infinities are possible. But Rufus's argument need not be affected by this change of view. If we postulate beginningless time, the number of days before today and the number of days before tomorrow are mappable infinite series and hence equal, not unequal, infinities. Rufus might still argue that if the world has no beginning, then we must give up the belief that less time transpires before earlier events than before later events.[37]

The version of this argument found in the works of Philoponus, al-Ghazzali, and William of Auvergne differs slightly.[38] These authors assume that more time transpires before later events than before earlier events. As they present the argument, the absurd conclusion to be rejected is that it is possible to add to an infinity, or that one infinity can be multiplied by another, so that one infinity would be greater than another by a determinate proportion. By contrast, the absurdity Rufus asks us to reject is that 'Today does not come sooner than tomorrow'.[39]

---

37. Rufus (?) In Physic. Aristot. 8.1–2: "Item, si esset tempus praeteritum infinitum ex parte ante, tunc numerus dierum usque ad diem istum esset ab unitate in infinitum. Iterum, numerus dierum usque cras esset ab unitate in infinitum. Sed talis numerus non est unus numerus maior alio nec minor, et sic non sunt pauciores dies usque ad diem illum quam usque ad diem crastinum, nec minus tempus. Et tunc non citius veniret ista dies quam crastina. Priori enim res, brevius tempus" (Erfurt, Amplon. 312, fol. 12ra).

38. Averroës Destructio Destructionum Philosophiae Algazelis, ed. Beatrice Zedler (Milwaukee: Marquette University Press, 1961), p. 78. William of Auvergne De universo 1.2.1: "Eodem modo est considerare de revolutionibus Saturni, quae sunt ad revolutiones solis in proportione unius ad trigenta. Similiter et de revolutionibus Jovis... in proportione unius ad duodecim.... Impossibile autem est infinitum esse, cujus partes certae comparationis, et proportionis ad ipsum inveniuntur, etc." (Paris ed. 1:688).

39. Richard Rufus almost certainly knew William of Auvergne. Whether Rufus had indirect access to Philoponus's version of this argument is uncertain. The current scholarship suggests that he did not. The most likely point of contact is in the works al-Ghazzali. Al-Ghazzali employed this argument in his refutation of Avicenna's views, The Destruction of the Philosophers, the second part of his Deliverance from Error.

Many of Rufus's other arguments employ Aristotelian premises to argue against Aristotelian conclusions. Rufus argues that Aristotle's belief in a first efficient cause commits him to the view that the world has a beginning.[40] If the time between nonbeing and now is infinite, then the number of intermediate causes between the first cause and the final effect is infinite, and there is no first mover. Rufus concludes that if Aristotle maintains that there is a first efficient cause, he must suppose that everything else has a beginning.

Rufus also adduces against Aristotle his statement that the infinite has no relation (*ordinatio*) to the finite. If past time is infinite, it has no relation to the finite, nor to this day. But in fact the past is related to today; therefore it is not infinite.[41] This was not simply an *ad hominem* argument. Rufus accepted the principle that infinite and finite cannot be ordered to each other. For this reason Rufus argues that an infinite God does not directly move the heavens. As an efficient cause, God acts mediately, by means of the Intelligences. If the heavens were moved directly by God's infinite power, they would move infinitely fast, and their motion would be instantaneous, not in time.[42]

The *Destruction* became available when Averroës' attack on it, the *Destruction of the Destruction*, was translated into Latin in 1328. Before 1328, however, most Latins knew only the first part of the *Deliverance*, a summary of Avicenna's views.

40. Rufus (?) *In Physic. Aristot.* 8.1–2: "Item, bene sumit Aristoteles quod primum fuit causa efficiens omnium, ergo educens de non-esse in esse.... Dicere ergo quod illud non-esse per infinitum tempus distat ab hoc nunc, est dicere quod positis extremis infinita sunt media [ut dicit] Aristoteles in lib. Posteriorum. Sic ergo videtur quod si ponat Aristoteles primum esse efficientem causam, quod ponat omnia alia incepisse" (Erfurt, Amplon. 312, fol. 12ra–12rb).

41. Rufus (?) *In Physic. Aristot.* 8.1–2: "Dicit [Aristot.] quod infinitum non habet ordinationem ad finitatem. Ex quo sequitur quod si tempus praeteritum est infinitum, non habebit ordinationem ad finitatem, ergo nec ad diem istum; sed habet ordinationem; ergo non est infinitum" (Erfurt, Amplon. 312, fol. 12ra).

42. Rufus (?) *In Physic. Aristot.* 8.10: "Praeterea, dicendum sicut dicit Commentator, quod oportet ibi esse duplicem motorem sicut intelligentiam creatam et primam causam. Quia enim motus est in tempore infinito, oportet ibi esse infinitam potentiam. Et quia non in instanti et similiter quia est ibi proportio motoris ad mobile, oportet ibi esse motorem finitae potentiae, ut dicamus quod potentia creata intelligens primum et informata per ipsum moveat, et ipsa sic considerata quodammodo est finitae potentiae, quodammodo infinitae. Et per hoc quod est ibi de potentia infinita, movet in tempore infinito, sed tamen quia illa potentia infinita movens mediante potentia finita, erit iste motus secundum possibilitatem potentiae finitae, et sic in tempore et non in instanti" (Erfurt, Amplon. 312, fol. 13vb).

Though he frequently argues against Aristotle, Rufus's attitude toward Aristotle and Aristotelian philosophy is very positive in the *Physics*-commentary. Rufus not only believes that reason makes evident that the world began in time, he also believes that many of the necessary arguments can be drawn from Aristotle's own works. In the *Physics*-commentary, Rufus even claims that it would be wrong to conclude that Aristotle held that the world is beginningless or eternal.[43] Rufus concedes only that perhaps Aristotle did believe that time is infinite. Aristotle may have been persuaded by Plato's authority to hold that the world was eternal *a parte post*—that is, having once begun, the world never ends. If so, Aristotle can be excused, for Plato's authority was linked to a good argument—namely, that willing destruction does not pertain to God. Pagan philosophers could be excused for believing that the world would not come to an end.[44]

CREATION EX NIHILO

Rufus even defends Aristotle's statement that the world was not created. Aristotle was arguing against Plato, who believed that the world was created from something preexisting, something with duration. According to Rufus, both Aristotle and Plato assumed that the statement 'The world was not created' was equivalent to the statement 'The world was not created from something preexisting'. Plato was mistaken to believe that before the world existed, something with the potential to become the world existed. In fact, the world was created from nothing, *ex nihilo*, as Scripture makes plain. Correctly interpreted, Aristotle was denying only that before the world existed there was a preexisting potential world, that the nonexistence of the world had duration, and that it was measured by some 'quasi-temporal' dimension. Aristotle was not arguing against the Christian view of

---

43. Rufus (?) *In Physic. Aristot.* 8.1–2: "Quia imponitur Aristoteli quod ipse intellexit mundum non incepisse, cuius oppositum apparet ex sua recapitulatione, videtur quod possumus concludere ex dictis Aristoteleis quod mundus incepit" (Erfurt, Amplon. 312, fol. 12ra).

44. Rufus (?) *In Physic. Aristot.* 6.1: "His et multis aliis rationibus contingit arguere ex dictis Aristotelis et per rationes physicas mundum incepisse. Sed forte crediderit mundum non habere finem iuxta illam auctoritatem Platonis: bona ratione coniunctum dissolvi velle non est Dei. Crediderunt enim mundum esse factum in optima dispositione, sed nos per fidem et vere credimus oppositum sicut resurrectionem et meliorem mundi dispositionem" (Erfurt, Amplon. 312, fol. 12rb).

16   REGA WOOD

creation—namely, that the world was created, and before creation nothing with the potential to become the world existed.[45]

Rufus's positive attitude toward Aristotle at this point in his career shows the influence of Alexander of Hales, whom Rufus knew at Paris before he joined the Franciscan order.[46] Alexander of Hales believed that there was no great danger in Aristotle's teaching. Aristotle and the ancient philosophers did not know about creation, which is above nature. But as far as their work went, ancient philosophers were correct. The world's existence and its motion are commensurate with the whole duration of time.[47]

THE METAPHYSICS-COMMENTARY (BEFORE 1238)

The picture presented in Richard Rufus's Metaphysics-commentary is similar in many respects to that of the Physics-

---

45. Rufus (?) In Physic. Aristot. 8.1–2: "Procedit enim ex suppositione huius 'si mobile est factum, hoc erat <er' E> per motum'. Et hoc non est verum nisi intelligamus factum ex aliquo praeiacente quod praeiacens erat in quiete et tempore praeiacente.... Sed tunc videtur peccare ratio Aristotelis quae dicit prius non-esse sine tempore, et sic non-esse mundi vel motus non praecedit esse. Si enim praecederet, tempus praecederet, et sic motus. Et possumus dicere quod ipse non sic intellexit, sed intendit ostendere quod non-esse non potest esse prius hoc /12ra/ modo ut in ipso non-esse cadit prius et posterius. Et ita posuerunt philosophi cum posuerunt mundum fieri ex aliquo praeiacente et non ex nihilo. Ipsi enim posuerunt non-esse mundi et motus cum quadam duratione.... Et debemus intelligere quod ipse [Aristoteles] non intendit quin tempus processit ex non-esse in esse. Sed hunc modum intendebat improbare eis ut eius non-esse esset cum dimensione aliqua et duratione. Et sic intellexit Platonem ponere, ut scilicet poneret non-esse mundi esse cum aliquo quod esset in potentia mundus. Sed durationem huius non vocavit plus tempus, quia non fuit motus. Posuit ergo [Plato] tempus processisse ex non-esse in esse, quod non-esse fuit divisibile. Et si esset divisibile, tunc possemus sumere primum instans in esse temporis.... Hoc ergo modo intelligamus et procedit ratio Aristotelis, nec concludit inconveniens, scilicet quod tempus non processit sic de non esse in esse, sed quod non-esse duraret per aliquam dimensionem ante eius esse" (Erfurt, Amplon. 312, fol. 11vb–12ra).

46. Rufus's many citations of Alexander of Hales's Glossa, an early work, are reported in the index of the 1951–1957 Quaracchi edition of Alexander.

47. Alexander of Hales De materia prima, in an unpublished translation by Richard C. Dales based on Paris, Bibl. nat. MSS lat. 15272 and 16406, and Bologna, Bibl. univ. MS 2554.

commentary. The first cause is an indivisible of infinite power.⁴⁸ As in the *Physics*-commentary, Rufus states that the heavens do not move in virtue of an intrinsic principle; they must be moved by an extrinsic principle—that is, the first principle, God. But God does not move the heavens directly, only mediately. The reasons adduced for this conclusion are substantially the same as those offered in the *Physics*-commentary—namely, that the heavens would move infinitely fast if moved directly by an infinitely powerful principle of motion.⁴⁹

The accounts in the commentaries on both the *Physics* and the *Metaphysics* indicate that the being and nonbeing of the world are not temporally ordered. There was no time before the world was created.⁵⁰ The now of eternity is an important explanatory concept in both works.⁵¹ Not every now is the beginning of a future and the end of a past.⁵²

But in some respects the picture has changed. Rufus's attitude toward Aristotle is much less positive; there is no defense of Aristotle on creation. Rufus's account of the beginning of time and motion has changed, and his defense of the view that creation does not imply

---

48. Rufus *In Metaph. Aristot.* 1a.1: "Et est illud indivisibile prima causa" (Vatican, Vat. lat. 4538; unpublished transcription by Gál, p. 14). 12.6: "[I]ntelligamus modo causam primam [esse in] indivisibili nunc aeternitatis." 12.7–8: "In speciali . . . declaratum est quod una substantia separata a materia aeterna [est]. De illa eadem declaratum est in fine octavi Physicorum quod nullam habet magnitudinem neque divisionem" (ed. Noone, pp. 186, 231–232).

49. *In Metaph. Aristot.* 12.8.6.4–5: "prima autem causa est motor remotus et non immediatus. Nam si sic, cum prima causa infinitam potentiam habeat, moveretur caelum in non tempore. . . . Prima causa nullo modo est sub tempore . . . oportet quod sit aliquid medium quod sit motor immediatus. . . . [D]e necessitate oportet quod sit intellectus movens caelum et non forma eius sic. Illud mobile per suum motum est causa cuiuslibet viventis in natura: vita vegetativa et sensitiva. Sed quidquid facit mobile, hoc facit per suum motorem. Motor enim est causa motus. Ergo motor est causa vitae. Oportet igitur quod sit res vivens" (ed. Noone, pp. 270–274). Rufus (?) *In Physic. Aristot.* 6.10 (Erfurt, Amplon. 312, fol. 13vb), as quoted above.

50. *In Metaph. Aristot.* 12.6.1.3–4: "esse et non-esse prout sunt termini creationis non distinguuntur tempore. Unde, etsi non-ese in creatione sit prius esse, cum [tamen] illud 'prius' non sit prius tempore sed natura solum, non sequitur quod tempus sit ante mundi generationem <*ita pro*: creationem>" (ed.Noone, p. 191).

51. *In Metaph. Aristot.* 12.6.1.3–4: "intelligamus modo causam primam [esse] indivisibili nunc aeternitatis." Compare 12.8–9.7.12 (ed. Noone, pp. 186, 317f.).

52. *In Metaph. Aristot.* 12.6.1.3–4: "Et ideo supposuit Aristoteles falsum quodlibet instans esse principium futuri et finis praeteriti" (ed. Noone, p. 186).

mutability in God is more elaborate and relies less on the traditional Boethian account.

THE BEGINNING OF TIME

Rufus abandons the quasi-Aristotelian position of the *Physics*-commentary that time has no intrinsic limit, only an extrinsic limit that is God's atemporal mode of being. Rufus no longer describes creation as flowing from the indivisible extrinsic limit, which is the creator. Instead, in the *Metaphysics*-commentary, Rufus allows that time has an intrinsic limit, that there is a first instant of time. God created the world *ex nihilo* at the first instant of time. Rufus dissociates himself from his former views by saying,

> Others wish to save Aristotle in another way. A line has an intrinsic beginning [*principium*]—namely, a point. But motion has an extrinsic, not an intrinsic, limit. And this is what Aristotle intended to say when he said that there is no first motion. For in motion there is nothing except having been moved or instants of motion [*motum esse*]. This reply is worthless, for Aristotle intends that time is infinite, and motion is infinite; <time> does not have any intrinsic beginning [*principium*]. For <every> now is the beginning of a future and the end of a past. According to Aristotle, an instant cannot be the beginning of time, so that before that instant there would be no other time. Hence he supposes that time has no end and no beginning, and neither does motion.[53]

Quite correctly, Rufus now sees that according to Aristotle's account, time has no beginning. All of time can have no limit, either intrinsic or extrinsic. On the Aristotelian account, an instant at the beginning of all time, or an intrinsic limit for time, before which there would be no time, is impossible.

---

53. *In Metaph. Aristot.* 12.1.2: "Alii volunt alio modo salvare ipsum sic. Linea habet principium intrinsecum sui, scilicet punctum. Motus autem habet principium extra se sed non intra, et hoc intendit Aristotles cum dicit quod non est motus primus. In motu enim nihil est nisi motum esse. Et illud nihil est, Aristoteles enim vult quod tempus sit infinitum et motus infinitus, et non habet principium intrinsecum aliquod. Quia nunc est principium futuri et finis praeteriti, et secundum ipsum instans non potest esse principium temporis, ita quod ante ipsum instans non sit aliud tempus. Unde ponit tempus non habere finem nec principium nec similiter motum" (ed. Noone, p. 181).

Rufus is no longer content to explain that Aristotle is fundamentally opposed only to the view that creation is a departure from an immediately previous state, not to theories of creation *ex nihilo*. Rufus has read a number of Robert Grosseteste's works, including *De libero arbitrio*, *Hexaëmeron*, *De cessatione legalium*, *De motu supercaelestium*, and *De scientia Dei*.[54] Grosseteste has convinced him that Aristotle really is opposed to the Christian account of creation; Aristotle cannot be excused. Rufus had always known that Aristotle claimed that every now is intermediate between a past and a future, but before reading Grosseteste he did not see this as a false imagination, the product of a clouded intellect. Grosseteste's views were in marked contrast to the optimistic tradition of Alexander of Hales, who indicated that pagan philosophers reasoned correctly in a limited sphere. Grosseteste taught, rather, that the errors of the philosophers were a necessary result of the bondage of their affections; so attached to transitory things, pagan philosophers could not attain an understanding of the simplicity of eternity.[55]

REFUTING THE ARGUMENT AGAINST *EX NIHILO* CREATION

In the *Metaphysics*-commentary Rufus offers no arguments which show that the claim that the world is beginningless leads to absurd conclusions. Instead he seeks to defend the doctrine of creation *ex nihilo* against Aristotelian attacks. Aristotle claims that there can be no change where there is no previous state. And Rufus fears that Aristotle may be right. "But now it seems that Aristotle spoke the truth. For since motion is not coeternal with God, ... the mover was not always in act. Therefore it was previously something moving *in potentia* and thereafter in act. Therefore it was changed from this disposition to that disposition."[56] Rufus also states the

---

54. Noone, "An Edition," p. 58.
55. Grosseteste *De finitate*, ed. Dales, pp. 261–264. Compare Grosseteste *Com. in VIII lib. Phys. Aristot.*, pp. 153–154.
56. In *Metaph. Aristot.* 12.6.1.2: "Sed modo videtur quod Aristotles dicat verum. Ex quo enim motus non est coaeternus Deo, ut ponimus, ergo non semper fuit motor in actu. Prius igitur erat in potentia transmovens et postea in actu. Ergo mutabatur ab hac dispositione in illam dispositionem" (ed. Noone, p. 181).

problem in symbolic terms.[57] Suppose we grant that *b* is the first mutation or indivisible change. Before that mutation there was something mutable whose disposition changed prior to *b*. Let *a* represent the change in the disposition of the mutable; *b* without *a* (or mutation without a prior change of disposition) is inconceivable. In reply to this objection, Rufus denies that *a* and *b* are distinct; rather, *a* and *b* are one and the same mutation. The beginning and end of mutations do not differ; in mutation 'It is being changed' implies 'It has been changed'. Because *a* is the beginning of *b*, and *b* is the end of *a*, and neither *a* nor *b* have parts, *a* and *b* are one and the same mutation. Because *a* is the same as *b*, *a* does not precede *b*.[58]

Rufus denies that before every mutation (*transmutatio*) there occurs change or motion (*motio*). Motion is change over time, a successive process. Mutation refers to instantaneous change, a change where there is no process, no distinction between the beginning of change and the completed change or the changed state. Unlike a first motion, a first mutation is possible because mutation is indivisible. There is no succession in creation, and hence it follows "*a* is [being] created, therefore *a* exists." In creation "coming to be made" and "having been made" do not differ.[59] Rufus concludes his argument by suggesting that this is the reply that should have been made to Aristotle's argument in *Physics* 8.[60]

---

57. His is an early medieval use of what is called the *argumentum in terminis*; Rufus is employing a manner of argument he found in Aristotle and Averroës. Compare Robertus Grosseteste, *De veritate propositionis* and *De libero arbitrio* 6(7), 8(9), and 9, as in Bauer, *Die philosophischen Werke des Robert Grosseteste*, BGPM 9 (Münster: Aschendorff, 1912), pp. 143, 170, 191–192, 196).

58. *In Metaph. Aristot.* 12.6.1.2: "[F]alsum est, quia haec transmutatio et *b* transmutatio, quae posita est prima, sunt una et eadem transmutatio. Et cum dicit *b* transmutatio est finis istius transmutationis, quia initium *b* transmutationis est finis alterius transmutationis, dicendum est quod initium *b* transmutationis et finis *b* transmutationis sunt unum et idem, quia *b* transmutatio est mutatio quae non est motus. Et in tali mutatione sequitur 'mutatur, ergo est mutatum'. Si igitur initium transmutationis *b* est finis illius transmutationis, igitur ista transmutatio et *b* transmutatio sunt una et eadem transmutatio. Ergo *b* transmutationem non praecedit alia transmutatio" (ed. Noone, p. 185).

59. *In Metaph. Aristot.* 12.6.1.3–4: "Unde sequitur '*a* creatur, ergo *a* est'. In creatione igitur non differt 'fieri' et 'factum esse', sed sequitur 'fit, ergo factum est' in creatione" (ed. Noone, p. 184).

60. *In Metaph. Aristot.* 12.6.1.3–4: "Penitus eodem modo respondendum est ad argumentum Aristotelis quod facit in octavo Physicorum" (ed. Noone, p. 185).

CREATION AND MUTABILITY

Rufus's response to the argument that creation necessarily implies mutability in the creator has undergone a similar development. As in the *Physics*-commentary, Rufus explains God's immutability in terms of the distinction between temporally prior and prior by nature.[61] But Rufus no longer claims that this is because of the simplicity of God's nature or because God's will remains unchanged. Rufus abandons this claim on the basis of the following argument:

> We could ask: When <God> created the world at the first instant of time, why didn't he create it before?[62] Either he willed to create the world before or he did not. If he did not, and he now wills to create the world, then there is a change [*diversitas*] in his will, and God is mutable. If God willed to create the world *ab aeterno*, and his will is his action, then he created the world *ab aeterno*.[63]

Here the objector has posed a dilemma. If the world is not coeternal with God, it came into existence at a particular point in time, at which point God's will changed. No one can claim that God's will is unchanged, and God chooses to act at the first instant of time, since God's will is identical with God's action. If, on the other hand, God's will dictated from eternity the creation of the world, why is the world not coeternal with God?

Rufus's reply to this objection allows that creation involves a change but denies that any change occurs in the creator. Rufus begins his reply to the objection by saying that the proposition 'God creates from eternity' is false. God speaks from eternity, but God does not create from eternity. Rufus distinguishes between God's making or creation (*facere*) and God's speaking (*dicere*). 'Making' differs from 'saying' in that it adds something to the object made—

---

61. *In Metaph. Aristot.* 12.6.1.3–4: "Unde cum quaerit 'quare non fuit mundus prius etc.,' cum illud prius non sit prius tempore sed natura, et mundus sit in universa creatura, hoc est quaerere quare non fuit creatura prior natura. Et hoc est quaerere quare non [est] mundus coaeternus Deo. . . . Et huic respondendum est quod Creator prior est natura omni creatura" (ed. Noone, pp. 190–192).

62. For a discussion of the "why not sooner" argument see Sorabji, *Time, Creation, and the Continuum*, pp. 232–238.

63. *In Metaph. Aristot.* 12.6.1.4: "Tum hoc potest quaeri: Cum creavit mundum in primo instanti temporis, quare non creavit ipsum prius? Aut enim voluit creare ipsum prius aut non. Si non, et modo vult, ergo diversitas voluntatis est in ipso. Ergo est transmutatio in ipso. Si voluit ab aeterno, et sua voluntas est sua actio, ergo ab aeterno creavit ipsum" (ed. Noone, p. 182).

namely, existence.[64] Rufus distinguishes types of predication about God. Predication about God's essence, absolutely considered, is distinguished from predication about divine essence as related to external objects.[65] Some predication about divine action is related to external objects in a way that implies nothing about whether the external object has material existence. Thus 'The first cause knows something' implies nothing about whether that thing exists.[66] On the other hand, 'The first cause makes something' and 'God creates something' imply that the object of the relationship has material existence.[67]

'Making' is a special kind of divine 'speaking', a kind which not only implies existence but which may also describe the time at which the thing is created. God's speaking always remains in the present tense, but what God says about the object may be that it has been or will be created. God is eternally present, but God's speech can

---

64. *In Metaph. Aristot.* 12.6.1.3: "Ad aliud dicendum quod huiusmodi propositiones sunt falsae: 'prima causa movet ab aeterno' et etiam 'creat ab aeterno' et similiter 'facit hoc ab aeterno'. Haec tamen vera 'dicit ab aeterno'. Et non est suum dicere suum facere. Nam si sic, cum quaecunque dicit dicit ab aeterno, ergo quaecunque facit facit ab aeterno, quod falsum est.// Sciendum est igitur quod facere et creare addunt aliquid supra suum dicere. Illa tamen additio cadit supra rem dictam ab eo et non super eum. Verbi gratia, intelligamus modo causam primam [esse in] indivisibili nunc aeternitatis, et similiter intelligamus omne praedicatum dicibile de ipsa dici de ea prout potest dici" (ed. Noone, p. 186).

65. Robert Grosseteste distinguishes what God knows about the divine substance absolutely and what God knows about divine substance in relation to variable substances. Knowing is a relation that varies when its terms vary. God's knowledge of variable substances establishes relations that are eternal but different from God because they are variable. Since relations have no essence apart from the essence of their terms, multiplying relations does result in an increase in entities. Grosseteste argues that he is not committed to postulating many eternal essences; there is only one eternal and indivisible essence which is God (*De libero arbitrio* 8[9] [ed. Dales, pp. 177f., 192, 196]).

66. The distinction between the 'knowing' and such verbs as 'creating' and 'governing' is also found in Grosseteste's *De libero arbitrio* 8(9) (ed. Dales, p. 184f). The relation established by knowing is indifferent to the existence or nonexistence of the thing known. On the other hand, the relation of creation implies the existence of the thing created. I owe these references to Grosseteste to Neil Lewis.

67. *In Metaph. Aristot.* 12.6.1.3: "Sciendum est quod, quando de ipsa causa prima praedicatur sua actio relata ad obiectum extra, et hoc per aliquam relationem dicibilem de ipsa...illud obiectum est indifferens sive sit actu in materia sive non. Et respectu alterius relationis quae exit a sua essentia et terminatur in obiectum extra, oportet quod illud obiectum non sit indifferens sed quod sit in materia extra in actu" (ed. Noone, pp. 187–188).

indicate what things will exist first, what things will succeed them, and what things will exist last.⁶⁸

How does this discussion answer the objection? First, God does not create from eternity; God speaks from eternity. Second, there is a change, but only in created things. God is eternally present and unchanging. When viewed from the perspective of created things, however, God's speaking and creation are not simultaneous. The world changes, and its changes are measured in a temporal succession dictated by God's eternal speech.

Rufus takes more seriously in the *Metaphysics*-commentary the challenge that Aristotle presents for the Christian account of creation. A less reliable authority than Rufus had previously thought, Aristotle is a more formidable philosophical opponent.

THE *SENTENCES*-COMMENTARY (C. 1250)

Rufus's *Sentences*-commentary represents a further stage in his development as an interpreter of Aristotle. Rufus confidently presents arguments against the eternity of time and for creation *ex nihilo*. He is no longer anxious to dissociate himself from the views expressed earlier in his *Physics*-commentary. Rufus once more advances the argument from the *Physics*-commentary that time must have a beginning: "All time before now is past. But . . . there is no past time which was not present. Therefore, any time which might be past had [already] been present, and thus the past is finite."⁶⁹

---

68. *In Metaph. Aristot.* 12.6.1.3: "Et similiter si dicam 'faciet hanc animam,' hoc est dictu 'dicit hanc animam fiendam esse, et hoc per suum dicere.' Similiter si dicam 'fecit hanc animam,' hoc est dictu 'dicit hanc animam factam esse, et hoc per suum dicere.' Et similiter si dicam 'creavit hanc animam,' hoc est dictu 'dicit hanc animam creatam fuisse, et hoc per suum dicere.' In omnibus his patet quod semper dicit praesentialiter de prima causa; futuritio et praeteritio cadunt super obiecta ad quae habent suae actiones relationem" (ed. Noone, pp. 188–189). For a further discussion of Rufus's views see Noone, pp. 129–133). Noone has also taken up these issues in his unpublished paper, "Richard Rufus, Franciscan, on Creation and Divine Immutability," delivered at Kalamazoo, 12 May 1990.

69. Rufus *Sent.* 2.1: "Sequitur contra aeternitatem motus et temporis aliquid dicere. Dico ergo quod totum tempus usque nunc, praeteritum est. Sed quidquid est praeteritum, aliquando fuit praesens; nihil igitur temporis est praeteritum quod non

THE BEGINNING OF TIME AND MOTION

In the *Sentences*-commentary, Rufus suggests that the description of motion found in the *Physics*-commentary may not be incompatible with the later *Metaphysics*-description. He asks: What is the beginning of motion? Does it have an intrinsic limit, as time has a first instant? He is not even sure time has a first instant. Perhaps the limit of time is extrinsic, as he had claimed in the *Physics*-commentary. Rufus asks: When we say something begins to move, don't we mean that now is the last instant that it is at rest?[70] Alternatively, as Rufus had maintained in the *Metaphysics*-commentary, a mutation is the beginning of motion—namely, the transformation from not moving to moving, whose beginning and end are one and the same mutation.

After claiming somewhat implausibly that these replies may amount to the same thing, Rufus decides in his *Sentences*-commentary for the account of the *Metaphysics*. Motion has a first mutation, an intrinsic limit, as time has a first instant. Before every motion there is a mutation. But it is not true to claim, as Aristotle would, that before every mutation there is motion.[71]

CREATION EX NIHILO

Though Rufus adopts the *Metaphysics*-commentary account, according to which motion has an intrinsic limit, the first mutation, he no longer uses this account of mutation to reply to

---

fuit praesens. Ergo praesens fuit antequam aliquid esset praeteritum, et ita praeteritum finitum est" (Oxford, Balliol College 62, fol. 105rb).

70. Compare Norman Kretzmann, "Incipit/Desinit," in *Motion and Time, Space, and Matter: Interrelations in the History and Philosophy of Science*, ed. Peter K. Machamer and Robert G. Turnbull (Columbus: Ohio State University Press, 1976); and Kretzmann, "Socrates Is Whiter Than Plato Begins to Be White," *Noûs* 11 (1977): 3–15.

71. Rufus *Sent.* 2.1: "Praeterea, illud supra tactum, quaeri potest quid sit principium initiale motus, et an aliquod habeat sui intrinsecum, sicut tempus habet instans primum.// Nescio an dicam quod ultimum non moveri sit principium motus. Verbi gratia: Incipit moveri, quid est hoc nisi nunc ultimo non movetur?// Aut aliter (sed forte in idem redit): Principium sive <(?)> initium motus est mutari, scilicet de non-moveri ad moveri. Et haec mutatio est subita, quia mutatio medium non habet.// Unde hoc patere potest, ut videtur, quod contra Aristotelem et alios philosophos: Omnem motum praecedit aliqua mutatio quae non est motus. Nam mutatum-esse praecedit motum, non tamen omnem mutationem praecedit vel mutatio vel motus" (Oxford, Balliol 62, fol. 105ra).

Aristotle's argument for a beginningless world. Rufus summarizes Aristotle's argument for the view that motion and the world could not begin *ex nihilo*: 'Everything that was not and afterwards is, was potentially'. In the *Sentences*-commentary Rufus does not present the solution advanced in the *Metaphysics*-commentary—namely, in the case of the creation of the world, 'The world has been created' follows from 'The world is being created'. Instead, in the *Sentences*-commentary he starts by invoking an argument from Alexander of Hales and Robert Grosseteste.[72] Any potential realized in creation is the active potential of the creator acting as an efficient cause. Implicit here is the claim that there is no material substrate in the case of creation, unlike generation. This distinction between creation and generation is found in the works of Alexander of Hales'.[73] It is emphasized by Richard Rufus in all three commentaries.

The more interesting solution Richard Rufus offers to this problem is taken almost verbatim from Robert Grosseteste's *De finitate*.[74] It involves careful distinctions about the meaning of the term 'after' when used to describe time and eternity. When we say, 'The first mutation was, after it was not', we should be precise about the word 'after'. If 'after' signifies a temporal order, then, given that there was no time before the first motion, the seemingly self-evident division "Either motion is perpetual or else it is after it was not" is in fact false, since motion does exist, and is not perpetual, but is also not temporally ordered 'after' its nonexistence. If, on the other hand, the

---

72. Alexander of Hales *De duratione mundi*: "Cum autem obicitur 'primus motus aut est factus aut est eternus,' dicimus quod factus est... sed non per viam naturae.... Nec est in creatis eductio de potentia in actum secundum quod haec eductio est materialis; potentia enim illa tunc esset potentia materiae sicut est in natura creata. Aut si fiat in potentia antequam educantur non sunt in potentia materiae, sed agentis tantum" (Paris, Bibl. Nat. lat. 15272, fol. 149va, cited in Dales, *Medieval Discussions of the Eternity of the World*, p. 70). Robert Grosseteste *De finitate*, "verum est quod mundus et tempus et motus fuerunt postquam non fuerunt; et priusquam essent, fuerunt in potentia... et 'potentia' non dicat potentiam causae materialis sed solum potentiam causae efficientis" (ed. Dales, p. 259). See also Grossseteste *Com. in VIII lib. Phys. Aristot.* 8 (ed. Dales, p. 150).

73. Alexander of Hales *De duratione mundi*, in Dales, *Medieval Discussions*, p. 70. Doubtless this distinction is found in many other authors.

74. Richard C. Dales quotes Grosseteste in the recent book *Medieval Discussions*, p. 73. Dales also notes Rufus's borrowing from Grosseteste (p. 79). The text as a whole is available in Dales's editions: *De finitate*, pp. 258–260; *Com. in VIII lib. Phys. Aristot.* 8, pp. 149–51.

word 'after' signifies the relation of time to eternity, then if the word 'is' signifies time or an instant, and the word 'was' signifies eternity, it is true that time, motion, and the world exist after they did not exist. Time and motion even existed potentially, provided we realize that the only potential that existed was the active potential of the creator and not any potential material cause. But this exposition of the term 'after' is forced. It would be appropriate if before time and the world began, there was time without beginning. But eternity is not the same as beginningless time; eternity is not temporally prior to the time the world began. So no potential world existed before creation.

The dictum 'Everything that was not and afterwards is, was potentially' is true, but its scope is limited. It applies only in cases where temporal priority makes sense, where both being and nonbeing are in time.[75]

Rufus's final tactic for defending *ex nihilo* creation involves an elaborate discussion of the word 'nothing'. As usual, Rufus's statement of the problem is pointed: "What is that nonbeing which is prior to being, and how is it prior if not in virtue of eternity?" Strictly speaking,

---

75. Rufus *Sent.* 2.1: "Et ad istud dici potest quod illa propositio falsa est: Omne quod est postquam non fuit, prius fuit in potentia nisi intelligatur de potentia activa creatoris. Potest et aliter dici quod cum dicitur prima mutatio fuit postquam non fuit, distinguendum est quod si haec dictio 'postquam' significet ordinem temporum <(!) B>, implicata est in hoc <h B> sermone contradictio, quia implicatur quod tempus praecessit primum motum. Et tunc non est haec divisio sufficiens: Motus aut est perpetuus, aut fuit postquam non fuit, quia sub neutra parte huius divisionis cadit motus, nec tempus, nec mundus.// Si autem haec dictio 'postquam' significet ordinem temporis ad aeternitatem, et hoc verbum 'est' consignificet tempus vel nunc temporis, et hoc verbum 'fuit' consignificet aeternitatem, verum est quod mundus et tempus et motus est postquam non fuit. Et priusquam essent, fuerunt in potentia, si designetur prioritas aeternitatis ad tempus, et potentia non dicat potentiam causae materialis sed causae efficientis.// Illa autem propositio 'omne quod de potentia priore exit ad actum' etc., vera est si significetur prioritas temporalis, et sic tenet eius probatio. Si autem significetur prioritas aeternorum ad temporalia, falsa est.// Item, illa ratio quod non esse mundi et eius esse dividuntur prioritate et posterioritate, et prius et posterius non sunt simul tempore, ergo ante mundum fuit tempus—In hoc sicut supra dictum est, puto quod sit error in eo quod non distinguitur inter prioritatem temporis et prioritatem quae significat ordinem aeternitatis ad tempus. Non-esse namque mundi et eorum quae cum mundo ceperunt non mensuravit tempus sine initio sed aeternitas. Non ergo fuit eorum non-esse prius tempore quam esse eorum. Sed fuit prius et in priori mensura quam eorum esse, quia eorum non-esse in aeternitate fuit, et earum esse in tempore" (Oxford, Balliol 62, fol. 105ra).

Rufus offers no reply. He tells us he is not sure that nonbeing is nothing. Perhaps it is an abuse of language to say that either nothing or nonbeing is prior to something or being. Or perhaps, loosely speaking, we might be allowed to say that nothing and nonbeing are prior by origin to something or being. But since being and nonbeing are never measured simultaneously, perhaps one cannot be prior to the other.[76] It may be that the only correct statement about the creation of the world is that 'it is, and it was not'.[77] Clearly, Rufus's scruple here has to do with the incommensurability of being and nonbeing. But he may also be concerned to avoid the possibility of anything even remotely resembling empty time, before the existence of the world.

MUTABILITY AND CREATION

In his discussion of mutability and creation, Rufus sets out to refute Aristotle by demonstrating that absurd conclusions

---

76. Rufus *Sent.* 2.1: "Quid ergo illud non-esse prius est quam istud esse, quomodo ergo prius si non aeternitate prius? Ecce aliquid fit ex nihilo, id est post. Ergo aliquid est post nihil, ergo nihil est prius illo aliquo, quomodo prius? Nescio an dicam quod illud non-esse, nihil est. Unde nec ipsum, nec nihil proprie loquendo prius est quam esse vel aliquid, et abusive solum dicitur illud prius, et hoc posterius.// An dicam quod sic improprie loquendo, nihil et non-esse quodammodo quasi origine prius sit quam aliquid et esse, et e converso aliquid et esse [sit] origine posterius quam nihil et non-esse.// Forte melius ad hoc dicetur sic: Mensuretur aeternitate illud non-esse. Mensuretur, id est contineatur. Subici enim scientiae Dei est contineri [vel] mensurari ab ipso Deo. Mensuretur et istud esse aeternitate <et *add*. B?>. Illud mensurabatur aeternitate quando ipsum fuit et istud mensuratur aeternitate quando ipsum est. Sed quando istud est, illud non est, nec quando illud fuit, istud fuit. Ergo sicut non simul sunt, sed unum alteri succedit, nec simul mensurantur aeternitate. Sed illud prius mensurabatur, et istud posterius mensuratur. Nec illud est aeternitate prius isto, quia non ambo simul sub aeternitate ordinantur. Nec istud est aeternitate posterius illo eadem ratione. Sed illud fuit prius mensuratum aeternitate quam istud. Et etiam illud aliquo modo dicendi origine prius est quam istud, et istud posterius origine.// Et similiter dicendum est de partibus temporis diversis.// Quid ergo proprie dici potest cum creatur nisi quod *a* est et non fuit *a*. Sic nulla erit improprietas in verbis" (Oxford, Balliol 62, fol. 105vb).

77. Allen W. Wood has suggested that Grosseteste and Rufus may not even be entitled to this formulation. Having given up the use of the terms 'before' and 'after' in the strict sense, they must give up the verb 'was' which cannot be expounded without the use of the term 'before.' A similar difficulty arises with respect to the term 'begin.'

follow from his views on the First Cause. As in the *Metaphysics*-commentary, Rufus sees Aristotle as claiming that the world is eternal and that God causes it, not a common position in Rufus's time.[78]

But there is a difference. In the giving accounts of the *Physics* and *Metaphysics*, Rufus had restricted himself to defending the Christian view that creation need not imply mutability in the creator. In the *Sentences*-commentary, Rufus takes the offensive; he seeks to show that unless Aristotle accepts the view that the world was created *ex nihilo*, he is committed to maintaining the absurd conclusion that God, or the First Cause, is mutable. Rufus seeks to show that Aristotle cannot consistently maintain both that the world is eternal and that God causes it:

> If God made the world, either it was made from something or from nothing. If it is made from nothing, then the world was nothing, and afterwards it had being; therefore in no sense is it eternal. Rather it has a beginning; it has being after nonbeing....
>
> If God made the world from something, then either it was made from God himself or from another nature. It cannot have been made from another nature, since there was no other nature. Therefore it must have been made from God. From this it follows that God is mutable and composite, and the world is of the same nature as God. For whenever something is made from anything, something is necessarily common to both. So if God made the world from God, God communicates something of God to the world, from which God fabricates the substance of the world. There is also something which God does not communicate to the world, and hence God is composite.[79]

---

78. Noone has pointed out that in this period this is a distinctive aspect of Rufus's interpretation of Aristotle ("An Edition," p. 28). But note that William of Auvergne, like Rufus, sees Aristotle as claiming that the world is eternal, and God causes it (*De universo* 1.2.8 [Paris ed. 1:690–692]).

79. Rufus *Sent.* 2.1: "Item, contra illum errorem qui ponit mundum Deo coaeternum, et tamen a Deo factum, opponitur sic: Si Deus fecit illum, aut ergo de aliquo, aut de nihilo. Si de nihilo, ergo mundus nihil fuit, et postea esse habuit, ergo nullo modo aeternus, sed initium habens, et esse post non esse.// Si de aliquo, aut de se Deo, aut de alia natura. Non de alia, quia nulla fuit alia, ergo de se Deo. Ex quo sequitur quod ipse Deus transmutabilis est et compositus, et quod mundus sit eiusdem naturae cum Deo.// Nam quando aliquid fit de aliquo, necesse est aliquid esse commune in utroque. /105va/... Si ergo Deus facit mundum de se Deo, aliquam partem sui mundo communicat, ex qua fabricat substantiam mundi et aliquid aliud mundo non communicat, et ita esset Deus compositus" (Oxford, Balliol 62, fol. 105rb–105va).

Here the conclusion—namely, that the substance of the First Cause is mutable and composite—would be as unpalatable to an Aristotelian as to a Christian theologian. Given the thorny problems Aristotle has set for the Christian account of creation, Rufus must have been pleased to have found an argument that seemed to show that unless Aristotle accepted *ex nihilo* creation, he must either give up the view that God causes the world, or else accept the view that God is mutable.

What will Rufus come up with next? I have not examined in detail Rufus's last work, the Paris commentary. But I note that Rufus repeats several of the arguments against the eternity of the world found originally in the *Physics*-commentary.[80] From the *Sentences*-commentary, Rufus takes the argument that the First Cause must be mutable if the world was not created *ex nihilo*; an immutable God cannot make the world from eternity.[81] Further examination would undoubtedly reveal exciting new arguments. Richard Rufus will not limit himself to repeating some of his own earlier arguments and adding to the discussion from Bonaventure's *Sentences*-commentary. Instead Rufus will take the dialogue with Aristotle a step further.

The exciting thing about Richard Rufus is how many interesting views he presented, apparently for the first time. He did not cultivate originality; he borrowed without hesitation from Alexander of Hales, Robert Grosseteste, and Bonaventure. Nevertheless, Rufus's own philosophical creativity was exceptional; he anticipated many of the classic Western replies to Aristotle on the eternity of the world.

Rufus was one of the first scholastic philosophers to face the conflict between Aristotle and the revealed doctrine of creation. For over a century after he wrote, Christian philosophers continued to explore

---

80. Rufus *Abbreviatio Bonav.* 2.1.1: "Si infiniti homines praecessissent.... Item, totum tempus usque nunc praeteritum est.... Item, impossibile est infinita ordinari.... Item, impossibile est infinita comprehendi.... Item, si mundus est aeternus cum nunquam fuit sine homine...." (Vatican, Vat. lat. 12993, fol. 132va–vb).

81. Rufus *Abbreviatio Bonav.* 2.1.1: "Item contra illos duos modos ponendi mundum Deo coaeternum, et tamen factum opponitur sic: 'Si Deus fecit mundum, aut ergo de aliquo aut de nihilo. Si de nihilo, ergo habet esse post non esse, ergo non est aeternus. Si de aliquo, aut ergo de se Deo, aut de alia natura. Non de alia, quia nulla sint alia. Ergo de Deo, ergo Deus est transmutabilis, mutabilis, corruptibilis, compositus etc. Et mundus eiusdem naturae est cum Deo, quae omnia absurda sunt'" (Vatican, Vat. lat. 12993, fol. 133ra).

these issues from a variety of standpoints and at a high level of sophistication. They engaged the best minds of the high Middle Ages, including Thomas Aquinas, John Duns Scotus, and William of Ockham. It is perhaps surprising, therefore, and certainly impressive, that Richard Rufus's treatment of these topics, clearly one of the earliest, already exhibits a subtlety and complexity comparable to the best of what was to follow.

St. Bonaventure University

Albert the Great on the Subject of Metaphysics and Demonstrating the Existence of God

TIMOTHY B. NOONE

In his comprehensive study of Thomas Aquinas's *Sententia super Metaphysicam*, James Doig introduces Albert the Great as one of the commentators whose interpretation of Aristotle's *Metaphysics* Thomas intended to challenge. In particular, Doig alleges that Albert's understanding of the formal object (or, in other terminology, the subject) of metaphysics is heavily indebted to the writings of Averroës, although the modern scholar acknowledges that Albert does not follow the Averroistic interpretation in all respects.[1] Furthermore, Doig contends that Albert's own *Metaphysica*, following Averroës's schema of metaphysical knowledge, contains no proof of the existence of God as the cause of being but simply relies on the proof of God as the cause of motion, as was developed in Aristotle's *Physics*.[2]

---

1. James C. Doig, *Aquinas on Metaphysics: A Historico-Doctrinal Study of the Commentary on the Metaphysics* (The Hague: Martinus Nijhoff, 1972), pp. 53–54, 125–152. The present paper originated as part of the author's licentiate thesis at the Pontifical Institute of Mediaeval Studies, Toronto. I would like to dedicate the paper to the late James A. Weisheipl, who directed the thesis, even as I acknowledge that he would have disagreed heartily with its conclusions.

2. For example, Doig, *Aquinas on Metaphysics*, pp. 202, 204.

In marked contrast to Doig's interpretation, Albert Zimmermann, in a monograph devoted to medieval conceptions of the subject of metaphysics, proposes that the main historical influence on Albert's teaching on the subject of metaphysics is not Averroës but Avicenna.[3] In light of these conflicting interpretations of Albert's position on the subject of metaphysics and the relation to metaphysics of proofs for God's existence, the present paper has a twofold purpose: first, to show that Albert's position on the subject of metaphysics, although original in many regards, is inspired by Avicenna rather than Averroës; and, second, to provide textual evidence that Albert maintains that there is a proof for the existence of God as a *causa essendi*, and not merely a *causa motus*, in his *Metaphysica*.

The immediate sources of inspiration for medieval discussions of the subject of metaphysics were the writings of Avicenna and Averroës, who had sketched out divergent theories of metaphysical knowledge.[4] Avicenna, applying to metaphysics the model of scientific knowledge that had been advocated by Aristotle in his *Posterior Analytics*, argued that the subject of metaphysics was being *qua* being, the being common to substance, accidents, and God. Yet Averroës found the Avicennian account of the subject of metaphysics to be both un-Aristotelian in inspiration and unsound in approach. Instead, Averroës contended that the proper subjects of metaphysics were the separate entities that functioned as the first and primary instances of substance or true being. Since the first task of this paper is to assess

---

3. Albert Zimmermann, *Ontologie oder Metaphysik?: Die Diskussion über den Gegenstand der Metaphysik im 13, und 14. Jahrhundert*, Studien und Texte zur Geistesgeschichte des Mittelalters 8 (Leiden and Cologne: E. J. Brill, 1965), p. 149. Doig seems to have been unaware of Zimmermann's interpretation. In another study, Zimmermann has argued that, although "Averroists" such as Siger of Brabant looked to Albert's writings for guidance in interpreting Aristotle and in distinguishing philosophical from theological knowledge, Albert by no means either shared their tendency to glorify Aristotle or embraced their distinctive doctrinal tenets. See Zimmermann, "Albertus Magnus und der lateinische Averroismus," in *Albertus Magnus: Doctor Universalis, 1280–1980*, ed. Gerbert Meyer and Albert Zimmermann (Mainz: Matthias-Grünewald, 1980), pp. 465–493.

4. On the background for the medieval discussions of metaphysics as a science, see Doig, *Aquinas on Metaphysics*, pp. 23–46; Zimmermann, *Ontologie oder Metaphysik?* pp. 85–119; Stephen F. Brown, "Avicenna and the Unity of the Concept of Being," *Franciscan Studies* 25 (1965): 117–150.

whether Albert the Great's account of the subject of metaphysics owes more to Avicenna or Averroës, we should acquaint ourselves, however briefly, with some of the finer points in each Islamic philosopher's position and the texts in which their theories were made available to Latin readers.

THE ISLAMIC BACKGROUND

AVICENNA

After discussing the general division of theoretical philosophy into its three branches of natural philosophy, mathematics, and divine science, Avicenna proceeds, in his *De prima philosophia*, to analyze the subject of divine science, or metaphysics. Although the phrase that he uses to describe metaphysics, "divine science," might lead one to believe that God would be the subject of metaphysics for Avicenna, in fact he explicitly rejects that possibility. His reasoning for doing so is concisely stated and shows the extent to which Avicenna had mastered the scientific methodology of Aristotle's *Posterior Analytics*.

For Aristotle, every science treats a subject whose existence is obvious but whose precise properties and attributes are unknown. Proceeding from the principles of the subject of the science and other generally understood principles as related to the subject, a given science shows which properties and attributes belong to the subject as such through reasoned argument or demonstration.[5] In light of such considerations, Avicenna points out, one and the same thing cannot both be the subject of a science and yet be sought (*quaesitum*) by the science, namely, be the conclusion of a demonstration, because this would entail that the same thing be presupposed and proved in the same science. Accordingly, if God is sought in metaphysics, God cannot be the subject of metaphysics.[6]

---

5. Aristotle *Posterior Analytics* 1.10.76a31–76b23.
6. Avicenna *Liber de philosophia prima sive scientia divina* 1.1.1, as in Avicenna Latinus 4 (Leiden; Louvain: E. J. Brill; E. Peeters, 1977), p. 4, lines 57–65. Hereafter Avicenna's work will be cited simply as *Metaph.*, and this edition will be cited in parentheses by volume, page, and line numbers.

How, it might be objected, do we know that God is sought in metaphysics? Avicenna anticipates such an objection by taking up and then examining the consequences of the hypothesis that God is not sought in metaphysics. If God were not sought in metaphysics, then either God's existence would be conceded for metaphysics, while established in another science, or God's existence would be granted in metaphysics and not established in another science. The former alternative cannot be true, because no other science even takes up the question whether God exists. In short, we know that God's existence is not sought in any other science by a type of induction, a simple recounting of the questions taken up in other branches of philosophy ("et tu scies hoc parva inspectione ex his quae multotiens inculcamus"), since the branches of philosophy are believed to be exhaustive of knowledge. The latter alternative also cannot be true, for it would imply either that God's existence were immediately known (*manifestum per se*) or were completely beyond human ken (*desparatum per se*), both of which Avicenna thinks are clearly false. God's existence cannot be immediately known, if, as is clearly so, some people are unaware of God's existence. Nor can God's existence be beyond human ken, if we perceive signs of God's existence (*signa habemus de eo*).[7]

Since every alternative underlying the hypothesis that God is not sought in metaphysics has proved to be false, the hypothesis itself must be false. Avicenna concludes that God is indeed sought (*quaesitum*) in metaphysics and, for that reason, is not the subject of metaphysics.[8]

Yet to state that God is not the subject of metaphysics is not to say what the subject of metaphysics is, as Avicenna well knows. Hence Avicenna devotes a number of pages to considering an alternative subject for metaphysics, the ultimate causes, and to exploring dialectically what requirements a candidate for the subject of metaphysics must meet. The possibility that the ultimate material, formal, efficient, and final causes, either singly taken or in combination, constitute the subject of metaphysics is rejected because of another requirement for scientific knowledge laid down in the *Posterior Analytics*: the subject of a science must be the common subject of investigation for every

---

7. Avicenna *Metaph.* 1.1.1 (4:4.64–5.79).
8. Avicenna *Metaph.* 1.1.1 (4:5.80–81).

part of the science.⁹ But, Avicenna reasons, metaphysics investigates matters such as the universal and the particular, potency and act, as well as the possible and the necessary, none of which fall under the notion of causality.¹⁰ Thus metaphysics cannot have as its subject the ultimate causes, whether these be taken singly or collectively. In exploring the logical requirements for the subject of metaphysics, moreover, Avicenna notes that the subject will have to be comprehensive enough to permit the metaphysician to study such divergent topics as the nature of body (in the sense of its ontological structure), the nature of substance, and the status of mathematicals, since no other science treats such matters, despite their manifest importance.¹¹

After these preliminary observations, Avicenna urges the conclusion that only being insofar as it is being is sufficiently universal and comprehensive to serve as the subject of metaphysics. Only being can function as something common to accidents and substance; only being can be the subject of discourse in discussions of unity and plurality, sameness and otherness.¹²

For our purposes, three things must be remembered from Avicenna's account of metaphysical knowledge: (1) He firmly and forthrightly rejects the opinion that God is the subject of metaphysics. (2) He posits being as common both to substance and to God as the subject of metaphysics. (3) He maintains that God's existence is shown only in metaphysics.

AVERROËS

Although Avicenna's account of the subject of metaphysics may seem to do full justice both to the requirements of Aristotelian science and to the nature of metaphysical inquiry, Averroës

---

9. Aristotle *Posterior Analytics* 1.28.87a38–87b4.
10. Avicenna *Metaph.* 1.1.1 (4:6.8–15).
11. Avicenna *Metaph.* 1.1.2 (4:10.79–12.13).
12. Avicenna *Metaph.* 1.1.2 (4:12.14–22). The reader may wonder why Avicenna uses *esse* here in place of the more usual *ens*. Part of the answer seems to be that the *ens* considered by the metaphysician is the fact of existence. (For a discussion of this point, see Doig, *Aquinas on Metaphysics*, pp. 24–29). Whatever may be the doctrinal significance of using *esse* in place of *ens*, Avicenna tends to use the expressions *esse inquantum esse* and *ens inquantum ens* interchangeably. Compare *Metaph.* 1.1.2 (4:12.28–32).

considered Avicenna's position to be fundamentally flawed. Where Avicenna had gone wrong, according to Averroës, was in failing to see that the first alternative following on the hypothesis that God is not sought in metaphysics is true: God's existence is conceded for metaphysics and is established in another science, namely natural philosophy:

> Accordingly, the consideration of forms belongs to two sciences. The first, natural science, discusses material forms; the second, which is the science of being as such, investigates the simple forms that are entirely separate from matter. But we should notice that the existence of this kind of being, namely, being separate from matter, is only discovered in this science, natural science. Moreover, anyone who contends that first philosophy tries to establish the existence of separate entities is mistaken. For such entities serve as the subject of first philosophy, and it has been stated in the *Posterior Analytics* that for a science to declare the existence of its subject is impossible. Instead, each science assumes that its subject exists either because the subject is evident in itself or because it has been demonstrated to exist in another science. Wherefore, Avicenna was gravely mistaken when he stated that the first philosopher demonstrates the existence of the First Principle and proceeded along these lines (which he deemed correct and even necessary) in his book *On the Divine Science*. Indeed, even the most certain of the arguments he employs in this book do not transcend the realm of probability.[13]

The elements of Averroës's solution to the problem posed by Avicenna are all contained in this text. Natural philosophy demonstrates the existence of separate entity through its proof that there must be an Unmoved Mover. Hence metaphysics does not need to show the existence of God or separate entity. Indeed, because, in Averroës's view, separate entity serves as the subject of metaphysics, metaphysics cannot show the existence of God and that for the very reason adduced by Avicenna—no science can prove the existence of its own subject.

What then is the subject of metaphysics for Averroës? In some texts, the question admits of a straightforward answer, but one easily

---

13. Averroës *In Phys. Aristotelis* 1 text 83, as in *Opera Omnia* 4 (Venice: Junta, 1550), fol. 22vb–23ra. Both from the context and the content of this passage, it is evident that Averroës intends to make a claim about the formal object of metaphysics, not just the material object.

misunderstood. For Averroës will say that being as such is the subject, or rather that *ens simpliciter* is the subject. Yet what Averroës means by *ens simpliciter* needs to be carefully interpreted, as is evident in the passage given immediately above. Notice that, in discussing the second science that deals with forms, Averroës states that it is a science treating of "being as such" (*de ente simpliciter*) and "simple forms separate from matter." Within a few lines, however, Averroës also claims that the subject of metaphysics is separate entity. Would the Commentator be suggesting here that there are two (or more) subjects for metaphysics? Probably not. The key to interpreting these divergent statements lies in Averroës's interpretation of the focal meaning of being in Aristotle's *Metaphysics*. According to Averroës, just as things which are said to be healthy are referred to the primary instance of health found in animals for their meaning, so the nine accidents are referred to substance.[14] Yet within substance there is an order of greater and less, according to priority and posteriority. Consequently, just as all things studied in natural philosophy have in their definition nature, so all things studied in metaphysics have in their definition God.[15] Thus ultimately, for Averroës, the study of being as such means the study of the divine being, or God, and this is why he can claim that separate entities serve as the subject of first philosophy.

In sum, Averroës's theory of metaphysical knowledge is characterized by the following claims: (1) The primary and truly apodictic demonstration of God's existence is found in natural philosophy in the form of the proof for an Unmoved Mover. (2) The science of metaphysics formally depends on the demonstration of God's existence in natural philosophy, since metaphysics receives its subject through this demonstration. (3) Metaphysics is the science of being as being in that it is the study of being in its first instance, God or separate entity, and the study of secondary instances as related to God, insofar as God is First Form and Last End.[16]

---

14. Averroës *In Metaph. Aristotelis* 4 text 2, as in *Opera Omnia* 8, fol. 31r-v; and 4 text 7, fol. 31vb. On the focal meaning of being in Aristotle's metaphysical thought, see G. E. L. Owen, "Logic and Metaphysics in Some Earlier Works of Aristotle," in *Aristotle and Plato in the Mid–Fourth Century*, ed. Düring and Owen, Studia Graeca et Latina Gothoburgensia XI (Göteborg, 1960), pp. 163–190.

15. Averroës *In Metaph.* 6 text 2, fol. 69rb.

16. Averroës *In Metaph.* 4 text 6, fol. 294vK-L.

ALBERT THE GREAT

Bearing in mind the Avicennian and Averroistic models of metaphysical knowledge, let us now turn to Albert's *Physica* and *Metaphysica* to determine which of the models he is more inclined to follow. We begin with the earlier *Physica* and then proceed to the *Metaphysica* as a way of checking for any change or development in Albert's position.

ALBERT'S PHYSICA

When Albert began to compose his Aristotelian commentaries around 1251, very little of Aristotle's philosophy had been expounded to the satisfaction of Latin readers.[17] In embarking on his work as Aristotelian commentator, Albert intended to fill this *lacuna* both by presenting a literal exposition of the Stagirite's words and by interspersing his expositions with careful and thorough discussions, entitled *digressiones*, of the philosophical issues at stake.[18] Albert

---

17. Albert *Physica* 1.1.1, ed. Paul Hossfeld, in *Opera Omnia* 4/1 (Munster: Aschendorff, 1987), p. 1, lines 9–14. Hossfeld dates Albert's composition of the *Physica* to c. 1251–1252 (p. vi). Since Albert taught theology at Paris before coming to Cologne, and so was more attuned to scholastic developments in Paris than elsewhere, it is not surprising to find him depicting the contemporary situation as one in which his brethren could not find a sufficient account of natural science. As a result of the proscriptions of Aristotle's writings promulgated in the early statutes of the University of Paris, very few commentaries on Aristotle's *libri naturales* were produced at Paris prior to the middle of the thirteenth century, after which the books of natural philosophy were included in the set of books to be read for university degrees. Nonetheless, one must remember that a considerable amount of valuable work had already been done on Aristotle's *libri naturales* at Oxford in the first half of the thirteenth century. Albert's statements about the lack of commentaries should not be taken as describing the entire Latin-speaking world. On the details of Albert's life and writings, see James A. Weisheipl, "Life and Works of St. Albert," in *Albertus Magnus and the Sciences: Commemorative Essays*, ed. Weisheipl (Toronto: PIMS, 1980), pp. 13–51. For the development of Aristotelianism at Paris, see Fernand Van Steenberghen, *Aristotle in the West: The Origins of Latin Aristotelianism*, trans. Leonard Johnston (Louvain: Nauwelaerts, 1970), pp. 89–138. The history of Oxford Aristotelianism is outlined briefly in the pioneering study of D. A. Callus, "The Introduction of Aristotelian Learning at Oxford," *Proceedings of the British Academy* 29 (1943): 229–281.

18. Albert *Physica* 1.1.1 (4:1.23–30). Despite Albert's obvious attempt to forward his own interpretation of Aristotle through the *digressiones*, there is some question of the extent to which one may legitimately read even the *digressiones* as Albert's own

meant to make available, eventually, the whole of what he termed *philosophia realis* (comprising natural philosophy, mathematics, and metaphysics). He began, according to the order he thought best suited to learning, with natural philosophy and ended with metaphysics.[19] Furthermore, from the very first of his Aristotelian commentaries, the *Physica*, Albert displayed the remarkable command of the newly translated Islamic and Jewish philosophical sources that made his commentaries popular in the thirteenth century and thereafter. In his *Physica* particularly, as the editor of the recently published critical edition has noted,[20] Albert makes frequent use of Averroës's *Commentarium*, although he often disagrees sharply with Averroës's interpretation of Aristotle's *Physics*.

If we turn our attention to the end of Albert's commentary on *Physica* 1, where, as we saw above, Averroës most forcibly criticized the Avicennian schema of metaphysics, we discover that Albert has taken due note of Averroës's criticism and has prepared his own rejoinder:

> There is another criticism that Averroës gives of Avicenna and this one is even less appropriate <than the one just mentioned>. For Avicenna speaks the truth when he says that the same thing is not both sought in a science and presupposed in it, and that, since God and separate substances or forms are sought in first philosophy, they cannot, for that very reason, truly be presupposed in it and thus cannot be the subject of first philosophy. Furthermore, I have no idea why Averroës criticizes Avicenna, since what Avicenna says is necessarily the case. For we know that, since being is the subject of first philosophy, the divisions and properties of being are the matters treated in first philosophy, namely *per se* and *per accidens*, potency and act, unity and multiplicity, and separate and nonseparate. And, since

---

philosophy. In other passages, Albert claims that he is doing no more than stating the position of the Peripatetics. For an account of the significance of such passages, see James A. Weisheipl, "Albert's Disclaimers in the Aristotelian Paraphrases," in *Proceedings of the Patristic, Mediaeval, and Renaissance Conference* 5 (1982): 1–27. Although the issue of the extent to which the Aristotelian commentaries represent Albert's personal thought deserves further attention and study, its ultimate resolution is not required for the present paper, which only proposes to examine Albert's role as Aristotelian commentator.

19. Albert *Physica* 1.1.1 (4:3.29–41).
20. Paul Hossfeld, "Die Physik des Albertus Magnus (Teil I, die Bücher 1–4): Quellen und Charakter," *Archivum Fratrum Praedicatorum* 55 (1985): 52–53.

separate is a difference and property of being, it cannot <itself> be the subject. Furthermore, when the metaphysician is said to be concerned with separate things, 'separate' is not understood in the manner in which the Intelligences are separate, but rather it is understood of those things that are separate in their definition and mode of existence. These, moreover, are the things which are considered in their simple quiddities, just as we stated in the foreword of this book.[21]

Several points should be noted in regard to this text. First, Albert's remarks are directly aimed at Averroës's *Commentum* 83 on the first book of the *Physics* and show unequivocally what Albert's general attitude is toward the disagreement between the two distinguished Islamic philosophers: Albert aligns himself with Avicenna. To state as much may seem to belabor the obvious, but the importance of doing so will be appreciated later when we encounter texts in which Albert uses language drawn from Averroës to express a doctrine rather different from that of the Commentator. Second, the reasoning that Albert gives for siding with Avicenna restates Avicenna's own reasoning but is made somewhat more precise through the introduction of the technical terminology of *differentia* and *passio* that is taken from the *Posterior Analytics*. 'Separate' cannot itself be the subject of a science, if it is shown to be the property of something else in that science. But this is precisely, Albert reasons, what happens in metaphysics. 'Separate' is demonstrated to be one of differences characteristic of being. The subject of metaphysics cannot, therefore, be a separate entity, whether the latter be identified with God, the Intelligences, or Separate Forms. Third, the notion of 'being' in the Albertian phrase 'being insofar as it is being' clearly does not carry the connotations associated with Averroës's phrase *de ente simpliciter*; the being with which the metaphysician deals does not signify primarily the separate entities. Lastly, there seem to be, by implication, two different meanings to the term 'separate'. 'Separate' denotes a difference and property of being, but 'separate' also describes a characteristic belonging to all the objects of metaphysical investigation. Yet no explanation of the latter is given in this text, and the reader is referred to the prooemium for further information.

21. Albert *Physica* 1.3.18 (4:76.37–56). Unfortunately, neither Zimmermann nor Doig seems to have known of this text, which provides the key to understanding Albert's whole position on the subject of metaphysics.

Returning to the prooemium, we find the appropriate place in a section wherein Albert is discussing the three parts of philosophy and the formalities of their respective objects. Things are purely intelligible, Albert tells us, which are abstracted from motion and matter both according to their definition and mode of existence (*secundum esse et diffinitionem*). Those things which are abstracted from motion and matter only according to their definition and not their mode of existence are both imaginable and intelligible. Finally, those connected with matter and motion both in definition and mode of existence are sensible, imaginable, and intelligible.[22] The objects so described, moreover, correspond respectively to the sciences of metaphysics, mathematics, and natural philosophy.[23] Furthermore, Albert gives substance as an example of an object that is purely intelligible, describing it in terms similar to those found in the text quoted above: "For if the definition of substance insofar as it is substance is given, it will be one abstracting from all magnitude and all sensible things. And, for that reason, its definition will be given through simple quiddities which are grasped by the intellect."[24] Added to what Albert has said elsewhere, this text implies that the intellect reaches a level of understanding at which it grasps what substance and other metaphysical notions are without adverting to the objects of sense or imagination. To be abstract in this manner belongs to the object apart from the mind's consideration (*secundum esse et diffinitionem*), yet clearly abstractness in this sense is not identified with the mode of existence belonging to God, angels, or separate souls. Instead, what abstract means in this context is that a given object is independent from matter and motion at least inasmuch as it instantiates such a notion as substance, since substance as such need not be in matter,[25] although in the instance of a physical thing it is in fact found in matter. Indeed, as we will see shortly, and as

---

22. Albert *Physica* 1.1.1 (4:2.51–59).
23. Albert *Physica* 1.1.1 (4:1.49–60). On the various *ordines* of the sciences in the thirteenth century, see Robert Kilwardby, *De ortu scientiarum* 63, ed. Albert G. Judy, Auctores Britannici Medii Aevi 4 (Toronto: PIMS, for the British Academy, 1976), lines 214–219.
24. Albert *Physica* 1.1.1 (4:2.59–63).
25. Albert *Physica* 1.1.1 (4:1.60–67).

Dähnert noted,[26] Albert tends to call objects of this metaphysical sort 'divine' and even refers to them as the immediate outpouring of God.

Nonetheless, a hermeneutical difficulty would seem to obtrude itself at this point, because Albert does not use 'separate' in the texts just discussed but, rather, 'abstract' or 'abstracted'. Fortunately, Albert himself connects 'separate' and 'abstract' while explaining in what sense the objects of natural philosophy are sufficiently stable and mobile to serve as objects of scientific knowledge:

> To understand this point, it is necessary to know that the things which are abstract or separate are abstracted in two modes, namely through their definitive nature—just as was said above—when the defining notes do not involve motion and sensibile matter, but are prior to these according to nature. And such a type of abstraction is found in nothing belonging to physics, whether the physical be taken as a subject or as a property proved to belong to a subject. There is, moreover, abstraction of the universal from this particular signate thing, such as occurs when we consider wood according to its nature and own mode of existence and not insofar as it is this wood, which is this cedar or this palm. And this type of abstraction is necessarily found in every science, since all science is concerned with the universal.[27]

In the first of the two modes of abstraction mentioned by Albert, the things abstracted are said to be such in their own nature which is understood to be prior to both motion and sensible matter. Such a mode of abstraction, moreover, is said to be outside the realm of physics. Clearly, what Albert intends by abstraction here is precisely what he means by abstract in the text quoted immediately above, except that here he explicitly connects abstraction with separation. Hence, we are justified in using both the latter texts to illuminate Albert's description at the end of the first book of the *Physica* in which he hinted that there were two senses of 'separate' in metaphysics, one a property and difference of being and another a characteristic belonging to all metaphysical objects. Furthermore, the texts on abstractness and separation in the prooemium of Albert's *Physica* give

---

26. Ulrich Dähnert, *Die Erkenntnislehre des Albertus Magnus: Gemessen an den Stufen der Abstractio* (Leipzig: S. Hirzel, 1934), p. 126, especially n. 51.

27. Albert *Physica* 1.1.2 (4:5.1–14). Note especially the phrase "ea quae abstrahuntur sive separantur."

us an insight into what he means by separate as a characteristic of all metaphysical objects. He teaches that in understanding any object metaphysically, the mind must grasp it without reference to, and apart from, matter and motion. Why? Because the object in its metaphysical nature transcends matter and motion—the object instantiates features that have nothing to do with, and are intelligible apart from, matter and motion. But to claim the latter is surely not to claim that a being or beings exist *tout court* apart from matter and motion, let alone to prove it. The latter, however, is exactly what is meant in metaphysics when *separatum* is used as a difference and property of being. Accordingly, Albert carefully distinguishes between the two senses of *separatum*, thereby implying that the origin of Averroës's mistaken analysis of the subject of metaphysics lies in his failure to make such a distinction.

If we summarize what we have learned from Albert's *Physica* regarding his position on the subject of metaphysics and the place within metaphysics for proofs for God's existence, we can state the following. First, with Avicenna, Albert explicitly argues that the existence of separate entity is proved in metaphysics and nowhere else. Second, Albert identifies the being of which the metaphysician treats not with the separate entities but in a manner similar to that of Avicenna. Accordingly, we may conclude that Albert's position in the *Physica* on the subject of metaphysics owes much more to Avicenna than to Averroës. Let us now turn our attention to Albert's *Metaphysica*, written some fifteen years later.

ALBERT'S METAPHYSICA

After a prooemium in his *Metaphysica* similar to that found in the *Physica*, Albert raises the question of what the subject of metaphysics is. He lists three opinions: one opinion according to which the ultimate causes are the subject; a second, according to which God and divine things are the subject; and a third, according to which being insofar as it is being is the subject. Clearly enough, this list of candidates for the subject of metaphysics derives from Avicenna's *De prima philosophia*,[28] but so too do many of Albert's

---

28. Compare Avicenna *Metaph.* 1.1.1, which also lists the same three possible subjects for metaphysics.

reasons for accepting the last candidate, being insofar as it is being, and rejecting the other two. What perhaps is more immediate to our purpose, however, is Albert's reasoning for rejecting the second opinion, for this, as we saw above, is the opinion of Averroës:

> That this opinion is mistaken is evident through this <argument>. No selfsame thing is both the subject and something sought in a science. God and separate divine things are sought in this science. Therefore, they cannot be the subject of this science.
>
> Furthermore, the parts of many things which are proved in this science are not reducible to God as to something commonly predicated of them, whether community be taken in the sense of a genus or in the sense of analogy.
>
> The properties, moreover, considered in this science, which were enumerated above, do not follow immediately upon God and divine things. Therefore, God cannot be the subject of this science.[29]

Albert shows no sign here of changing his mind regarding the opinion that God or separate entities are the subject of metaphysics, although he does not mention Averroës's name in connection with this opinion as in the *Physica*. Instead, Albert seems to have elaborated even more thoroughly his reasons for rejecting such an opinion by reducing his objections to two tersely stated syllogisms and an enthymeme. Each of these syllogistic arguments, moreover, points out a respect in which metaphysics would fail to meet the criteria of scientific knowledge laid down in the *Posterior Analytics*, if God or separate entities were posited as its subject. The first argument shows that if God were the subject, metaphysics would be a science in which the same thing is presupposed and proved. The second claims that if God were the subject, metaphysics would have no common predicate in its demonstrative syllogisms, contrary to the Aristotelian canon of *dici de omni*. The third indicates that if God were the subject of metaphysics, the Aristotelian rules of *dici per se* and *dici de primo* would be broken, since many of the properties demonstrated in metaphysics do not follow immediately upon God or divine things.[30]

---

29. Albert *Metaphysica* 1.1.2, ed. Bernard Geyer in *Opera Omnia* 16 / 1 (Münster: Aschendorff, 1960), p. 4, lines 38–50.

30. On the conditions for scientific knowledge, see Aristotle, *Posterior Analytics* 1.4.73a21–74a4. For Albert's account of these conditions, see his *Posteriora Analytica* 1.2.7–15, ed. Auguste Borgnet, in *Opera Omnia* (Paris: Vivès, 1890), pp. 36–59.

But to provide evidence that Albert still rejects the opinion that God or separate entity is the subject of metaphysics in the *Metaphysica* is not, in itself, a sufficient indication of Albert's own position on the subject of metaphysics or what place proofs for God's existence occupy within his notion of metaphysical knowledge—although the passage quoted immediately above might be sufficient to indicate his continued dependence on Avicenna. For information on these matters, we must turn, instead, to Albert's positive descriptions of the subject of metaphysics and to his account of book lambda of Aristotle's *Metaphysics*.

Albert's *ex professo* solution to the question about the subject of the *Metaphysica* is quite similar to the description of metaphysics given at the end of the first book of his *Physica*. The true subject of metaphysics is said to be being insofar as it is being (*ens inquantum est ens*) and the things following upon being as such are claimed to be the properties (*passiones*) of being. The items listed as properties of being are cause and effect, substance and accident, potency and act, and, significantly, separate and nonseparate.[31]

Likewise, in the very first chapter of his *Metaphysica*, Albert contrasts metaphysics with the other speculative sciences in much the same way he does in his *Physica*. But in the course of doing so, Albert also gives us a brief account of the sense in which metaphysics is transcendent and divine:

> This science is called transphysical because that which is a nature determined by quantity or contrariety is based upon the principles of simple being [*esse simpliciter*], which <principles> altogether transcend everything called physical. <This science> is called divine, moreover, because all such principles are divine and best and first, giving to all other things the fullness of their being. For the being [*esse*] which this science considers is not conceived as confined to this <thing> or that, but rather insofar as it is the first outpouring of God and the first created thing prior to which nothing else has been created. . . . Among the theoretical sciences, moreover, the divine science which we now are treating excels <others> in that it provides the basis for the subjects, principles, and properties of all the other sciences and is not based, in turn, on any other. And this <science> is the perfection of the divine intellect within us in that it is about objects of thought [*speculationibus*] which are not connected with

---

31. Albert *Metaphysica* 1.1.2 (16:4.51–56).

the continuum and time but are simple, being pure from things such as these which overshadow the divine being [*esse divinum*] and firm in that they are the basis of others, yet are not based on others in turn.[32]

Despite the manifest similarity between this text and the *Physica* in regard to the transcendence of being, a new note is introduced here. The being treated by the metaphysician is identified with the first created thing of the Pseudo-Aristotelian *Liber de causis* and is described in Neoplatonic overtones as the immediate outpouring of God. Hence, although Albert also employs the phrase *ens simpliciter* derived from Averroës, the meaning of that phrase is not at all the same as the one intended by Averroës. The being studied in metaphysics does not refer primarily or absolutely to separate entity or God, but to the first creature of God, being. This being is simple so far as it is no way connected with time and the continuum, a clear parallel to Albert's contention in the *Physica* that the objects of metaphysical speculation universally have the characteristic of being separate in the sense of being intelligible apart from motion and magnitude.

Furthermore, the connection of simple being (*esse simplex*) to being insofar as it is being is expanded upon by Albert in a later section of the *Metaphysica*. Metaphysics is claimed to be about four things: being insofar as it is being and its parts; the things following upon being as such, namely, unity and multiplicity; physical and mathematical entities inasmuch as they have their source in the principles of simple being; things wholly separate and ubiquitous in their existence, such as God and the Intelligences. Moreover, metaphysics retains its unity as a science, despite the diversity of the different items with which it deals because it treats all the things ennumerated under one formality,

---

32. Albert *Metaphysica* 1.1.1 (16:2.88–3.25). On the notion of *esse simplex*, see Leo Sweeney, "The Meaning of *Esse* in Albert the Great's Texts on Creation in *Summa de creaturis* and *Scripta super Sententias*," in *Albert the Great: Commemorative Essays*, ed. Francis J. Kovach and Robert W. Shahan (Norman: University of Oklahoma Press, 1980), pp. 65–95; and Sweeney, "Are Plotinus and Albertus Magnus Neoplatonists?" in *Graceful Reason: Essays in Ancient and Medieval Philosophy Presented to Joseph Owens, CSSR*, ed. Lloyd P. Gerson, Papers in Mediaeval Studies 4 (Toronto: PIMS, 1983), pp. 177–202. Albert's notion of *esse primum creatum* has been thoroughly explored in two other studies by Sweeney, "*Esse primum creatum* in Albert the Great's *Liber de causis et de processu universitatis*," *Thomist* 44 (1980): 599–646; and "A Controversial Text on *esse primum creatum* in Albert the Great's *Liber de causis et processu universitatis*," *Proceedings of the Patristics, Medieval, and Renaissance Conference* 5 (1982): 137–149.

which is their having being not bound up with the continuum and time ("secundum esse non conceptum cum continuo et tempore").[33]

What do these texts tell us about Albert's conception of metaphysical knowledge in the Metaphysica? As in his Physica, Albert maintains that the subject of metaphysics is being insofar as it is being (*ens inquantum est ens*), and he conceives being along Avicennian lines as something common, although his conception of being is much more indebted to Neoplatonic sources such as the *Liber de causis* than to Avicenna.[34] Furthermore, in the midst of Albert's descriptions of the subject and scope of metaphysics, we once again seem to encounter two different senses of 'separate'. The first, here equated with *esse simplex*, is a characteristic belonging to all objects of metaphysical speculation precisely because of their independence from material conditions such as time and the continuum. The other is a division or property of being instantiated only in some beings studied in metaphysics. The language of property (*passio*), moreover, hearkens back to the *Posterior Analytics* and reminds us that, just as Albert himself stated in the key text at the end of the first book of his *Physica*, separateness in the second sense must be demonstrated to be a property of being. In looking to Albert's commentary on book lambda of the *Metaphysics*, therefore, we would expect Albert to claim that metaphysics attains a distinctive knowledge of God as an *ens separatum*.

Do we find such a claim in Albert's account of book lambda? Certainly Doig could find no trace of one. He argued, partially on that basis, that Albert's scheme of metaphysical knowledge was Averroistic in its conception. Here, however, we must distinguish two issues. As has already been established, Albert's conception of metaphysical knowledge is sufficiently Avicennian to require that he attribute a unique knowledge of God to the metaphysician, a knowledge of God in some way consequent upon the metaphysician's unique subject matter and entirely distinct from any knowledge of God as First Mover in natural philosophy. Consequently, the first issue is whether Albert does claim that metaphysics attains to a knowledge of God

33. Albert *Metaphysica* 1.2.11 (16:28.61–90).
34. Ludger Honnefelder, "Der zweite Anfänge der Metaphysik: Voraussetzungen, Ansätze und Folgen der Wiederbegründung der Metaphysik im 13./14. Jahrhundert," in *Philosophie im Mittelalter: Entwicklungslinien und Paradigmen*, ed. Beckmann, Honnefelder, et al. (Hamburg: Felix Meiner, 1987), p. 172.

independent of the vicissitudes of natural philosophy, a demonstration of God as *causa essendi* and not merely as *causa motus*. Yet another issue is at stake, and it is on this also that Doig based his interpretation of Albert's position on the subject of metaphysics. That issue is whether Albert, in fact, offers any such proof of God's existence in his account of book lambda. Although this second issue deserves consideration, its solution is not necessary for determining Albert's position on the place of proofs of God's existence in the scheme of metaphysical knowledge, since Albert may consistently claim that metaphysics demonstrates God to be the cause of being without himself giving such a demonstration in his commentary. In turning to Albert's commentary on book lambda, then, we shall seek to settle only the first issue, whether Albert claims that metaphysical knowledge of God is knowledge of God as a *causa essendi*.

After explaining that the whole focus of the inquiry in book lambda is on substance and the principles and causes of substance, Albert introduces Aristotle's threefold division of substance. The division, Albert tells us, proceeds by distinguishing two primary types and then distinguishing two subtypes. The primary division is into sensible substance and supersensible substance, but the former category is further subdivided into corruptible and incorruptible. In regard to this division of substance, the ultimate task of metaphysics is to show the relationship among these types of substances. Albert describes how metaphysics accomplishes that task:

> And thus there are three <substances> in general: sensible, incorruptible, but mobile; sensible, corruptible, and mobile; supersensible, immobile, and separate; and we must discuss all of these according to the method and mode of this wisdom. For we shall show which is the immobile and separate <substance> and how it is the principle of mobile, incorruptible substance, and we shall show how immobile, separate substance is also the principle of sensible, corruptible, and mobile substance through the motion of incorruptible, sensible substance. And in this will be the end and fulfillment of this work which is called wisdom, since then we shall know completely true being in itself and in its parts and according to its own properties [*passiones*].[35]

Here Albert claims that metaphysics must identify separate entity and then show the connections among the three types of substance.

---

35. Albert *Metaphysica* 11.1.3 (16:462.28–40).

Showing the connections seems to amount to indicating how separate substance is the principle of both types of sensible substance. Furthermore, Albert's language indicates that he still considers a knowledge of separate entity to be an intimate part of metaphysics, for, as in the *Physica*, he uses the term *passio* to describe how the knowledge of separate entity fits into the scope of metaphysical knowledge.[36]

Yet one might attempt to argue that Albert's intention has changed from the earlier *Physica* to the commentary on book lambda, since the text given here from book lambda does not close off the possibility of an Averroistic reading. After all, Albert does not speak unreservedly of metaphysics demonstrating the existence of separate entity in the text I have quoted immediately above but, rather, of metaphysics' identifying separate entity ("quae est immobilis et separata"). Perhaps, then, what Albert has in mind is not a demonstration of separate entity at all, despite his use of *passio*. Perhaps all metaphysics does here is to identify more clearly the properties of God, whose existence has already been established through the proof of the Unmoved Mover, by showing how God is a principle of all other substances.

That such an Averroistic interpretation of Albert's commentary on book lambda is mistaken, however, can be readily seen from two other passages in which Albert takes pains to distinguish the metaphysician's knowledge of God from that of the natural philosopher. In the first passage, Albert comments on Aristotle's remark that it is incumbent upon the metaphysician to ascertain the elements of incorruptible, mobile substance (at 1069a32–33):

> For although in the physical <treatises> the elements of mobile substance have been taken up <for discussion>, nonetheless these elements have been understood of substance as mobile, not of substance as substance. But here we shall take up the elements of <mobile> substance so far as it is substance flowing from the First Formal <Principle> and Ultimate End; for this wisdom properly considers these causes. In the physical <treatises>, moreover, we considered both matter and efficient <causality>, and if we also spoke of form this was only of the form of the mobile and the end insofar as end is a term of the motion of a mover. Here, however, we shall show that the First and *per se* Efficient <Cause> is the Universal End and that from him flow all mobile substances and that he bears the

---

36. On Albert's use of *passio* to describe how separate entity is included under the subject of metaphysics, see above, note 22.

same relationship to the remainder of the universe that a general does to his army. For this <way of argument> is proper to this science and in this way we shall not at all be indebted to natural philosophy. Indeed, although we showed there through <a study of> motion that the First Mover is Unmovable, nonetheless we have not made clear that he is the Cause of all being [universi esse] both as a Form and as an End, and in this way we shall investigate the First Mover here.[37]

Likewise, in response to Averroës's argument that metaphysics only considers formal and final causes, Albert states:

> Nor should we say, as certain people do, that the philosopher of nature considers <only> efficient and material causes and the metaphysician formal and final causes. Because, although we have already shown in the third book of this wisdom that the first philosopher principally considers form and end (through which he demonstrates according to the proper mode of his wisdom, in that these causes especially give us scientific knowledge), nonetheless both the metaphysician and the natural philosopher consider all four causes. But the natural philosopher considers these <causes> insofar as they are the principles of mobile <substance>, whereas the metaphysician traces back [reducit] efficient <causality> into the First Form and Last End; and in this way He is the Cause of all being [universi esse] both as a Form and as an End. Furthermore, if the First Cause is shown to exist [accipiatur] through motion, this is not so that he may be known as the Mover of such a motion, but rather insofar as he encompasses in his Power and Form both the mobile and motion, the former of which is <but> the instrument of the outflowing of all being from Him [fluxus totius entis ab ipso]. And in this way, the natural philosopher does not consider Him.[38]

Albert's intention in these texts is unambiguous. He wishes to distinguish the natural philosopher's knowledge of God from the metaphysician's. On what basis does he do so? Albert contends that the metaphysician, proceeding in the science of being as being, knows God as the cause of being (*causa universi esse*), and not simply as the cause of motion. Indeed, Albert elaborates the last point in the second text quoted so as to avoid all confusion; God may be known through motion but God is known in metaphysics not as Mover but as the Source of being. Motion simply serves as the means by which we know that God is the cause of being, just as, in the entitative order,

---

37. Albert *Metaphysica* 11.1.3 (16:462.53–71).
38. Albert *Metaphysica* 11.1.3 (16:462.81–463.10).

motion serves as the instrument by which God communicates being to the universe. As expected, therefore, Albert does attribute a unique knowledge of God to the metaphysician in that Albert claims the metaphysician knows God to be the cause of being and not simply the cause of motion. Moreover, if we examine these texts for information regarding what type of proof or proofs a metaphysician would use to show the existence of God, they seem to require arguments in the orders of formal and final causality, but also, according to the second text, efficient causality.[39] Yet to trace where or how Albert gives proofs of this sort would exceed, as was already pointed out, the scope and theme of this paper.

After considering all the pertinent texts, we must conclude that Albert's position on the subject of metaphysics is much more indebted to Avicenna than to Averroës. With Avicenna, Albert denies that God is the subject of metaphysics, contends that the subject of metaphysics is being insofar as it is being, and reserves the knowledge of God as the cause of being to the metaphysician. The texts in which Albert describes the metaphysician's knowledge of God, moreover, indicate that Albert believes there to be proofs for God's existence in the orders of efficient, formal, and final causality distinct from the proof of an Unmoved Mover in natural philosophy. Yet there is a certain tension unresolved in Albert's position on the subject of metaphysics, a tension first described by Zimmermann, but more recently studied by Thomassen and Honnefelder.[40] Although Albert continues to use

---

39. Albert hinted in the *Physica* that the metaphysician would use efficient causality as one of the means by which to reach the First Cause. In commenting on the natural philosopher's use of efficient causality, he writes, "Et ideo omne principium physicum et omnem causam physicam accipit et colligit [sc. physicus], sed tamen non omnem causam efficientem nec omnem finem. Si enim acciperet omnem causam efficientem, oporteret, quod extenderet se ad aliquid non-physicum, *quoniam prima causa est efficiens per essentiam suam, et de illa non intendit physica, sed prima philosophia*. Eodem autem modo est de fine ultimo, qui est finis universitatis et est in prima causa sicut in duce exercitus." See Albert *Physica* 1.1.6 (4:9.60–69; emphasis mine).

40. Zimmermann, *Ontologie oder Metaphysik?* p. 155. Although his book is mainly devoted to studying how metaphysics fits into Albert's theory of human intellectual development, Thomassen makes some perceptive remarks. See Beroald Thomassen, *Metaphysik als Lebensform: Untersuchungen zur Grundlegung der Metaphysik im Metaphysikkommentar Alberts des Grossen* (Münster: Aschendorff, 1985), pp. 61–82, especially pp. 77–79. Examining the various conceptions of the subject of metaphysics

the language of *passio* to describe how discussions of separate entity fit into metaphysics, he also claims that God and divine things are included under metaphysics as principles of the subject, as principles of being.[41] Such language, anticipatory as it may be of Thomas Aquinas's position on the relationship of God to the subject of metaphysics, is rather difficult to relate to Albert's idea that 'separate' is a property of being. It is perhaps even more difficult to reconcile the language with Albert's notion that metaphysics has a single subject. For Albert never explains how discussions of God would fit into metaphysics, if God is taken up in metaphysics not only as 'separate entity' but also as the principle of the subject of the science.[42] Nonetheless, despite troublesome passages indicating that Albert had other ideas on the subject of metaphysics which he never integrated into a coherent theory, the substance of Albert's views, as has been made clear from the present paper, derive from Avicenna.

St. Bonaventure University

---

throughout the High Middle Ages, Honnefelder traces the tension described here back to Aristotle, labeling it 'onto-theological'. See Honnefelder, "Der zweite Anfang der Metaphysik," pp. 164–167 and 171–177.

41. Albert *Metaphysica* 6.1.3 (16:305.75–306.4). See also note 33, above.

42. Indeed, in at least one place Albert shows his reluctance to confine God to any of the divisions of being which he usually gives by suggesting that antecedent to any of them is the division of being into *ens a seipso* and *ens ab alio*. See Albert *Metaphysica* 1.4.8 (16:57.62–79).

Towards a Narrative Understanding of Thomistic Natural Law

PAMELA M. HALL

I wish to discuss Thomistic ethics in this essay in a way that seeks to integrate Aquinas's natural law teaching with his treatment of the virtues, most particularly with the virtue of *prudentia* or practical wisdom.[1] Natural law's importance in the moral philosophy of Saint Thomas has been given undue and autonomous emphasis in my view; I want to make a case that any account of natural law that neglects the role of practical wisdom—and of the other virtues as well—in the natural law's development and application simply falls into incoherence. But there have been philosophers who have seen problems with reconciling practical wisdom and the natural law within Aquinas's moral teaching, and I will begin with a discussion of some of the difficulties they have seen.[2]

---

1. *Prudentia* is the Latin translation of Aristotle's *phronesis*. I take the term "practical wisdom" to best translate *phronesis* and *prudentia*, words that, as I say below, are roughly synonymous; I suggest some differences later in my essay. When I use the English word "prudence," I mean it as a synonym for Thomas's *prudentia*.

2. In the discussion that follows, I will restrict comment to only a few philosophers writing on Aristotle and Aquinas. Of course, a massive body of scholarship addresses Aristotle's ethics as well as Thomas's natural law theory. It is my desire in this essay to speak incisively and clearly about a specific set of issues. I believe this can best be done by addressing the primary texts in Aquinas himself, without repeated

Students of Aquinas have long been troubled by apparent incompatibilities between Thomistic and Aristotelian ethics. Foremost among these incompatibilities is the tension between the standards of right action that they employ. Aristotle holds *phronesis*, the practical wisdom of the fully virtuous person, to be the chief determinant of right action; further, he says very little, and that little is obscure, about natural or nonconventional justice. Aquinas, on the other hand, propounds the doctrine of natural law precisely in order to describe a nonconventional standard of justice accessible to all rational creatures. In this context Thomas recalls the remarks of Paul in Romans 2:14: "where the gentiles who have not the law do by nature those things that are of the law."[3] Aquinas sees this Pauline teaching as presupposing a natural law, one consistent with divine law but not requiring special revelation. Aristotle and Aquinas thus appear to hold different, and perhaps incompatible, standards of justice. This difference of opinion goes beyond a possible disagreement between Aquinas and the pagan philosopher he so esteemed; Thomas imports the standard of practical wisdom, what he calls "prudence," into his own ethics. There then look to be two distinct standards of right action within Thomistic ethics itself. If these standards are separate and unintegrated, Thomas faces the charge of a naive or immature eclecticism. If these standards are not only separate but incompatible, Thomas faces the far more serious charge of internal inconsistency. What I want to defend is an interpretation of Aquinas that reconciles practical wisdom and the natural law; such an account may also render his ethics more deeply Aristotelian than it is sometimes taken to be.[4]

---

reference to other interpretations and perspectives. I invite Nussbaum and Goerner into the discussion because their particular interpretations, which are also concerned with connections between practical wisdom and law in some sense, help to draw out important issues that I wish to address. I do not pretend, of course, that theirs are the only important interpretations of Aristotelian practical wisdom or of Thomistic natural law.

3. Quoted by Thomas in the *Summa theologiae* 1-2.91.2. Translations from the *Summa* are my own unless otherwise noted. The Latin text from which I am working is that of the Leonine edition of *Opera omnia* (Rome, 1882–).

4. In all of this presentation, I acknowledge my indebtedness to Alasdair MacIntyre, whose discussion of these issues in chapters 9 and 10 of *Whose Justice? Which Rationality?* (Notre Dame: University of Notre Dame Press, 1988) taught me a great deal.

A NARRATIVE UNDERSTANDING OF NATURAL LAW 55

Let me now describe further the potential incompatibilities between prudence and natural law.

I am taking Aristotelian *phronesis*, roughly synonymous with Thomistic "prudence," to be a capacity for judgment in individual cases that takes account of the particular circumstances of each situation. This excellence is dependent, as are all the virtues on Aristotle's view, on the proper early moral education provided by the community of the *polis*. Well-developed *phronesis* is the virtue that completes all the other virtues. That is to say, it makes out of what is originally mere habituation, the stuff of early moral training,[5] action that is rational and fully deliberate. Practical wisdom governs an agent's deeds in such a way that he or she always acts to achieve the good in individual circumstances. It thus perfects all other virtues because it determines their exercise at any particular time; for this reason the other virtues are immature and, as it were, without proper counsel if *phronesis* is lacking. While desire for the proper end is secured by habituation primarily, these ends would never be achieved without the deliberations of *phronesis* regarding the means to those ends.[6] Further, the virtuous agent possessed of practical wisdom recognizes the good that he or she seeks to achieve as good; this is to say that the phronetic person sees the point of his or her earlier habituation. What I want to emphasize in this short summary of Aristotelian teaching are the following points. First, *phronesis* is chiefly a capacity for judgment about how to achieve the good with respect to a particular circumstance, i.e., it must needs attend to particulars in securing these means. Second, its development presupposes the moral training provided by a specific kind of community, the *polis*; this training sets the ends at which phronetic deliberation aims. Yet only with the acquisition of practical wisdom comes a right appreciation of the goods into desire of which the agent has been habituated.

Let me now proceed to a brief exposition of Thomistic natural law. In doing so, I will postpone more sophisticated exegesis until later. I take what I will say here to be more or less uncontroversial, i.e., to be acceptable according to most understandings of Thomistic natural law. I base my remarks chiefly on that section of the *prima*

---

5. See *Nicomachean Ethics* 2.3.1104b9–13. The translation is my own.
6. See *Nicomachean Ethics* 6.13.1145a5–6.

secundae of the *Summa theologiae* that treats of laws; I will refer as well to other portions of the *Summa*. Natural law, on Aquinas's view, derives from certain claims about human nature a set of exceptionless rules with respect to types of actions.[7] If one then adopts the standard of natural law, one must ignore all but the relevant type-differences when deliberating about actions in any particular situation. Of course, any action and any situation can be described in an infinite number of ways; for the natural law theorist, what matters is whether or not any part of the description of a given action falls under the natural law's prohibitions or prescriptions concerning kinds of actions. For example, if a proposed action counts as a genuine instance of adultery, or murder, or lying, then that action is forbidden, on Thomas's view, no matter what additional descriptions might be supplied. There is then a *prima facie* philosophical incompatibility between these two standards, insofar as a morality which attends to the particulars of a situation, as does Aristotle's, might be seen to conflict with a morality that judges according to general types or categories of actions.

Lest I be accused of addressing a contrived conflict, I note here that recent philosophers have cited this difference between Aristotle and Aquinas in criticisms of Aquinas. Martha Nussbaum in particular has found fault with Thomas's rule-following ethics over and against what is on her view the superior standard of the Aristotelian virtues, with its stress on perception and moral imagination.[8] On her view, an ethics of exceptionless rules must fail to do justice to the unique particulars

---

7. Ultimately I do not want to refute this traditional view but, rather, to reshape it; it is to the core sense of natural law, the *inclinationes*, that primary emphasis belongs. Traditional interpretations of Thomas's natural law theory have unduly emphasized the role that rules play and, I will argue, neglect an explanation of their origin. For the following point about crucial issues for the natural law theorist, and Thomas in particular, I am indebted to Herbert McCabe's clarity in his own formulation of this point; see his *What Is Ethics All About?* (Washington, D.C.: Corpus Books, 1969).

8. The dim view that Martha Nussbaum takes of Aquinas is most explicit in an early work, her commentary on Aristotle's *De motu animalium* (Princeton: Princeton University Press, 1978), in the essay "Practical Syllogisms and Practical Science." But her critique of any ethics employing exceptionless rules continues in even her more recent work. See her "The Discernment of Perception: An Aristotelian Conception of Private and Public Rationality," in *Proceedings of the Boston Area Colloquium in Ancient Philosophy*, ed. John J. Cleary, vol. 1 (Lanham, Md.: University Press of America, 1986).

of a given situation; likewise such a system underemphasizes the role that "right emotion" must play in mature moral action. She wishes to allow for a certain "improvisation" even within rule following itself. But there are also others who, with greater sympathy for Aquinas, find the standard of natural law inferior. In his exegesis of Thomistic ethics, E. A. Goerner has stressed the superiority of practical wisdom over natural law, calling natural law "the bad man's view of Thomistic natural right."[9] According to Goerner, natural law secures the success of divine providence by fear of penalty, through consequences that flow naturally from violations of the law.[10] Practical wisdom, on the other hand, is embodied in the judgment of the virtuous person who acts through love of the good, not through fear of penalty. This standard of prudence is intrinsically superior to natural law, on his view, because of the nobler intentions of the agent and because the standard permits and requires attention to particulars. Such an attention will allow for variations on how the good is achieved; variation would not be possible should the natural law itself be taken as the primary standard of right action. Thus both Nussbaum and Goerner, from quite different starting points, find fault with the standard of Thomistic natural law understood in terms of a code of absolute rules. Nussbaum views prudence and the natural law to be separate and incompatible standards of right action. Goerner takes them to be at best functionally compatible standards, the natural law serving as a kind of initiation into the life of full virtue.

But what I am arguing for is an understanding of Thomistic natural law that in fact requires the activity of prudence in the application of the law's precepts and that requires prudence even for the discovery of the law. This issue of discovery is critical insofar as Thomas claims for this law a kind of promulgation independent of special revelation; this law must be accessible in some sense to everyone. Indeed Thomas's own general definition of "law" explicitly requires as much. In defining law *per se*, Aquinas assigns it four characteristics: "it is nothing else than an ordinance of reason for the common good, made by the one

---

9. See Goerner's "On Thomistic Natural Law," *Political Theory* 7 (1979): 101–122, and his "Thomistic Natural Right," *Political Theory* 11 (1983): 393–418.
10. For a discussion and critique of Goerner's interpretation of natural law, see my "E. A. Goerner on Thomistic Natural Law," *Political Theory* 18 (1990): 638–655.

who has care of the community, and promulgated."[11] Since the natural law is binding on all human beings, it needs must be satisfactorily published to them.[12] Thus, in a way different from Aristotle, Aquinas wishes to make progress in the moral life available to all people, regardless of individual community or history. Not that Thomas abolishes all operative notions of community: he simply creates a new kind, a community rooted in the essential characteristics of a species.

The natural law is thus primarily, on his view, the rational creature's "participation"[13] in eternal law, the law by which God governs the entire cosmos; the community to which the natural law pertains is the community of rational creatures. Indeed, law as Thomas treats of it in the *prima secundae* is an analogical term, and the heart of the analogy is the eternal law. All other forms of law of which Aquinas speaks (natural, human, divine) are in one way or another related to it. I shall focus primarily on how the natural law functions as the means by which rational creatures are subject to eternal law.

What does Thomas mean when he speaks of our "participation" in eternal law? Within his initial discussion of natural law, Thomas links it chiefly with God's providential ordering of the cosmos. Natural law is what orders us to our "proper act and end" by natural inclination;[14] this is to say that natural law, whatever else it involves, is primarily how we are directed to our end, which is ultimately God. This direction is not coercive or without sense for the rational creature; Thomas calls the guidance law gives "instruction,"[15] and he claims that it is the "light of natural reason," permitting us knowledge of good and evil, that so instructs us in natural law.[16] Thomas's own emphasis on the natural law is in terms of *inclinationes*, ways of being directed to one's end, not in terms of any set of rules.

---

11. *Summa theologiae* 1–2.90.4.
12. This definition of law (in 1–2.90.4) occurs in the most general treatment of law; Thomas proceeds in subsequent questions to extend the definition in specifying laws of many different kinds. The definition, being generic, cannot be adequate for understanding any particular form of actual law.
13. *Summa theologiae* 1–2.91.2.
14. *Summa theologiae* 1–2.91.2: "per quam habet naturalem inclinationem ad debitum actum, et finem."
15. *Summa theologiae* 1–2.90 prologue.
16. *Summa theologiae* 1–2.91.2.

All of this having been said, let me go on to flesh out my own interpretation of Thomistic natural law. I seek to bring together Aquinas's use of exceptionless rules and his new community of rational creatures within the natural law with his (more Aristotelian) emphasis on the virtues, especially the virtue of practical wisdom or prudence. I believe that the way in which Thomas speaks of natural law shows clearly that it is principally forms of directedness toward our proper ends or goods; this much has been noted already. But, and moreover, if one takes the rational character of this law seriously, then necessarily natural law also affords us understanding of the goods to which we are so directed. We must see and assent to the goods to which we are inclined by our natures. In this sense, natural law clearly is meant to have some of the components of Aristotelian *phronesis*, which also enables the appraisal and recognition of certain ends as good.

In question 94 of the *prima secundae*, Thomas discusses natural law and its most fundamental characteristics. He begins with a description of the way in which natural law is a habit;[17] natural law is a *habitus* insofar as we hold the fundamental principles of this law by the habit of synderesis. These principles form the core knowledge of natural law within us, and these principles, held by synderesis, are "indelible," persisting in even the most vicious.[18] Practical reason pertains to action, and so its first principles must pertain to what is to be sought or avoided within action.

> ... so good is that which first falls under the apprehension of the practical reason, which is ordered to action: since every agent acts for an end, which has the aspect of a good. Therefore, the first principle in the practical reason is that which is founded on the aspect of good, that good is that which all things desire. Hence this is the first precept of law, that good is to be done and pursued, and evil is to be avoided.[19]

Every rational creature has this much of an apprehension of good and evil, even babies and the damned.[20] Thomas also claims that

---

17. *Summa theologiae* 1–2.94.1.
18. *Summa theologiae* 1–2.94.6: "Quantum ergo ad illa principia communis, lex naturalis nullo modo potest a cordibus hominum deleri in universali."
19. *Summa theologiae* 1–2.94.2.
20. *Summa theologiae* 1 2.94.1 sc.

synderesis is infallible,[21] although application of its principles can be in error. I understand by this claim of infallibility a fundamental link with synderesis and what Thomas says regarding the will: that it chooses always under the formal aspect of goodness, the *ratio boni*.[22] I grant that this explanation of synderesis makes Aquinas's claim of synderesis's freedom from error peculiar. It may just be peculiar. I see its function as conceptual, determining how we consider actions, choices, objects of desire—i.e., in terms of goods and evils.

But why is synderesis so important for Aquinas? It is a Neoplatonic import within Aquinas's largely Aristotelian epistemology. Its presence seems therefore problematic and has certainly vexed Thomas's defenders to nightmare.[23] The importance of synderesis, on my view, springs from the crucial starting point it provides for any inquirer in the moral life; it is impossible, given this capacity, for an agent completely to lack guidance in the moral life. He or she has even initially some root, inerrant apprehension of the good with which to begin the moral life and moral deliberation. We begin with at least the necessary conceptual equipment. Notice that by adopting synderesis Aquinas suggests a possible solution to a problem set him by an inadequacy (from the Christian perspective) of Aristotelian ethics: How does one make participation in the moral life available to every human being, regardless of community, and yet answer the need for moral education? One begins to do this by synderesis, which provides the most basic tutelage in reasoning about action; it secures, infallibly, that the right questions will be asked, that actions will be reasoned about under the descriptions of good or evil.

Indeed I see synderesis, when coupled with the *inclinationes* that are primarily the natural law, as taking the place of the Greek *polis* in the role of providing initial moral training of the desires. The habit of synderesis alone is by no means sufficient for ethical guidance. The forms of directedness give practical content to the conceptual

---

21. *Summa theologiae* 1.79.12 ad 3: "quod huiusmodi incommutabiles rationes sunt prima principia operabilium, circa quae non contingit errare, et attribuuntur rationi, sicut potentiae, et synderesi sicut habitui: unde et utroque, scilicet ratione, et synderesi, naturaliter iudicamus."

22. *Summa theologiae* 1–2.10 and 18 in particular.

23. Witness the cottage industry John Finnis and Germain Grisez have built up in explaining the first principles within synderesis.

apprehensions of good and evil provided by synderesis. Thus there are on Aquinas's view activities and states that are naturally understood to be either goods or evils. This much can be counted on no matter what sort of human community it is to which one belongs. Such seems to be Thomas's claim when he says that the natural law, in its most general (*communissima*) principles, are known to all and cannot be erased from the human heart.[24]

Thomas speaks as well of the primary precepts of the natural law, which pertain to the goods to which our inclinations direct us by nature (recall this is the primary sense of "natural law" for Aquinas).

> ... thus it is that all those things to which the human being has a natural inclination, reason naturally apprehends as goods and consequently as things to be pursued, and their contraries as evil and things to be avoided. Therefore the order of the precepts of the natural law is according to the order of natural inclinations.[25]

In this secondary sense of natural law, the sense of its exceptionless rules, there are three sets of precepts according to Aquinas.[26] These correspond to the hierarchy of the *inclinationes* themselves. First is a set of precepts governing the preservation of human life, a good that we share with all living things. Second are precepts pertaining to the begetting and rearing of offspring, a good that we share with other animals. Finally, there are precepts governing the goods to which humans incline as specifically rational beings; Thomas mentions in particular our desire "to know the truth about God and to live in society."[27] Significantly, Aquinas, in his core treatment of the contents of the natural law, does not so much as spell out some of the actual rules of the natural law. Instead, what he is concerned with is establishing a fundamental link between any precept of the natural law and the goods to which these precepts are ordered. Thomas does not here tell us which rules are necessary for human beings to achieve the good of

---

24. *Summa theologiae* 1–2.94.6. Such a claim is easy to make but hard to prove; I suspect the only sort of proof possible would be phenomenological in kind. Simone Weil, in her writings about the "human personality," might provide a good example of such a proof. See the *Simone Weil Reader*, ed. George A. Panichas (New York: Moyer Bell, 1977), pp. 313–339.
25. *Summa theologiae* 1–2.94.2.
26. *Summa theologiae* 1–2.94.2.
27. *Summa theologiae* 1–2.94.2.

living in society; he tells us that some rules will be necessary to this end.[28] I emphasize this in the light of the characterization by many philosophers of Thomas as a legalist and of his natural law as chiefly rule oriented.

In what way are these precepts arrived at? What are their actual contents? I wish to maintain that they involve an articulation of which actions are conducive towards, or destructive of, those goods to which our *inclinationes* direct us. They are then further articulations of what we mean by good and evil; as such, they enrich the conceptual apprehensions of good and evil afforded by synderesis. But they may also enrich our understanding of the forms of directedness themselves insofar as they specify what is minimally necessary to attain those goods of our nature; indeed, the discovery and observance of these precepts may in part constitute these goods.

This discovery of the natural law occurs by way of reflection on the goods to which we are directed by our natures and then by discovery of the necessary means for achieving or constituting these goods. I want to stress that this inquiry takes place within a life, within the narrative context of experiences that engage a moral agent's intellect and will in the making of concrete choices. In attention to what makes up one's experience and in the making of choices, both good and bad, a human being augments understanding of his or her own nature and of what most promotes the flourishing of that nature. This process of inquiry is then one of practical reasoning, practical reasoning that can be carried on individually and communally. And in so mentioning practical reasoning, I do mean to imply the operation of some measure of phronetic, i.e., of prudential, deliberation.[29]

Such an understanding of natural law at least escapes the pitfalls of treating the rules of the natural law as though they were self-evident; the process I am describing would be far more rough-and-ready, also

---

28. Bear in mind that *praeceptum* need not mean "precept" in our sense of an actual rule.

29. Thomas's treatment of the actual reasoning of natural law in the later articles of question 94 shows just how far his understanding of the function of natural law is from a mechanical, legalistic understanding (see, e.g., 1–2.94.4). Not only do we need prudence to apply the "rules" of the natural law, but also the principles of the natural law are very general and must be specified and amplified before they are (practically) useful in guiding actual human choices.

far more historical. Discovery takes time. There is certainly warrant for such a reading of Aquinas, who repeatedly stresses how human custom and moral disposition can impact our knowledge of the natural law. In mentioning the "German robbers" who failed to recognize the prohibition against theft, Thomas mentions passion, evil custom, and an evil disposition of nature as damaging our ability to reason about our good.[30] To assert then that reasoning about our good at all, let alone the achievement of excellence in it, is deeply influenced by personal and social history hardly seems radical. Indeed, the presence of the moral virtues also disposes us well to discovery of the law of our nature.

This understanding of natural law also emphasizes its rational character. Only by the free exercise of our practical rationality could we discover the natural law, and this discovery would involve in part doing over again the work of the first legislator, God. In that sense, God first manifests God's providence through the eternal law (in which natural law participates) and so directs all creatures to God's own self. Just so, men and women imitate (and yet obey) divine providence by directing themselves in discovering and pursuing their good. Indeed, this renders intelligible Aquinas's claim, earlier in the *Summa*, that human prudence is included within the providence of God.[31]

It is essential to note that an understanding of particular rules of the natural law, e.g., "Never murder,"[32] is inseparable from an understanding of the rules' point and purpose. What the prohibition against murder prevents is the kind of disrespect for human life that would be destructive of life in community; without this law, a community could not exist in such a way as to pursue the various goods constitutive of social life. And such an understanding of the end or purpose of law can be given only by practical wisdom, on the Aristotelian and the Thomistic views. Thus to divorce natural law from the virtues is to misunderstand how both the law and the virtues

---

30. *Summa theologiae* 1–2.94.4.

31. *Summa theologiae* 1.22.2 ad 4. Note also that *providentia* and *prudentia* are linked etymologically. I make exactly this point as well in my critique, "E. A. Goerner on Thomistic Natural Law," p. 645.

32. I take an example from the Decalogue. Thomas notes in *Summa theologiae* 1–2.100.1 that the moral precepts of the Old Law really amount to the natural law, i.e., what we should have known anyway.

conduce human beings to their proper goods and is to misunderstand how one arrives at the specific rules of the natural law in the first place. Given that only practical wisdom can yield a realization of the ends we pursue as genuine goods, some degree of it must operate in the discovery of the natural law.

Aquinas says as much in his own discussion of prudence (practical wisdom).[33] Aquinas follows to some extent Aristotle when he says that moral virtue sets the ends for prudence.[34] But Thomas also states that prudence relates to synderesis, as "natural reason determines the ends of the moral virtues by what is called synderesis."[35] Thus prudence ultimately takes its goals from synderesis; indeed, Thomas goes on to state that prudence reasons from synderesis, "just as understanding of [first] principles moves scientific knowledge."[36] Here he seems to me to suggest that prudence precisely involves insight into synderesis even as it reasons from it. Such a reading would be much in accord with the account I have sketched concerning our "natural" knowledge—begun in synderesis but continued by a deliberative prudence—of good and evil. Prudence on this view functions, even in imperfect exercise, within our discovery of the natural law, helping to generate the very rules it will then work to apply and extend. For no rule, let alone those of the natural law, can be applied or constituted without an accompanying understanding of the rule's point as given by practical wisdom. This is so because to know how to apply a rule or even to know which rule to apply requires the exercise of practical judgment; such judgment would have to pick out of the situation at hand the relevant particulars in order to know which rule is appropriate for it. For example, even applying a rule as absolute as the prohibition against murder requires some grasp of what constitutes murder and a grasp of which situations fall under that prohibition, a task that is not always easy. Witness contemporary debates on the ethical status of abortion, capital punishment, and nuclear deterrence. One cannot intelligently select and apply a rule without some (prudential) grasp of the good that the rule is seeking to secure or protect. And some rules must be exceptionless, for example,

---

33. *Summa theologiae* 2–2.47–50 in particular.
34. *Summa theologiae* 1–2.47.2.
35. *Summa theologiae* 2–2.47.6 ad 1, to which compare 1.79.12.
36. *Summa theologiae* 2–2.47.6 ad 3.

the rule against murder, because certain goods are so crucial for an attainment of our end and because certain actions, such as murder, operate so as to destroy these goods.

Indeed, in his discussion of the moral precepts of the Old Law, codified in the Decalogue, Thomas says that these precepts are reducible to the natural law because they are accessible to natural reason.[37] The Decalogue then articulates what we should, as it were, have known anyway. He explicitly rejects the possibility that these laws could ever be dispensed with because

> the precepts of the Decalogue contain the very intention of the legislator, namely God. For the precepts of the first table, which are ordered to God, contain the very order to the common and final good, which is God. The precepts of the second table contain the order of justice to be observed among human beings, namely that no one do what is undue, and that to each should be returned what is owed: for in this manner are the precepts of the Decalogue to be understood. On this account, the precepts of the Decalogue are entirely indispensable.[38]

It is clear in this passage that Aquinas understands the precepts of the Decalogue, also of the natural law, to be in part articulations of what virtue is as it pertains to God and to life in human community. (Recall what he says in the *prima secundae* 94.3 about all acts of virtue being of the natural law.) These rules do not express merely contingent means to the good; they constitute in part what it is to be just to others and to worship God rightly. When observed in the spirit of the natural law, out of the desire for the goods to which the law directs us, these rules help to specify what virtue is and observance of these rules is constitutive of virtue.

That for Aquinas *phronesis* and the rules of the natural law stand independent of one another cannot then be so. Neither can it be that they are incompatible. We need practical wisdom in order to discover and apply the rules of the natural law; but we also gain our knowledge of the goods to which these rules should conduce from our essential and dynamic directedness towards these goods. This directedness is Thomas's primary sense of natural law. I hope it has become clearer in what ways certain current interpretations of Aquinas fall

---

37. *Summa theologiae* 1–2.100.1.
38. *Summa theologiae* 1–2.100.8.

short. Nussbaum, her emphasis on the virtues notwithstanding, fails to understand that the virtues themselves presuppose a fundamental orientation to the good; this orientation makes them means to, and also constitutive of, human flourishing. This is simply how Aquinas understands the natural law, not in terms of a code of rules. Likewise, Nussbaum fails to see in what way rule following, even of the kind she criticizes, requires some measure of prudence. A more careful reader of Aquinas but in a vein similar to Nussbaum, Goerner characterizes natural law persistently in terms of absolute rules; he, too, thereby neglects the more fundamental form of natural law in the *inclinationes*. By this neglect, he then fails also to see how the natural law and prudence are interdependent. Thus, by too completely severing the natural law from prudence, he does more than badly misinterpret Aquinas: he makes it impossible to understand how the natural law could function as a pedagogical tool (which is precisely the role on which Goerner lays stress). Without some understanding of the goods to which they are inclined by their natures (which would be given in prudential reflection), the Germans could never learn to recognize the "penalties" from which they suffer as penalties for the violation of the natural law. The natural law might be their scourge; it could never be their teacher.

I have thus far spoken of our knowledge of the natural law, aided by prudence, as a knowledge that is progressive and historical; we work to acquire understanding of our natures, and of the means for the flourishing of our natures, through a process of inquiry that goes on over time individually and communally. But in making this last point, I run the risk of treating natural law in isolation from another form of law from which it can never be wholly separate: human law. For human life is always lived in community, on Thomas's view, and thus the general principles of the natural law must be further articulated (and supplemented) according to the special needs of individual communities; human law is the law of specific communities. All such law should be derived from the natural law, Thomas argues. That derivation can occur in two ways:

> in one way, as conclusions from principles; in another way, as determinations of certain generalities. The first way is similar to that by which

demonstrative conclusions proceed from principles in the sciences. The second way is similar to that by which, in the arts, common forms are determined to a certain particular case.[39]

As an example of the first way, the way of conclusions from more general principles, Thomas offers the move from "Do harm to no one" to "Do not kill." As an example of the second way, the way of further specification, Thomas explains that while the natural law dictates that offenders should be punished, it does not say how; human law has the job of determining what the punishment should be for particular crimes.

Thus to speak of natural law as a guide for action by itself is a mistake; on Thomas's view, it is the responsibility of human law, the law of actual communities, to restate and to specify further what the natural law teaches. Indeed, natural law serves as the standard of justice for those making civil law. Thomas states that human law in discord with the natural law is "a corruption of law."[40] To go against the natural law is to act against the human good; thus, civil laws that are not ordered to the human good are, Aquinas says, more like "violence rather than laws."[41] Natural law is clearly intended to work always in tandem with human law in communities; all law is intended to make people good, Thomas says,[42] and both the natural law and human law command acts of all the virtues.[43]

Thus in his treatment of the human law Thomas again acknowledges the specific social forms of human life; natural law does not work in isolation, as a generic, and wholly adequate, moral standard applied in the same way across all communities. Instead, natural law requires further specificity in order to be effective as a guide to right action; this specificity is given in human law, as formulated by prudent legislators. At the same time, the natural law is the standard for judging the justice of human laws; this act of criticism is accomplished in part by

39. *Summa theologiae* 1–2.95.2. I acknowledge the help of the English Dominican Fathers' translation in guiding my own.
40. Ibid.
41. *Summa theologiae* 1–2.96.4.
42. *Summa theologiae* 1–2.92.1.
43. *Summa theologiae* 1–2.94.3 and 96.3. Not all the vices are punished under human law, however, lest the law become too burdensome and contempt for it be taught (96.2 corp. and ad 2).

assuring that the ends of human law coincide with the ends to which we are ordered by the natural law.

I want to break stride at this point by going back to a description I have given concerning discovery of the natural law. I have said that the process of discovering the natural law is a gradual one: it is a "historical narrative" involving reflection on who we are as a species and within community, reflection that is ongoing and corrigible. Such a process entails the activity of practical reason operating both on the level of the individual moral agent and, also importantly, on the level of the legislators and leaders of whole communities (within the scope of human law as well). Let me try to make some more specific remarks about this narrative process, and about what facilitates this process. My remarks here can only be open-ended and provisional; they will diverge from exegesis of Aquinas at key points, but (it is to be hoped) only to return with illumination.

First, determining what we are as a species must be a historical business. Knowledge of human nature is acquired gradually, by experience and reflection. No simple or intuitive path can arrive at an adequate account of what we are as creatures and of what conduces to our flourishing. Thus of course is there even less a way to derive precepts in a simple manner from knowledge of our natures. There can be no "reading off" of what to do from claims about our essence or character. Such claims are hard-won and subject to revision; what practical guidance such claims yield to us is likewise only carefully drawn out.

Second, discovery of the natural law, as I take Thomas to describe it, is extended through time and involves ongoing experience on both the individual and social levels. This narrative process of discovery coincides with, or rather presupposes, the narrative structure of human experience itself. The life of an individual, or of a community, is best represented in the terms of a story: this is the genre that most aptly captures the form of human experience. As Augustine notes in the *Confessions*, the very fact that our experience is distinguished in terms of past, present, and future is a wonder and a puzzle. Our lives are not only made up of a continual flow of sensations. They are also characterized by the intentions and projects that link the moment of the present with past and future actions, intentions, and projects.

In this regard, characterizing our temporal experience as a series of atomistic "moments" is unhelpful and obtuse. The "feel" of our time is not atomistic. It has duration, as well as linkage with the past and projection into the future.[44]

Likewise, it may only be by the living out of our plans and intentions that we can come to understand what we were seeking in those very plans and intentions. As Abigail Rosenthal puts it, "At minimum, a story is a purpose transformed into enough experience to allow that purpose to understand itself a little better."[45] This helps us to see why discovery of the natural law must be time-bound (and why our conclusions about it must be open to revision). It is in the pursuit (and, often, possession) of goods that we learn about what we did or did not really desire. This is of course a kind of self-discovery. Also important to remember is that our conceptions of goods, let alone our conceptions of the virtues, are always themselves particularized within a community or at the least a life. Reasoning, then, about what we need to flourish will, then, always be reasoning about particular goods in particular contexts. This is part of the practical nature of this inquiry.

Third, can we say anything general about the nature of these particular inquiries? Alasdair MacIntyre, in his own discussion of narrative in *After Virtue*, notes that the narrative stories of our individual lives share at least two common features: they are teleological, i.e., they aim at an end or goal; and they are unpredictable, i.e., subject to chance and to the intervention of others. Thus MacIntyre goes on to claim that the moral life is essentially a quest, a quest searching for what the good is for us, both as individuals and as members of humanity. He notes rightly that "a quest is always an education both as to the character of that which is sought and in self-knowledge."[46] For this

---

44. I wish to acknowledge my indebtedness in these matters to Stephen Crites, "The Narrative Quality of Experience," *Journal of the American Academy of Religion* 39 (1971): 291–311. My discussion compresses many of the points he makes at greater length.

45. Abigail Rosenthal, *A Good Look At Evil* (Philadelphia: Temple University Press, 1987), p. 13. Rosenthal uses in this book the notion of narrative as a way of describing different sorts of evil human "types."

46. See Alasdair MacIntyre, *After Virtue* (Notre Dame: University of Notre Dame Press, 1981), p. 204. My discussion of MacIntyre is drawn from his chapter 15.

reason MacIntyre gives the virtues such emphasis: they enable us to live out our questions well, to succeed at our quest. For reasoning well about our good (discovering the natural law in my understanding of Aquinas) as a quest is not a process that goes on in a vacuum. We do this work in the midst of, and about, the experiences and choices that constitute and shape our lives. This work occurs within and about the joys and sorrows, the suffering, the anxiety, the exhilaration, the ambiguity, and even the terror of living the moral life. Quests are taxing, trying affairs. About this Nussbaum has been right to stress the need for courage and for tolerance of ambiguity in the moral life. Behind or beneath this, however, I want to stress the commitment necessary to make possible the kind of inquiry I am describing. One must first believe the inquiry has a point, that how we live matters (and perhaps this is what MacIntyre means when he says that our lives are teleological). Quests, after all, are undertaken; we must begin by accepting the charge of inquiry. Our commitment to the inquiry begins to make possible the process of reflection, let alone the fear and trembling, of the discovery of the natural law.

Fourth, we began with claims concerning the narrative structure of experience and the narrative discovery of the natural law. But as we all learn, one fundamental aspect of our experience, and the fate of all plans we make and live out in experience, is the role of fortune in completing or confounding our plans. And if human experience is subject to chance, then we must wonder to what degree Fortune plays a part. MacIntyre himself opens up this question in *After Virtue*, in part to suggest that individual quests for the good may go unfinished, being interrupted by death.[47] But how seriously may misfortune impair our pursuit of the inquiry about the good? Recall that Aquinas denies that all knowledge of the natural law can be expunged from the human heart; he concedes that human community and passion can obscure the "particulars" of the law.[48] We are back in some way to the old Aristotelian problem concerning the necessity of proper moral upbringing for progress in virtue. If we give tragedy its full due, is it not possible that certain personal histories are too bereft of right teaching, too full of corrupt influence, to engender the questions that launch us on the quest for our good? About the natural law, we might

---

47. See MacIntyre, *After Virtue*, pp. 197–198.
48. *Summa theologiae* 1–2.94.4. The word Aquinas uses for "particulars" or "details" is *propria*.

ask if it can produce a just person from an unjust city.[49] My sense is that Thomas would deny this contingency; God's providence governs even Fortuna. Thomas certainly does deny the possibility of simple moral perplexity, in which a moral agent, without prior fault, cannot help but do wrong. I am not satisfied with this profession of faith in providence, so I raise it as a question.

In conclusion, let me multiply the senses of narrative to be recognized in Thomas. I have spoken in this essay of the natural law and the ongoing, narrative acquisition of knowledge of it. It is ongoing (1) in our coming to understand more about our natures and (2) in our coming to understand what means to choose in constituting the flourishing of our natures. Thomas repeatedly indicates that our inquiry regarding the natural law takes place socially and over time. Such indications include how prudence, which requires experience, is necessary for knowledge of the natural law. They also include his remarks about the Germans and how cultural (and moral) impediments to our knowledge of the natural law can exist.[50] Add to this the fact that human law is needed to articulate and to specify the natural law for particular communities. Thus citizens of communities will encounter present understandings of the natural law within the rules (and customs) of their own societies.

But my scenario of ongoing acquisition of (our knowledge of) the natural law is too simple as it now stands. Thomas builds into his account of law a fourth type, one that also is derived from the eternal law (divine providence), but that stands in curious relationship to the natural law itself. This fourth type is the divine law, the law that is revealed by God. This revelation comes in two distinct parts, the Old Law and the New Law. It is necessary, Thomas tells us, because natural law does not suffice to order us to God; although our *inclinationes* direct us to "connatural" goods, God alone can completely satisfy us, and God is utterly beyond the reach of our powers. Thus the divine law aids us so that we may attain God.[51]

Moreover, humankind suffers under the burden of sin, one manifestation of which Thomas also characterizes as a quasi-law.[52] The *lex fomitis* is the law of concupiscence (literally, the law of tinder

---

49. Or, to name a community even more proximate, from an unjust family?
50. See *Summa theologiae* 1–2.94.4 and 6.
51. *Summa theologiae* 1–2.91.4.
52. *Summa theologiae* 1–2.91.6.

or kindling—the fire in the flesh that is not completely subject to reason). It is a consequence of our primordial rejection of God, and thus the unruliness of our passions constitutes a further block to our pursuit of the good, even as understood in terms of the natural law. Thus our natural powers are not only limited; they are infirm. Divine law is necessary as a remedy for the effects of sin.

Thomas thus stresses not only the general social and historical nature of our inquiry and pursuit of the good; he indicates that there is one very specific community and history to which we all belong. We are children of Adam and Eve, and the history of us all is located within salvation history. Thus the narrative of Scripture is authoritative in its explanatory power of our condition (and that condition's remedy).[53]

Going one step further: Is there in Thomas a place for the deployment of stories within the work of ethics? Recall what was said earlier regarding the narrative structure of human experience itself. It would then seem that stories, speaking now of human constructs apart from Scripture, are powerful shapers and informers of the self-understanding of individuals and communities, being reflective of the fundamentally narrative character of human experience. These might serve as imaginative guides for us in the structuring and interpreting that must make up personal and communal histories. That Scripture is clearly the most authoritative story for Thomas need not entail the exclusion of other stories (either creative artifacts or histories) as influences or educators. Indeed, such stories would resemble Scripture in their use of metaphor and example.[54] Still there is a question: Does Thomas's own understanding of moral theology accommodate such a use of narrative? Can it as well supply an account of how such narratives would stand in relation to, or be integrated into,

---

53. See, for example, how Aquinas "reads" the infidelity of the Hebrews to the Decalogue (reducible to the natural law): "[God] decided to give human beings a Law which they could not fulfill of their own power so that, when they relied upon themselves they would discover that they were sinners, and, humiliated, would have recourse to the help of grace" (*Summa theologiae* 1-2.98.2 ad 3, after the Blackfriars translation). What we discover in reflection upon our natures is not just the natural law but also the fact that we cannot, and will not, do what we know is our good.

54. See Thomas's remarks about the appropriateness of the use of metaphor in Scripture, *Summa theologiae* 1.1.9.

philosophical argument *per se*? These concerns take us well beyond the scope of this present essay, but an answer to them would contribute to a richer understanding of Thomistic ethics as well as Thomistic method.[55]

Emory University

---

55. I gratefully acknowledge the support of the University Research Council of Emory University in giving me the leave time to pursue my study of Thomistic ethics. In a work in progress I am pursuing this last question regarding the senses of narrative in Aquinas.

St. Thomas Aquinas on Satisfaction, Indulgences, and Crusades

ROMANUS CESSARIO, O.P.

In order properly to elucidate the church's doctrine on indulgences, the theologian must study the practice of granting indulgences in the contexts of the satisfaction of Christ and of penitential works undertaken by Christian believers.[1] In his treatment of indulgences, Thomas Aquinas is concerned to explain how Christ's redemptive sufferings can spiritually benefit the members of the mystical body. Aquinas understands that, through indulgences, the church allots certain spiritual benefits to those who collaborate by one means or another in building up the mystical body.[2] In his view, then, the theology of indulgences simply develops the general theological axiom that one person can share according to some determined measure in

---

1. For the historical development of indulgences, see Bernhard Poschmann, *Der Ablaß im Licht der Bußgeschichte* (Bonn: Peter Hanstein, 1948).

2. For example, Nikolaus Paulus, *Indulgences as a Social Factor in the Middle Ages*, trans. J. Elliot Ross (New York: Devin-Adair, 1922), illustrates how the church related indulgences to various aspects of ecclesial communion. See the sections entitled "Indulgences for Ecclesiastical and Charitable Objects" and "Indulgences for Socially Useful Temporal Objects."

SATISFACTION, INDULGENCES, AND CRUSADES   75

the good deeds of another person. To put it differently, as much as Christians ought to pray for and help one another, indulgences are a way of giving concrete expression to the communion of saints.

Aquinas undertakes a broad, multifaceted study. Besides analyzing the nature of indulgences, he also illustrates their connection to the sacrament of reconciliation, defines the proper authorities for granting indulgences, and examines the necessary conditions for gaining an indulgence.[3] In the course of these discussions, Aquinas gives clear evidence that he appreciates how the thirteenth-century church had made canon law a principal means of establishing the principles of pastoral care. But since his theological project is not restricted simply to questions of jurisprudence and pastoral practice, Aquinas normally discusses such issues, including the canonical aspects of indulgences, within the broader contexts of soteriology and ecclesiology; as a result, his conclusions throw more than historical light on the meaning of an indulgence.

For a complete appreciation of St. Thomas's doctrine, two texts in his theological corpus merit special attention. The principal places where Thomas deals with the theology and practice of granting indulgences include his *Scriptum super libros Sententiarum* 4.20.1.3–5 and *Quaestiones de quolibet* 2 8.2. To be sure, the editors of the *Supplementum* to the *Summa theologiae* assembled three questions on indulgences, but Thomas himself set aside work on the *Summa* before he was able to confront the questions within its original framework.[4] The two *ex professo* discussions that he did complete belong to different periods in his career; they also represent different literary genres. In his "writings" on the *Sentences* of Peter Lombard, which Aquinas composed at Paris between 1252 and 1256, we recognize a

---

3. Peter of Bergamo's tabulation, *In Opera Sancti Thomae Aquinatis Index Seu Tabula Aurea Eximii Doctoris* (Rome: Editiones Paulinae, n.d.), distributes the thirty subjects related to indulgences under four headings: "In communi," "Ecclesiae," "Agens," "Quibus." The *Index Thomisticus* shows that the vast majority of this material occurs in Aquinas's *Scriptum* 4.

4. See *Summa theol*. suppl. 25, "De indulgentia secundum se"; 26, "De his qui possunt indulgentias facere"; 27, "De his quibus valent indulgentiae." James A. Weisheipl, *Friar Thomas d'Aquino*, 2d ed., with corrigenda and addenda (Washington, D.C.: The Catholic University of America Press, 1983), p. 362, explains that "the Supplement, intended to complete the *Summa*, is 'put together with scissors and paste from pieces cut out of Aquinas's writings on the *Sentences* (especially Bk. 4).'"

systematic treatment from a young theologian. But *Quaestio de quolibet 2*, recorded at Paris around 1270, gives us an insight into how the seasoned university professor handled the subject in open debate. In addition, the *De quolibet* 2 8.2 gives witness to a certain growth and change of theological perspective that, according to the opinion of some scholars, marks Aquinas's thinking during the second half of his academic career.[5]

Although I take into account pertinent material from the earlier treatment in the *Scriptum*, the text *De quolibet* 2 8.2 is the principal focus for this study. I also refer to Aquinas's teaching on merit and satisfaction, especially his mature treatment of those subjects in the *Summa theologiae*.[6] Still, the brief exposition in *De quolibet* 2 incorporates many of the basic theological principles that Aquinas considers indispensable for a comprehensive understanding of indulgences.[7] The crusading indulgences, as we shall see, afford him the occasion for articulating a theory concerning the place that indulgences occupy in the church's sacramental economy.

As a principal element of his analysis, Aquinas employs a traditional metaphor. He speaks about the spiritual treasure chest that contains the good works of Christ and the saints: the *thesaurus ecclesiae*.[8] Even if such language presents an unwieldy metaphor for

---

5. For example, R.-A. Gauthier, "La date du Commentaire de saint Thomas sur l'*Ethique à Nicomaque*," *RTAM* 18 (1951): 103, n. 91, argues that during the second Parisian regency, Aquinas was induced to "mitigate the excessive intellectualism that he had earlier displayed." See also Santiago Ramirez, *De hominis beatitudine* 3 (Madrid: CSIC, 1947), p. 192.

6. See Cessario, *The Godly Image: Christ and Salvation in Catholic Thought from Anselm to Aquinas*, Studies in Historical Theology 6 (Petersham, Mass.: St. Bede's, 1990), for an interpretation of Aquinas's texts on soteriology and Christian satisfaction.

7. *De quolibet 2* 8 contains two articles, each of which treats the forgiveness of sins. The first article asks whether the sin against the Holy Spirit remains unforgiveable. The second carries the title: "Utrum crucesignatus qui moritur antequam iter arripiat transmarinum, plenam habeat peccatorum remissionem?" I have consulted Sandra Edwards's translation, *Quodlibetal Questions 1 and 2*, Medieval Sources in Translation 27 (Toronto: PIMS, 1983). Edwards gives a general introduction to this literary genre and the issues discussed in the two questions.

8. Carl J. Peter, "The Church's Treasures (*Thesauri Ecclesiae*) Then and Now," *Theological Studies* 47 (1986): 251–272, examines the history and contemporary significance of this concept.

Christ's charity, Thomas nonetheless clearly distances himself from both mercantile views of redemption and physicalist interpretations of grace. In brief, he does not consider indulgences as a spiritual deposit-and-withdrawal system for building up heavenly merits, as if they were so much interest in a bank account.[9] Indeed, we can uncover no justification in Aquinas's theology for the well-known abuses of the later Middle Ages, especially the so-called sale of indulgences by professional "pardoners." One might even argue that if Aquinas's theological finesse in treating indulgences had shaped the practice of the church in the sixteenth century, they might not have been one of the issues that provoked Protestant reform. For Aquinas consistently demonstrates that indulgences form an integral part of the church's mission to communicate both the merits of Christ's sacrifice and his satisfaction to believers in the truth of the gospel.

HISTORICAL BACKGROUND: PARIS, 1269–1272

The historical circumstance that links the granting of indulgences to the church's promotion of the crusades serves as background for *De quolibet* 2 8.2. Aquinas inquires whether a crusader who dies before setting forth for the Holy Land and thereby escapes the hardships and duress of fighting the infidels actually gains a full remission of his sins.[10] The church had formally begun the practice of

---

9. To be sure, we have examples where Aquinas's language lends itself to such an interpretation, as when he suggests in the *De quolibet* 5 7.2 that meritorious deeds can remain with us "quasi apud Deum deposita," but the context clearly indicates that the idiom is suggested by the Vulgate, as for example in 2 Timothy 1:12, "Scio enim cui credidi, et certus sum quia potens est depositum meum servare in illum diem."

10. The twelfth-century Latin term is *crucesignatus*. Du Cange renders it as "Qui sacrae Crucis militiae nomen dabant," *Thesaurus* 2:1175–1176. Compare J. F. Niermeyer, *Mediae Latinitatis Lexicon Minus* (Leiden: E. J. Brill, 1976), who translates it as "croisé" in French and "crusader" in English. Although it could be argued that, given the terms of the theological discussion in article 2, a crusader who has taken the vow remains a crusader-designate until he actually completes the crusade, I have kept the term "crusader" throughout. For more on the history and significance of *crucesignatus*, see Maureen Purcell, *Papal Crusading Policy: The Chief Instruments of Papal Crusading Policy and Crusade to the Holy Land from the Final Loss of Jerusalem to*

granting plenary indulgences as part of its strategy for popularizing the crusades.[11] Admittedly, the exact nature of Pope Urban II's promise at the Council of Clermont (1095) remains a matter of dispute among medieval historians. Nevertheless, the record appears to show that the pontiff promised remission of all penitential practices incurred by the crusaders provided they confess their sins.[12] In an important study, Maureen Purcell points to a difference between the language allegedly used by Urban II at Clermont, "a full remission of enjoined penance," and the statement by the Fourth Lateran Council in 1215, which promises a "full remission of sin."[13] Either way, we can suppose that a certain confusion between what an indulgence accomplished and what constituted the actual remission of sins enveloped popular views on these matters.[14]

---

the Fall of Acre, 1244–1291, Studies in the History of Christian Thought 10 (Leiden: E. J. Brill, 1975), p. 5, n. 4; and Michael Markowski, "Crucesignatus: Its Origins and Early Usage," Journal of Medieval History 10 (1984): 157–165.

11. Nikolaus Paulus, Indulgences as a Social Factor, pp. 62ff., includes the crusades among other worthy enterprises that the church promoted through the granting of indulgences. For a comprehensive study of the relationship of indulgences to crusading, see Jonathan Riley-Smith, The First Crusade and the Idea of Crusading (Philadelphia: University of Pennsylvania Press, 1986), especially chapter 1.

12. See Mansi, SCC 20:816. The actual words quoted are "iter pro omni paenitentia reputetur." For a detailed analysis of the documentation concerning Pope Urban's famous speech at Clermont on 27 November 1095, see James A. Brundage, Medieval Canon Law and the Crusader (Madison: University of Wisconsin Press, 1969), pp. 30ff.

13. Purcell, Papal Crusading Policy, p. 36. For the text of Ad Liberandam Terram Sanctam of Lateran IV, see Antonio García y García, Constitutiones Concilii Quarti Lateranensis Una cum Commentariis Glossatorum, Monumenta Iuris Canonici, series A: Corpus Glossatorum 2 (Vatican City, 1981), pp. 110–118: "plenam suorum concedimus ueniam peccatorum."

14. Generally speaking, before Albert the Great indulgences were considered above all a commutation of poena, but afterwards theologians came to define them as a remission pure and simple. See Albert's Scripta Super Sent. 4.20.E.16: "Dicendum, quod diffinitiones datae satis possunt sustineri. Si quis tamen hanc dare vellet, scilicet quod 'indulgentia sive relaxatio est remissio poenae injunctae ex vi clavium, et thesauro supererogationis perfectorum procedens': puto, quod melius diffiniret." Albert completed this work before 1249. On the whole question of what indulgences were commonly understood to mean, see Hans Eberhard Mayer, The Crusades, 2d ed. (Oxford: Oxford University Press, 1988), pp. 293–295, n. 15.

Whatever Pope Urban's true intentions may have been, the fact remains that until the thirteenth century, developments in the doctrine of indulgences were almost wholly implicit in theological teaching on the sacrament of penance. By that time, theologians generally understood indulgences as supplying for the satisfactory works that ordinarily form part of the sacramental discipline. In the *tertia pars* of the *Summa theologiae*, written shortly after the *De quolibet 2*, Thomas explains that contrition, confession, and satisfaction are suitably designated as the parts of penance.[15] Indeed, penitential works such as prayer, fasting, and almsgiving—all of which can serve as works of satisfaction—gradually rectify the disorders of soul that result from a person's sinful actions. Even in his *Scriptum* on the *Sentences*, Aquinas introduces his treatment of indulgences towards the end of the tract on the sacrament of penance.[16] A century earlier, however, Peter Lombard had not considered the topic of indulgences important enough to include in the *Sentences* themselves (1155–1158). Still, the connection among the sacrament of penance, works of satisfaction, and indulgences remains important for appraising correctly the practice of granting indulgences in the thirteenth century.

Since physical participation in a military campaign inevitably involves personal hardships, such an enterprise easily could serve as a sort of satisfaction for sins. Accordingly, medieval inquiry normally included as a matter of course such questions as we find posed in *De quolibet 5* 7.2 (held in Paris at Christmastime 1271), "Whether

---

15. *Summa theol.* 3.90.2: "Sic igitur requiritur ex parte poenitentis, primo quidem voluntas recompensandi, quod fit per contritionem; secundo quod se subjiciat arbitrio sacerdotis loco Dei, quod fit in confessione; tertio quod recompenset secundum arbitrium ministri Dei, quod fit in satisfactione. Et ideo contritio, confessio et satisfactio ponuntur partes Poenitentiae." In addition, see Poschmann, *Der Ablaß*, especially pp. 36ff.

16. *Scriptum super Sent.* 4.20.1 a.3, "Utrum per indulgentiam possit aliquid remitti de poena satisfactoria"; a.4, "Utrum quilibet sacerdos parochialis possit indulgentiam dare"; a.5, "Utrum indulgentia valeat existentibus in peccato mortali." All in all, book 4 devotes nine distinctions to the sacrament of penance. The *quaestio unica* of the twentieth distinction includes two other articles on the effects of sin in the life of the believer, namely, a. 1, "Utrum aliquis in extremo vitae suae poenitere possit"; and a. 2, "Utrum poena temporalis, cujus reatus post poenitentiam manet, taxetur secundum quantitatem culpae." For a historical study of indulgences during the early scholastic period, see Nikolaus Paulus, "Die Ablaßlehre der Frühscholastik," *Zeitschrift für katholische Theologie* 34 (1910): 433ff.

a crusader who dies on the way to the Holy Land dies in a better state than one who dies on the return trip?" or, in *De quolibet* 2 8.2, "Whether a crusader who dies before he can take the journey across the sea has full forgiveness of sins?" Although today such queries may at first seem arcane, they nonetheless facilitate Aquinas's discussion of a range of issues related to Christian satisfaction. For example, he turns again and again to the merits of Christ himself, to the meritorious works of the saints, to the meaning of the *thesaurus ecclesiae*, to the purpose of satisfaction in the Christian life, and to the conditions that permit a person to gain an indulgence.

The quodlibets report public question-and-answer sessions that took place within medieval universities. At Paris, such quodlibetals were held only during Advent and Lent. Perhaps the exercise was considered penitential for the masters. Palémon Glorieux argues that such unprecedented public discussion first came about at Paris in the mendicants' schools, probably during the student strike of 1220–1231.[17] Scholars usually date *De quolibet* 2 from the beginning of Aquinas's second Parisian regency (1269–1272).[18] In the article presently under consideration, Thomas entertains the question whether a crusader who dies before undergoing the hardships of fighting the infidels actually benefits from the crusading indulgence.

Perhaps the question was not purely hypothetical. In fact, the second article may reflect an earnest concern for the French church of the mid–thirteenth century. We know that the French king, Louis IX, came back from his first crusade in 1254. After an unsuccessful campaign, during which he had been imprisoned for about a month, he returned disappointed over the results of his labors. The very next year, Louis had to dispatch a company of royal archers to protect the

---

17. Palémon Glorieux, *La littérature quodlibétique de 1260 à 1320* 1 (Kain: Revue des sciences philosophiques, 1925), 2 (Paris: J. Vrin, 1935), pp. 9–50. For a fuller discussion of Aquinas's use of the quodlibetal questions, see Leonard E. Boyle, "The Quodlibets of St. Thomas and Pastoral Care," *Thomist* 38 (1974): 232–256, reprinted in his *Pastoral Care, Clerical Education, and Canon Law, 1200–1400* (London: Variorum Reprints, 1981), pp. 232–265.

18. The exact dating of the *De quolibet* 1–12 remains a matter of dispute among scholars. See Weisheipl, *Friar Thomas D'Aquino*, pp. 367–368. In "The Quodlibets of St. Thomas," Boyle also gives a summary of the different opinions concerning the dating of the quodlibetal questions. Sandra Edwards follows Weisheipl and Boyle in her *Quodlibetal Questions*, especially pp. 5–10.

Dominican convent from the Parisian crowds because they had been turned against the newly arrived mendicants by partisans of the secular masters, who strongly opposed sharing university privileges with the friars. Despite the antagonism generated by established members of the Parisian intellectual community, Louis remained a strong supporter of both the Franciscans and the Dominicans. And, according to William of Tocco, the king especially liked Brother Thomas Aquinas.[19]

Historical evidence lets us suppose that Thomas had his royal patron in mind when responding to the question How does an indulgence affect a man who has not had the chance to endure in his own person the hardship for which the indulgence had been granted. In 1267, with events in the East growing worse for the Christian community, Louis IX once more took the cross. But in little more than a month, after setting sail from Aigues-Mortes in July 1270, the king died in Tunis. Admittedly, one commonly accepted date for *De quolibet 2* is Christmastime 1269. Still, scholars recognize that the dating of certain quodlibetal questions remains only probable. For example, Franz Pelster asserts that *De quolibet 2* was actually held at Christmastime in 1270.[20] Accordingly, this suggestion seems quite reasonable: The fate of the French king had indeed raised interest in the relationship between the remission of punishment and the actual endurance of a stipulated penalty for sin, to the extent that at the very next quodlibetal session, a student might well have posed the question to Magister Thomas Aquinas.

As I have already noted, the plenary indulgence gained prominence in the church's practice as a result of the tactical objective of recovering the Holy Land. The crusading decree of Lateran IV, *Ad liberandum* (1215), clearly states the cause for receiving the plenary indulgence. Note, however, the exact terms of the decree: the document promises

---

19. For example, William of Tocco, *Hystoria beati Thomae de Aquino*, no. 36, records that "de illustri rege Franciae S. Ludovico dicitur, quod semper in rebus arduis dicti Doctoris [scil., Thomae] requirebat consilium, quod frequenter expertus fuerat esse certum: ut utriusque in hoc perpenderetur sanctitas, et illustris regis in dubiis Doctorem consulendum requireret et sancti Doctoris, qui divino doctus Spiritu, quod esset utilius, responderet."

20. Franz Pelster, "Literarische Probleme der Quodlibeta des hl. Thomas von Aquin," *Gregorianum* 28 (1947): 78–100; and 29 (1948): 62–87, especially pp. 63–69.

full pardon of repented sins properly confessed to "all who in their own person shall undergo this burden [of the Crusade] at their own expense" ("omnibus qui laborem istum in propriis personis subierint et expensis").[21] This decree, in turn, formed the basis for two subsequent documents, *Afflicti corde* (Lyons I, 1245) and *Zelus fidei* (Lyons II, 1274).[22] We can assume that Aquinas was aware of the first two decrees. His quodlibetal text acknowledges that a papal letter exists that promises full remission of the punishment due to past sins for those who are willing to undertake the hardships and dangers of a medieval crusade.

THE THEOLOGICAL ARGUMENT

But what does it mean to affirm that a member of the church obtains a remission of the punishment due to sin? How can the church replace punishment for sin with the hardships of a military campaign? And what theological grounds exist for making such a claim within the Christian church? In order to discover Aquinas's answers to these questions, we must now turn to a close examination of his text.

ARGUMENTS

Aquinas presents four arguments. Two support the thesis that a dead crusader receives the promised indulgence even if he never reached the Holy Land; two others (the so-called *sed contra* arguments) offer reasons for thinking otherwise. Each of the arguments, of course, supposes the traditional threefold elements of sacramental reconciliation: *contritio cordis, confessio oris, satisfactio operis*. Judged from one point of view, indulgences constitute commutations of satisfactory works attached to particular deeds, such as prayers, pilgrimages, or other burdensome actions, including the risky and painful undertaking

---

21. See García y García, *Constitutiones*, p. 117.
22. See the text in *Conciliorum Oecumenicorum Decreta*, ed. J. Alberigo et al. (Freiburg: Herder, 1962), pp. 273–277; 285–290. Purcell, *Papal Crusading*, pp. 187–199, also reproduces the decrees of 1245 and 1274. The single extant version of *Zelus fidei* was first published by H. Fincke, "Constitutiones pro Zelo Fidei," in *Konzilienstudien zur Geschichte des 13. Jahrhunderts* (Münster, 1891).

of military combat. Accordingly, the indulgenced deed, the necessary condition of the indulgence, theoretically accomplishes the same good in the sinner that otherwise would have been brought about by the sacramental penance or satisfaction.

The first two arguments represent what we might call the juridical point of view. The first points out that the canonical requirements for gaining an indulgence have been met once the crusader has fulfilled the stipulated conditions. What are these requirements? The text mentions two: first, the crusader must confess his sins with true contrition; and, second, the indulgence must come from the pope, who alone has jurisdiction over the punishment involved. If these conditions are fulfilled, the suddenly deceased crusader should benefit from the indulgence.

> 1. For anyone to receive an indulgence, it suffices, as stipulated in the papal letter, that he be truly repentant and that he confess his sins. But a crusader who dies before he leaves for the crusade has fulfilled all those things set forth by the official document in order to receive a plenary indulgence for sins. Therefore he does receive it fully.
> 2. Furthermore, only God forgives the offense of sin. When the pope, therefore, gives a plenary indulgence, this is not to be referred to the offense but only to the totality of punishments. Now according to the stipulations of the papal document, the one who accepts the crusader's cross will not suffer punishment for his sins. Thus, he will escape punishment immediately, having achieved the full remission of sin.[23]

These arguments appraise the disorder of sin as something marginal to the psychological capacities of the human person. In order to adjust the punishment due to sin, the church must supply nothing more than the proper legal formality. As a purely legal convention, an indulgence absolves the guilty party from whatever penalty he or she stands liable to suffer.

In other words, the two affirmative arguments simply propose that in order to gain the indulgence, it suffices that a person possess true interior contrition for past sins and have confessed these sins to the priest. Moreover, in accord with the terms of the papal letter, the actual indulgence results from accepting the crusader's cross. In other words, on the assumption that God alone forgives sins (what the Scholastics referred to as *culpa*), the pope simply grants remission of

---

23. *De quolibet* 2 8.2 ob.1–2 (ed. R. Spiazzi [Turin: Marietti, 1956], pp. 36–37).

sin's punishment (what the Scholastics called *poena*) to those willing to accept the burdens of a crusade. The two arguments clearly consider the punishment due to sin as a juridical reality over which the pope holds authority in the same way that an appellate judge can commute the sentence meted out to a convicted prisoner.

The second set of arguments takes up the question from another point of view that reflects the Augustinian teaching on sin as a deformation of the image of God that remains to some extent even in the baptized. In particular, the second *sed contra* argument raises the parallel of forgiveness within the sacrament of reconciliation. In the sacrament, the person who confesses and displays sorrow for his or her sins receives absolution from the offense of sin through the ministry of the priest. Still, the tradition also holds that the penitent remains bound to satisfactory works that must be accomplished either during this life or in purgatory. In brief, satisfaction readies one to see God.

> 1. Augustine says in *De Trinitate* 15 that to take out the arrow is not the same as to heal the wound. The arrow of sin is removed by the remission of sin; the wound, however, is cured by the restoration of the image [of God], which satisfactory works alone accomplish. But the crusader who dies before he undertakes the actual crusade has undergone nothing for the restoration of the image. Therefore, the wound is not yet healed; and thus he would not enter glory immediately without suffering the punishments of purgatory.
>
> 2. Furthermore, any priest uses these words, "I absolve you from all your sins." If therefore the dead crusader escapes all punishment for sin, by the same token anyone who receives absolution from a priest should also. This, however, would be unsuitable.[24]

The first of these arguments especially provokes Aquinas to interpret indulgences from what we might nowadays call a personalist standpoint. Since sinful actions disregard the in-built teleologies of human nature, sin affects the psychology and character of the whole person. Only a sort of remedial discipline can redirect human energies towards virtuous activity, that is, fully heal what are described metaphorically as sin's "wounds." Can Aquinas supply a theological explanation that demonstrates why the practice of granting indulgences does not involve an inconsistency with this notion of sin? How does an indulgence respect that sin represents something more

---

24. *De quolibet* 2 8.2 sc.1–2 (ed. Spiazzi, p. 37).

than the simple infraction of a divine rule or the breach of moral conventions?

As I have explained, a particular theology of sin controls Aquinas's approach to this matter. Sin conforms our psychological powers to purposes that fall short of incarnating God's goodness in the world. Since this sinful deformity implies disordered attachments to created goods, conversion entails satisfactory works. In fact, satisfaction finds its explanation in the human need for reordering our appetites towards morally good objectives instead of bad ones. This alone accomplishes the restoration of the original godly and godward image in the human creature.

The contrary arguments do not suppose that God assigns punishment for sin after the manner of a courtroom proceeding. Rather, the punishment due to sin arises from the very nature of sin itself. As Augustine reminds us, the effect of every disordered action remains its own punishment. Appropriately, Thomas cites Augustine's text from *De Trinitate* 15, "non est idem abstrahere telum, et sanare vulnus." Aquinas interprets this saying to mean that it is one thing to forgive sin (according to the metaphor, to remove the arrow) and another to heal the wounds caused in our human character by sin. This latter process, the restoration of the image of God in the human being, can only come about as a result of spiritual discipline. And Aquinas ascribes this task to works of satisfaction. Now the crusader who dies without performing the equivalent of such satisfaction has not undergone the purgation required to be able to behold the face of God.

Furthermore, the deceased crusader, according to the second argument of this set, does not seem to be in any different position from the ordinary Christian who receives sacramental forgiveness. And it would be unfitting to infer from the case of the unfortunate crusader that satisfaction held no place in the scheme of Christian conversion and renewal. However, if the forgiven sinner or the indulgenced crusader were excused from all of sin's *poena*, this would imply that the restoration of the image of God occurs without human effort or personal commitment.

THEOLOGICAL PRINCIPLES

In the body of the text, Aquinas begins to establish the theological basis for granting a commutation of the rectification that works of satisfaction ordinarily accomplish in the repentant believer. First Thomas enunciates a basic principle of Christian soteriology, namely, that one person can satisfy for another. Christ accomplished precisely such a work. So Aquinas begins:

> For the resolution of this question, it should be noted, as was said above, that the work of one person can be satisfactory for another, whom the doer's intention designates.
> But Christ shed his blood for the church, and did and underwent many other things which are to be judged of infinite value by reason of the dignity of [his] person. Thus it is said in Wisdom 7:14 that in it "there is infinite treasure for human beings." Likewise all the other saints had the intention in those things which they suffered and did for God that such would be for the well-being not only of themselves, but for the whole church.[25]

The notion that the quality of the person directly affects the value of whatever sufferings he or she undergoes finds its antecedent in certain provisions of Roman law. Because of the sovereign dignity of Christ's personhood, Christ's work, one can argue, possesses a kind of infinite value. In a way similar to Anselm's argument in *Cur Deus homo?* Aquinas applies the principle here to account for the universal efficacy of Christ's passion. Or, as the canonical scriptures express it, Christ died "once for all" (Hebrews 7:27).

Aquinas argues next that all Christians can participate in this spiritual good insofar as they form one body in the church. Although the good deeds of the saints possess such a value only insofar as they themselves remain united with Christ, the personal actions of Christ and the saints are said to constitute the *thesaurus ecclesiae*, the treasury of the church. In order to concretize this notion, however, Aquinas recalls the canon that the one who presides over the universal church on earth possesses authority to dispense this treasury to everyone who remains united in the same bond of charity. In accord with the traditional terminology, Aquinas refers to the authority of the Petrine office as the "power of the keys."

> Therefore, dispensation of this treasure belongs to the one who is in charge of the whole church; hence the Lord gave to Peter the keys of the kingdom of heaven [Matthew 16:19]. Accordingly, when either the well-being or absolute necessity of the church requires it, the one who

---

25. *De quolibet* 2 8.2 corp. (ed. Spiazzi, p. 37).

is in charge of the church can distribute from this unlimited treasure to anyone who through charity belongs to the church as much of the said treasure as shall seem to him opportune, either up to a total remission of punishment or to some certain amount. In this case, the passion of Christ and of the other saints would be imputed to the member as if he himself would have suffered whatever was required for the remission of his sins, as happens when one person satisfies for another, as has already been explained.[26]

The union in charity forms the ultimate ground for the possibility of sharing in the good works associated with Christ and the saints. When Aquinas speaks about imputation, he rather intends the sort of loving communication among the members of the church that forms them as if into one person.[27] In a certain manner of speaking, indulgences help formalize the participation by one member of the church in the good works of another member.

Accordingly, whether by a total remission, or by only a partial remission, of the punishment due to sin, the beneficiary of an indulgence relies on the sufferings of Christ and of the saints as if having undergone personally the same suffering for sin. As Aquinas puts it in *De quolibet 2* 7.2, "All who are in charity are like one body, and just as the hand is devoted to the whole body and likewise to any member of the body, so the good of one redounds to all."[28] Aquinas argues that charity, which represents the highest perfection that a human person can achieve, and the ecclesial bond that charity generates are to be considered of greater significance in establishing the grounds for indulgences than the requirements that strict justice would impose.

Now Aquinas can resolve the question of the crusader who dies before he reaches the Holy Land. First, Thomas summarizes the three canonical conditions for receiving an indulgence: (1) the work must involve a cause pertaining to the honor of God or the needs of the

---

26. *De quolibet* 2 8.2 corp. (ed. Spiazzi, p. 37).
27. For instance, see Aquinas's discussion of this point in *Summa theol.* 3.49.1. Compare Cessario, *Godly Image*, pp. 159ff.
28. In *De quolibet* 2 7.2, Aquinas is explaining why the prayer of one can benefit another. He affirms that "omnes qui sunt in caritate, sunt quasi unum corpus; et ita bonum unius redundat in omnes, sicut manus deservit toti corpori, et similiter quodlibet corporis membrum." Aquinas refers back to this explanation in the text of 8.2.

church; (2) the indulgence must be established by a duly constituted authority; (3) the one who receives the indulgence must already enjoy that union of charity in which the whole reality of the church consists.

> For an indulgence to benefit anyone, however, three things are required. First, a cause that appertains to the honor of God, or for the necessity or utility of the church. Secondly, authority in him who grants it: the pope principally, others insofar as they receive either ordinary or commissioned, that is, delegated, power from him. Thirdly, it is required that the one who wishes to receive the indulgence should be in the state of charity. And these three things are designated in the papal letter. For the appropriate cause is designated in that one is sent forth to help the Holy Land; the authority, in that mention is made of the authority of the apostles Peter and Paul, and of the pope himself; charity, in the recipient, in that it is said: "to all truly sorry and confessed." It does not say, "and to those who have satisfied," because the indulgence does not excuse from contrition and confession, but does take the place of satisfaction.[29]

The medieval canonists freely incorporated elements of moral and dogmatic theology into their various efforts to organize the administration of the church.[30] As the text above makes clear, the canonical outlook governed even such strictly theological topics as divine charity, Christian satisfaction, and the Petrine office.

Second, Aquinas replies to the actual case by insisting on a close reading of the terms given in the papal letter. On the one hand, if the text mentions the actual undertaking of the crusade, as is so in the decrees of 1215 and 1245, then the dead crusader does not gain the indulgence. On the other hand, if the mere intention to go on crusade (*votum itineris*) constitutes the condition, then the dead crusader has fulfilled what is required.

> So, for the question proposed: if according to the provisions of the papal document the indulgence is granted to those taking the cross for a military expedition to the Holy Land, the crusader immediately gains the indulgence, even if he should die before he actually leaves for the crusade. In this case, of course, the condition for the indulgence remains a vow to go and not the actual undertaking itself. If, on the other hand, in the

---

29. *De quolibet* 2 8.2 corp. (ed. Spiazzi, p. 37).
30. For a discussion of *poena* and *culpa* in the work of the canonists, see Stephan Kuttner, *Kanonistische Schuldlehre*, Studi e testi 64 (Vatican City: Biblioteca Apostolica, 1935).

phrasing of the document it is stipulated that the indulgence should be given to those who actually cross the sea, then the one who dies before he makes the crossing has not fulfilled the condition for the indulgence.[31]

At this point in the discussion, Aquinas establishes that he is conversant with the pertinent canonical legislation and that these legal distinctions play a role in his theological judgment about how indulgences work.

In considering the live crusader, we can easily understand how one who actually endures the hardships of the crusades qualifies for the indulgence. For example, in *De quolibet 5* 7.2, composed after the text presently under consideration, Aquinas simply affirms that the crusader who dies upon returning from the crusade, all other things being equal, dies with greater merit than he would have done before experiencing the hardships because such a person has personally endured the difficult undertaking. At the same time, Thomas acknowledges that from the point of view of the moral nature of the action, to go on a crusade is more meritorious than merely to return from one.[32]

But Aquinas also undertakes the more difficult case of explaining why the crusader who dies on route to the Holy Land can benefit from the indulgence. How can a merely juridical act, even one issued by the competent authority and fulfilled according to stipulations set down in the papal brief, ready a soul for beatitude? Elsewhere Aquinas explains that the purification of a soul by the punishment of purgatory constitutes nothing else than the expiation of the guilt of punishment required for entering glory.[33] Given Augustine's presuppositions, the person who has not undertaken such a purification cannot see God because the sinner's personal dispositions remain disproportionate to divine beatitude. But how can an indulgence change our dispositions?

---

31. *De quolibet 2* 8.2 corp. (ed. Spiazzi, p. 37).
32. *De quolibet 5* 7.2: "Manifestum est autem, quod ille qui moritur in redeundo de ultra mare, ceteris paribus, cum pluribus meritis moritur quam ille qui moritur in eundo: habet enim meritum ex assumptione itineris, et ulterius ex prosecutione, in qua forte multa gravia est passus. Et ideo, ceteris paribus, melius moritur ille qui moritur redeundo; quamvis ire sit magis meritorium quam redire, genus operis considerando."
33. *Scriptum super Sent.* 4.45.2.2.2 ad 3: "[P]urgatio animae per poenas purgatorii non est aliud quam expiatio reatus impedientis a perceptione gloriae."

In order to follow Aquinas's reasoning, we need to recall that the general principle for sharing in the spiritual goods of another person differs depending on whether we are talking of merit or of satisfaction. Since merit directly entitles a person to a reward, merit remains incommunicable. On the other hand, the members of the church can share works of satisfaction; just as a person can pay the debts of a friend, so a person can consign satisfaction to another believer. The eminent satisfaction of Christ and the superabundant satisfaction of Mary and the saints form a treasure that the church guards and administers through indulgences: "All the other saints had the intention in those things which they suffered and did for God that such would be for the well-being not only of themselves, but for the whole church."[34] So if the crusader has endured nothing difficult or dangerous, the grounds for allowing him pardon for sin's punishment without his having duly performed penitential activity find their ultimate explanation in the supreme satisfaction that results from Christ's charity.

This explanation develops a theme that Aquinas frequently employs in discussions of Christian redemption. He upholds the principle that one person can satisfy for another. For example, in the *Scriptum* we find the assertion, "unus pro alio satisfacere potest."[35] In *De quolibet* 2 7.2, Aquinas further specifies the basis for this sort of interchange: "one is able to satisfy for another, if the former intends this."[36] We now recognize that the metaphor of the treasure graphically symbolizes that the members of the church satisfy for one another. As a result, the church can oversee and regulate the conditions for this exchange. The church indulges those persons who, for whatever reason, have not actually undergone a painful process of spiritual regeneration by themselves. "The reason," writes Aquinas, "why indulgences work remains the unity of the mystical body, in which many perform penitential works beyond the measure of their debts and patiently bear

---

34. See above, note 25.

35. *Scriptum super Sent.* 4.20.1.2.3. In this instance, however, St. Thomas makes a distinction between satisfaction and merit. In the latter case, as *Summa theol.* 1–2.114.6 clearly teaches, no one can merit grace for someone else in strict equivalence (*ex condigno*) except Christ alone.

36. *De quolibet* 2 7.2: "sed secundo modo opus unius valet alteri per modum satisfactionis, prout unus pro altero satisfacere potest, si hoc intendat."

many unjust treatments, through which a multitude of punishments are able to be expiated."[37] Although the reason remains implicit in the quodlibetal text, Aquinas holds that Christ's love remains powerful enough to alter what the sinner himself did not have the occasion (or perhaps the will) to do for himself.

Accordingly, the satisfaction of Christ remains the principal source of this thesaurus. In the *De quolibet* 2, Aquinas makes the point that the dignity of Christ's personhood accounts for the exceeding value that his sufferings produced in the church. Of course, this leads us to consider the supreme charity and obedience with which Christ lived his life. In the *Summa contra gentiles*, for example, we find a complete discussion of these dispositions in Christ. There Thomas explains the universal benefits of Christ's passion by citing the dignity of the person who suffers, "ex dignitate personae patientis," and also by appealing to the charity with which Christ embraced his salvific mission, "ex maiori caritate procedens."[38] Obviously, these affirmations remain crucial for the present discussion.

Aquinas reasons that Christ's heroic love can overcome even the habitual sinner's resistance to godly living. So, the duly indulgenced sinner who dies without undergoing the actual restoration of the divine image is ready for the beatific vision. In another theological opusculum, the *Collationes super Pater Noster*, Aquinas insinuates a reason to explain why this can happen within the mystical body. He affirms "that the Lord strengthens us against temptation by the fervor of charity, because any charity no matter how small can resist sin."[39] All in all, the incarnation remains the underlying reason

---

37. *Scriptum super Sent.* 4.20.1.3: "Ratio autem quare valere possunt, est unitas corporis mystici, in qua multi operibus poenitentiae supererogaverunt ad mensuram debitorum suorum et multas etiam tribulationes injuste sustinuerunt, per quas multitudo poenarum poterat expiari."

38. See *Summa contra gentiles* 4.55.

39. *Collationes super Pater Noster*, Petitio 6: "Regit autem hominem ne inducatur in tentationem per fervorem caritatis: quia quaelibet caritas quantumcumque parva, potest resistere cuilibet peccato." Aquinas gave these Lenten sermons in Naples in 1273. Earlier (c. 1270) in the *Summa theol.* 1–2.114.6, he had made a similar point: "Sed anima Christi mota est a Deo per gratiam, non solum ut ipse perveniret ad gloriam vitae aeternae, sed etiam ut alios in eam adduceret, inquantum est caput Ecclesiae et auctor salutis humanae, secundum illud ad Heb., 'Qui multos filios in gloriam adduxerat, auctorem salutis' etc."

for our spiritual progress and well-being; and this communication of divine goodness can overcome whatsoever indisposition sin may generate in us.

REPLIES

According to scholastic practice, the replies to the opening arguments provide Aquinas with an opportunity to supply further clarifications on the topic under discussion. Aquinas addresses each of the four original arguments in turn. The first reply simply asserts the obvious conclusion that a close reading of the stipulations in the papal letter implies. If the condition of the indulgence requires that one actually journey to the Holy land, then, Aquinas rejoins, "it should be pointed out that in this last case, the crusader who dies lacks what is most important for an indulgence, namely, its necessary condition."[40]

On the other hand, the reply to the second argument clarifies two distinctions that have emerged in the course of the argument. The first distinction concerns the offense (*culpa*) of sin and the punishment (*poena*) that results from sin. The second distinction points out the difference between mediated divine authority, associated with the sacrament of holy orders, and the power of jurisdiction which, according to the customs of the time, even a noncleric may exercise. First of all, Aquinas recalls a basic premise of all sacramental theology: Only God exercises the principal agent's causality in a sacramental action.

> To the second: It should be noted that only God possesses the authority to forgive sin's guilt. But mediately it also belongs to the priest, insofar as he offers the sacrament of the forgiveness of sins, for example in baptism or penance. Nevertheless an indulgence does not embrace the forgiveness of sin's guilt, since it is not a sacramental reality; thus it belongs not to order but to jurisdiction. For even a nonpriest can grant an indulgence if he be commissioned to do so. Therefore, the punishment is totally remitted if the condition is fulfilled, not, however, if it is wanting.[41]

Even though other mediators participate in the divine authority, only God can forgive the actual offense of sin; indulgences only

---

40. *De quolibet* 2 8.2 ad 1 (ed. Spiazzi, p. 37).
41. *De quolibet* 2 8.2 ad 2 (ed. Spiazzi, p. 37).

concern sin's punishment. While from a theological point of view sin's punishment directly affects the character of the believer, a juridical aspect to these punishments still remains. As a theological metaphor, the *thesaurus ecclesiae* combines this juridical aspect of indulgences with the theological reality of participation in the satisfaction of Christ. Since the church can regulate the juridical punishments—for example, in prescribing certain works of satisfaction for particular transgressions—the appropriate persons can establish the conditions for allowing a sinner to benefit from the *thesaurus ecclesiae*. As we have seen, Aquinas considers it especially fitting that, since the Roman pontiff presides over the universal church, he alone can establish these conditions.

In the reply to the third argument, Aquinas throws still further light on the important distinction between satisfaction as a juridical act and as a theological reality. In this text, we find the clearest expression of the reason why an indulgence can supply for the actual restoration of one whose life has not been reformed by penitential activity. Aquinas's resolution does not depend here simply on technicalities of language in a papal decree. Again, satisfaction can be considered in two ways: as punitive inasmuch as it belongs to retributive justice; and as remedial or healing insofar as it forms part of the sacramental system. Strictly speaking, then, indulgences supply for satisfaction only in its punitive aspect.

> To the third: Satisfaction is both punitive, inasmuch as it remains an act of vindicative justice, and restorative, inasmuch as it is in a certain sense sacramental. An indulgence therefore takes the place of satisfaction insofar as it is punitive: because the punishment that another undergoes is imputed to this one as if this one had undergone it, therefore the guilt of punishment is removed. An indulgence does not, however, take the place of satisfaction insofar as it is medicinal, since there still remains the proneness to sinning left from prior sins, the cure of which necessarily entails the work of satisfaction. Accordingly, the crusader, while he lives, should be counseled not to omit satisfactory works, insofar as they serve to guard against repeated sin, even though the guilt of punishment stands totally removed, nor does this require any labor; for the labor of Christ's passion suffices. For one dying, of course, such prevention is not required, only liberation from the guilt of punishment.[42]

42. *De quolibet* 2 8.2 ad 3 (ed. Spiazzi, p. 37).

Clearly, the power of Christ's love works differently in one who is still a member of the church on earth than it does in one who has died. The need for spiritual discipline and reformation of life implies that the first one must continue on as part of the church on earth, for death marks the end of a person's deliberate involvement in the process of salvation. And since the good works of one individual do not appreciate another's spiritual discipline, Aquinas counsels penance even for the individual who does survive the crusade. Even though the successful completion of the indulgenced work replaces the punitive satisfaction, the crusader still needs to do penance for spiritual growth and maturity.

Satisfactory works in the church serve a dual purpose. First of all, since sin results in a state of alienation from God that requires redress on the part of the sinner, satisfaction—which Aquinas construes formally as love and obedience, and materially as bodily suffering—can restore the relationship. Of course, Aquinas clearly recognizes that the alienation lies in the sinner and not in an injured God. Because the sinner needs to redress the imbalance caused by sinful disorder, theology can still speak about vindicative satisfaction. On the other hand, satisfaction also possesses a therapeutic function. For the sinner willingly undergoes certain exacting exercises that reorder his or her psychological powers towards godly living. Undoubtedly, an indulgence can only satisfy the vindicative aspect of satisfaction. An indulgence cannot assure that the beneficiary receives the benefits of spiritual training in virtuous living. But if someone dies, the spiritual communion of the church insures that the indulgenced soul enjoys passage to the beatific vision without undergoing the ordinary purifications.

The final reply again treats the relationship of an indulgence to the sacramental system. Aquinas has already indicated that satisfaction possesses a certain (*quoddam*) sacramental power. Thus, he recognizes that theology can only apply in an analogical way the concept of sacrament to satisfaction, and the indulgence that supplies for it. Aquinas restates the principle that the priest mediates God's forgiveness for the offense of sin. While a partial forgiveness for only some sins would impugn the totality of loving communion required by divine charity, sacramental absolution nonetheless leaves some of the punishment due for sin intact. On the other hand, an indulgence can remove all of the punishment for sin, as happens in

SATISFACTION, INDULGENCES, AND CRUSADES 95

the crusader's indulgence, because of the spiritual authority exercised by the pope.

> To the fourth: The words of the priest saying, "I absolve you from all your sins," do not refer to punishment, but to the offense of sin, for which the priestly office authorizes absolution. Now no one can be absolved from one offense without being absolved from all of them. But punishment can be dismissed either totally or partially. For punishment is dismissed partially by sacramental absolution; totally, however, by the spiritual grace of an indulgence: as the Lord himself says [John 8: 11] to the adulterous woman, "I do not condemn you; go, and sin no more."[43]

Significantly, in his *De regimine principum*, Aquinas even identifies this ecclesial authority with the very primacy of Christ's headship over the church.[44] In this text, Thomas's "personalist" orientation embraces the New Testament teaching on the divine authority which Christ communicates to Peter and his successors.

The citation from John, which brings the article to a conclusion, both intimates Aquinas's evangelical outlook and inspires his procedure in the whole discussion. According to the Gospel account, Jesus speaks to the adulterous woman the words that form the basis for the ministry of reconciliation in the church: "Neither do I condemn you; go, and do not sin again." In Thomas's commentary on this passage of the Gospel, he points out that Christ shows himself to be both a lover of justice and a dispenser of mercy: to be sure, he forgives the woman her sin; however, he also instructs her to use this experience as an opportunity to grow in virtue.[45] In effect, this reflects Aquinas's principal concern in developing a theology of indulgences. We find a remarkable phrase in the third reply that seems to suggest that indulgenced pardon for sin is not burdensome because "the labor of Christ's sufferings suffices." In this way, Aquinas brings the discussion

---

43. *De quolibet* 2 8.2 ad 4 (ed. Spiazzi, p. 37–38).

44. *De regimine principum* 3.10: "Cum enim summus Pontifex sit caput in corpore mystico omnium fidelium Christi, et a capite sit omnis motus et sensus in corpore vero; sic erit in proposito. Propter quod oportet dicere in summo Pontifice esse plenitudinem omnium gratiarum, quia ipse solus confert plenam indulgentiam omnium peccatorum, ut compleat sibi quod de primo principe Domino dicamus, quia *de plenitudine eius nos omnes accepimus*."

45. See *In Joan.* 8.1.6: "Sed Dominus culpam non amans, peccatis non favens, ipsam damnavit culpam, non naturam, dicens, 'Amplius noli peccare': ut sic appareat quam dulcis est Dominus per mansuetudinem, et rectus per veritatem."

back to its proper christological center, which he fully recognizes must ground any theology of indulgences.

This quodlibetal question is a good example of the distinguished theological craftsmanship that Aquinas had achieved by the time he began his second teaching assignment at Paris. The question of penitential satisfaction had occupied theological investigation since the end of the eleventh century, when Anselm finished his celebrated *Cur Deus homo?* Although some authors slight Thomas's singular achievement in this area, he makes a significant contribution to the transformation and revitalization of the concept of Christian satisfaction.

Aquinas's theology of indulgences clearly represents his seasoned theological insight. In his mature years, he recasts the institution known as indulgences by emphasizing how they form part of the God–man relationship. At the same time, Thomas illustrates the central role that Christ and his intention plays in the actual life of the believer. Aquinas explains all human effort within the church as a result of Christ's capacity to communicate the effects of his own sufferings to his members, "quia sufficit labor passionis Christi." In Aquinas's "personalist" theological perspective, the mystery of God's love draws all men and women to God. Because the church is a communion of charity and belief, indulgences validly express the unity and grace that mark the visible reality of Christ's body. As a matter of fact, Aquinas's teaching on indulgences continues a primitive intuition expressed far earlier by St. Cyprian in his *Treatise on the Lord's Prayer*:

> We do not say "My Father, who art in heaven," nor "Give me this day my daily bread." It is not for oneself alone that each person asks to be forgiven, not to be led into temptation or to be delivered from evil. Rather, we pray in public as a community, and not for one individual but for all. For the people of God are all one.[46]

A similar ecclesiological vision undergirds Aquinas's views on indulgences.

Dominican House of Studies,
Washington, D.C.

---

46. *De dominica oratione* 8 (CSEL 3/1:271).

On the Purpose of 'Merit' in the Theology of Thomas Aquinas

JOSEPH WAWRYKOW

I aim in this essay chiefly to provide an adequate answer to the following question: why does Thomas Aquinas affirm the theological notion of 'merit'?

On the face of it, the answer to this question appears simple. Conditioned by Reformation debates, we are apt to think that merit-talk must be designed primarily to advance a set of claims about the dignity and achievement of the human person. By 'meritorious' action, a person establishes a right to spiritual reward from God; the affirmation of merit before God would thus testify to the ability of the person to contribute in a meaningful way to his or her own salvation. While Aquinas throughout his career agrees that human beings do contribute by their actions to their own salvation, in this article I shall argue that by the time of the *Summa theologiae* this aspect of merit-talk has receded to secondary importance. Rather, the principal focus of the mature discussion of merit lies elsewhere, in the depiction of the God who is revealed in striking fashion through the salvation of human beings. By the time of the *Summa theologiae*, the doctrine of merit is primarily designed to allow Thomas Aquinas to speak most appropriately about God.[1]

---

1. In an article entitled "John Calvin and Condign Merit," to appear in the *Archiv für Reformationsgeschichte* (1992), I have examined in some detail the principal

The article falls into three distinct parts. First, I will delineate the main contours of Thomas's mature discussion of 'merit' in the *Summa*, here noting the chief differences between this analysis and that offered much earlier by Thomas in the *Scriptum* on the *Sentences* of Peter Lombard. Then, I shall try to account for these differences, paying particularly close attention to the developments between the *Scriptum* and the *Summa* in Thomas's understanding of grace, as well as in his sense of the purpose of God's creating and redeeming. Finally, I shall make some wholly tentative observations about the originality of the mature Thomas's treatment of merit, especially as this pertains to my claim about the principal purpose of merit-talk in the *Summa*. The careful examination of Thomas's construction of the mature teaching on merit will concomitantly shed light on Thomas's theological procedure, and so suggest, in turn, the general shape of a responsible reading of his theological work.

DIFFERENCES IN THOMAS'S DISCUSSIONS OF 'MERIT'

While there are numerous references in passing to 'merit' throughout the Thomistic corpus, Thomas has provided us with extensive analyses of 'merit' in only two of his works, conveniently located, however, near the beginning and near the end of his theological career.[2] As we would expect, the treatments of merit in the early *Scriptum* and in the later *Summa* share a number of features. In both, human existence is viewed in terms of a 'journey' which begins in the conversion from sin to grace, runs through the morally good and graced actions that are pleasing to God and bring one closer to God,

---

objections raised by Luther and Calvin to the Catholic affirmation of merit. I have also argued that despite his polemic against merit, Calvin in fact approximated, especially in his analysis of sanctification, a teaching on condign merit as found in the later Aquinas.

2. The discussion of merit in the early (1252–1256) *Scriptum* on the *Sentences* of Peter Lombard is found in 2.27.1.3–6. I have used the edition of P. Mandonnet and M. F. Moos (Paris: Léthielleux, 1929–1947). Thomas considers merit in the *Summa theologiae* (1266–1273) in the final question of the *prima secundae*, 1–2.114. I have used the version in the Leonine edition of the *Opera Omnia* (Rome, 1882-).

'MERIT' IN THE THEOLOGY OF THOMAS AQUINAS 99

and, culminates, in the next life, in the beatifying vision of God. The *Scriptum* and the *Summa* similarly agree about the principal rewards of the actions done in grace: eternal life itself; and an increase in the habitual grace that is required to perform acts pleasing to God.

Even more striking than the common elements, however, are the differences that distinguish the earlier and the later accounts of merit. The *Summa*'s discussion of merit differs in two main ways from the *Scriptum*'s. The first emerges in Thomas's discussions of the possibility of merit.[3] In both the *Scriptum* and the *Summa*, Thomas demonstrates a keen sense of the difficulties involved in affirming merit. 'Merit' means to put another in one's debt. But God cannot be a debtor to anyone, and so human merit before God would seem to be excluded.[4] Similarly, merit presupposes an equality between what is done and what is given as reward. But nothing that people can do could possibly be equal to the reward of eternal life, thus again placing merit before God in doubt.[5] While the concerns about the possibility of merit remain the same, Thomas meets these concerns in each work in remarkably different ways. In the *Scriptum*, his basic move is to determine the type of justice that pertains to merit before God, arguing that it is not commutative justice (which would demand a quantitative equality between our act and God's reward), but rather distributive justice that is here in force—God renders to people who are equally deserving the same reward for their works.[6]

Thomas as well has a second move in the *Scriptum* to establish the possibility of the merit of eternal life, one to which he simply refers here in passing: the promise of God.[7] God has, in freedom, committed God to render the reward of eternal life for human merit. In this light, then, it is incorrect to speak of meritorious action placing God in a person's debt. Rather, by the promise, God has placed God

---

3. In the *Summa theologiae*, Thomas has devoted a separate article (1–2.114.1) to the consideration of the possibility of meriting before God. In the *Scriptum*, his comments on the possibility of merit occur in the course of his examination of the condign meriting of eternal life (*Super Sent.* 2.27.1.3).

4. *Super Sent.* 2.27.1.3 ob. 4; *Summa theologiae* 1–2.114.1 ob. 3.

5. *Super Sent.* 2.27.1.3 ob. 2; *Summa theologiae* 1–2.114.1, to which compare 1–2.114.3 ob. 3.

6. *Super Sent.* 2.27.1.3 sol., to which compare ad 1 and ad 4.

7. *Super Sent.* 2.27.1.3 ad 4.

in debt to God, and in rendering reward to us God is simply being faithful to God.

In the discussion of the possibility of merit in the *Summa*, on the other hand, Thomas's earlier preoccupation with the kind of justice that is involved in merit has simply fallen away. In its place, he now affirms a divine ordination as the ground of merit: merit before God is possible because God has ordained that acts done in grace will be meritorious of eternal life. By virtue of the divine ordination, the difficulties raised in the objections lose their force. Of course there is an infinite distance between God and people. But God's ordination simply bridges the gap: God has ordained that what human beings do, despite its intrinsic inferiority, will nevertheless be treated as deserving of eternal life.[8] Similarly, the divine ordination removes the 'debtor' objection. In rewarding our action, God is being faithful to God's freely made ordination. To the extent that there is a 'debt' here, on the basis of the divine ordination the debt is owed by God to God.[9]

The divine ordination thus assumes in the *Summa* great significance. By explaining the possibility of meriting, it renders feasible the subsequent dicussion of the particular rewards of this meriting. It is one thing, however, to detect importance; it is quite another to assert the precise meaning of this crucial term. Now a variety of meanings for 'ordination' have in fact been proposed in the literature on merit;[10] it will be of the utmost importance to my claim about

---

8. *Summa theologiae* 1–2.114.
9. *Summa theologiae* 1–2.114.1 ad 3.
10. In general, students of Aquinas's teaching about merit have tended either to construe the *Summa*'s *divina ordinatio* too narrowly, restricting it to a single meaning, or to underplay its significance, failing to see that it is the foundation of the distinctive analysis of merit offered in the *Summa*. For examples of the former, see Otto H. Pesch, "Die Lehre vom 'Verdienst' als Problem für Theologie und Verkündigung," in *Wahrheit und Verkündigung: Festgabe* M. *Schmaus*, ed. Leo Scheffczyk et al. (Paderborn: Ferdinand Schöningh, 1967) 2:1904, which assimilates *ordinatio* too closely to the Scotist *acceptatio*; and B. Hamm, *Promissio, Pactum, Ordinatio* (Tübingen: J. C. B. Mohr, 1977), pp. 312–313, 334–336, which relates the divine ordination that makes merit possible to the inner teleology of grace. For an example of the latter error, see W. D. Lynn, *Christ's Redemptive Merit: The Nature of Its Causality According to St. Thomas* (Rome: Gregorian University, 1962). Lynn recognizes (e.g., p. 43) that the term '*ordinatio*' covers a wide range of meanings, but fails to recover all of these meanings or to accord *ordinatio* the prominence and centrality that it enjoys in the mature teaching.

the main purpose of merit-talk in the *Summa* to attain a greater familiarity with this concept. Still, at this stage in the investigation, we are simply not in position to grasp the full range of meaning of this term as used in the first article of the question on merit in the *Summa*; that must wait until later in this essay. For the moment, let it suffice to say that at an absolute minimum the 'ordination' that grounds merit in the *Summa* refers to the 'promise' that had figured momentarily in the related discussion in the *Scriptum*. We can 'merit'—that is, can deserve a reward from God—because God has freely determined to treat our actions done in grace as 'meritorious' of reward.

In addition to the enhanced prominence of the divine ordination, there is a second way in which the *Summa*'s treatment of merit differs from that in the *Scriptum*. Thomas's discussion of merit in the *Scriptum* is a rather straightforward account, that concentrates on the actual objects or rewards of merit. Hence, it is concerned to demonstrate in this distinction that by their good acts people can merit not only the end of the spiritual life, God, but the increase of grace and even the conversion of another person as well.[11] In the *Scriptum*, Thomas is not interested in telling us which features of the spiritual life, if any, elude merit. The only possible exception in the *Scriptum* is his discussion of conversion, the first entry into the state of grace: in this distinction, Thomas appears reluctant to concede that the human person can merit the first grace.[12] However, I believe that this is only an apparent exception to the claim that in the *Scriptum* Thomas deals only with the actual objects of merit. In this writing, Thomas affirms the *facere quod in se est*, according to which God grants grace to a sinner who by his or her freely initiated and performed actions tries to amend his or her life.[13] Moreover, although he stresses that congruent merit is an imperfect merit that falls short of merit in the strict sense—that is, falls short of the condign merit that is governed by justice—in this writing Thomas does admit that congruent merit is a real merit, and in fact he discusses the *facere* in terms of such a

---

11. Thomas considers the meriting of beatitude in *Super Sent.* 2.27.1 article 3, of the first entry into the state of grace in article 4, of the increase of grace in article 5, and for another in article 6.

12. *Super Sent.* 2.27.1.4.

13. See, for example, *Super Sent.* 1.48.1.3 sol. and ad 1, 2.4.1.3 sc., 2.27.1.4, and 2.28.1.3 ad 3.

congruent merit.[14] Thus, in his discussion of the merit of the first grace in the present distinction, all Thomas probably wants to do is to exclude the condign merit of first grace, while wishing us to understand that the sinner nevertheless does merit this grace congruently.[15]

The situation is rather different in the *Summa*. Thomas naturally enumerates in 1-2.114 the rewards that do fall under merit, and again tells us that people can merit the end of the spiritual life, as well as the increase of habitual grace and conversion for another.[16] But in the *Summa* Thomas is not content just to tell us which rewards Christians can merit by their acts. He also devotes considerable attention to telling us which aspects of the spiritual life cannot be merited through good action. Thus, for example, whatever hesitations he might have had on this question in the *Scriptum*, Thomas unequivocally rejects in *Summa theologiae* 1-2.114.5 any merit of the first grace. In keeping with his affirmation of gratuitous election to salvation, in this article Thomas stresses that conversion itself is worked freely by God alone, apart from any kind of merit of the sinner. Similarly, in the ninth article, Thomas argues for an unmerited grace of perseverance.

Thomas's attitude toward perseverance in the earlier *Scriptum* is difficult to document, precisely because he hardly discusses the question. However, it is most likely that his position in the earlier work is that the one who perseveres on the path to God is the one who acts freely in accordance with the inclination of the habitual grace received in justification; perseverance in grace is left, as it were, in the hands of the justified. In the *Summa*, on the other hand, perseverance is a free gift of God by which God applies a person to good action and keeps the person away from sin. The result of Thomas's inclusion of these unmerited graces of conversion and perseverance in his description

---

14. In *Super Sent.* 4.15.1.3, Thomas recalls the view that the disposition for grace is sometimes said to be congruently meritorious of that grace, but he adds that congruent merit is not really or properly 'merit'. In other texts (2.27.1.4 ad 4, 2.27.1.6), he reports that some theologians explicitly link the *facere* to congruent merit. Thomas does not indicate any disapproval of such a claim.

15. For the claim that Aquinas did in fact teach a congruent merit of the first grace in the *Scriptum*, see J. Rivière, "S. Thomas et le mérite 'de congruo'," *Revue des sciences religieuses* 7 (1927): 641–649.

16. Thomas treats the meriting of eternal life for those who possess grace in *Summa theologiae* 1-2.114 articles 2–3, the congruent merit of first grace for another in article 6, and the increase of habitual grace in article 8.

of merit is a more nuanced account. Their inclusion helps us to perceive the limits of meritorious action by bringing to our attention those features of spiritual existence that fall outside of merit. And, most significantly, this revision of his teaching on merit underscores the ultimate gratuity of salvation: that one gets into grace and then stays there is due to God's free decision to provide these graces to the person.

REASONS FOR THE DIFFERENCES IN THOMAS'S DISCUSSIONS

Once we have described the chief differences between Thomas's two discussions of merit, the question naturally arises: why has Thomas revised his teaching in these ways?

Considerable progress in accounting for these differences will be made by recalling the immediate context of the discussions of merit. In both works, the discussion of merit comes in the course of the general discussion of grace. Thomas's understanding of grace had been significantly modified between the composition of these two works.[17] In the *Scriptum*, his teaching about grace is rather close to that of other thirteenth-century theologians. Grace is conceived exclusively as habitual grace; the need for grace is constituted principally by the 'ontological difference' between creatures and the God who is their beatifying end. Relatively little consideration is given to the problem of sin, thus making it possible to ascribe conversion and perseverance to human initiative.

By the time of the *Summa*, however, Thomas advanced a markedly different conception of grace. Greater sensitivity to the pervasive effects of sinfulness has led the mature Thomas to look as much at the healing, as at the elevating, function of grace.[18] Thomas had

---

17. For orientations to the developments in Aquinas on grace, see Henri Bouillard, *Conversion et grâce chez s. Thomas d'Aquin* (Paris: Aubier, 1944); and Bernard J. F. Lonergan, *Grace and Freedom: Operative Grace in the Thought of St. Thomas Aquinas*, ed. J. Patout Burns (New York: Herder and Herder, 1971).

18. This is apparent in the discussion of the need for grace in *Summa theologiae* 1–2.109. From the second article on, Thomas is very much concerned to show the dire effects of the fall and of sin in general. In the later articles of the question

meanwhile discovered a second form of grace, the grace of *auxilium*, to complement the earlier-affirmed habitual grace, the two forms of grace being equally involved in the healing and elevating of the human person. The developments in Thomas's thinking about grace are evident in what is arguably the single most important text in the treatise on grace, 1–2.111.2.

This passage neatly gathers up the insights of the preceding questions on grace while furthering the discussion by showing that grace as understood by the Thomas of the *Summa* can be interpreted in terms of the Augustinian categories of 'operative' and 'cooperative'. The corpus of this article is divided into two sections. In the second, shorter section, Thomas explains that his habitual grace can be both 'operative' and 'cooperative'.[19] Operative habitual grace is responsible for 'being', taken in both a moral and a supernatural sense. By operative habitual grace God both forgives the person's sin, and so grants the individual a new moral stature before God, and elevates the person to the supernatural level, orienting the person to God as to his or her beatifying end. 'Cooperative habitual grace', on the other hand, is responsible for 'operation'. While Thomas's meaning is somewhat obscure, it is likely that 'operation' here refers to an inclination or disposition to act. By cooperative habitual grace, the person who has been made pleasing to God is now disposed to act in the way conducive, both morally and supernaturally, to attaining eternal life.

The discussion of *auxilium* in terms of the traditional Augustinian categories in the first section of the corpus is more extensive, probably reflecting Thomas's own greater interest in working out the implications of his discovery of this form of grace.[20] Earlier in the treatise

---

(especially 109.8–9), Thomas insists that the tendency to sin remains active even in the justified and must be overcome by subsequent healing graces.

19. *Summa theologiae* 1–2.111.2.

20. Lonergan, *Grace and Freedom*, chapters 4–6; see also Mark D. Jordan, "The Transcendality of Goodness and the Human Will," in *Being and Goodness: The Concept of the Good in Metaphysics and Philosophical Theology*, ed. Scott D. MacDonald (Ithaca, N.Y.: Cornell University Press, 1991). Jordan highlights Aquinas's use of an extra-Christian source, the Pseudo-Aristotelian *Eudemian Ethics*, in the refinement of his ideas about the interplay of divine and human causality, including in the construction of his mature teaching on grace (see pp. 138 ff., especially p. 148).

on grace, Thomas had argued for the need of a grace of *auxilium* to explain action. Habitual grace provides the capacity, the possiblity, for morally correct and supernatural action. What is in potency to act does not move itself, but must be applied to its action by what is already in act. Thus, by the grace of *auxilium* God must realize the potential established by habitual grace, applying the possessor of such grace to act.[21] In the present article, by explaining that *auxilium* can as well be understood in terms of the distinction between 'operative' and 'cooperative', Thomas further specifies how God through *auxilium* applies individuals to their action.[22] Thomas begins this stage of his analysis by defining 'operative' and 'cooperative' as used of *auxilium*. In operative *auxilium*, the will is simply passive, moved by God to its appropriate act; in cooperative *auxilium*, the will is both passive and active, moved by God in such a way that it also moves itself. Thomas then relates these definitions of operative and cooperative *auxilia* to his treatment earlier in the *prima secundae* of the main stages of the complete human act.[23]

---

21. On the need for both forms of grace, see *Summa theologiae* 1–2.109 in general. For the claim that habitual grace provides the capacity (*virtus*) for morally correct and supernatural action, see 1–2.109.2. Thomas argues the need for divine assistance for human action to occur from the first article of that question. See as well 1–2.109.2 ad 1, where, employing the passage from the Pseudo-Aristotelian *Eudemian Ethics*, Thomas proposes the need for divine *auxilium* even in the mind healed of sin. Thomas repeats that such *auxilia* are required in the life of the justified in 1–2.109.9. Incidentally, habitual grace is first received at the end of a process initiated by an (operative) *auxilium*; see 1–2.109.6 corp. and ad 3, as well as 1–2.112.2 and 1–2.111.2. The sequence of graces is therefore this: an operative *auxilium* that works conversion; followed by the infusion of habitual grace, operative and cooperative, and the subsequent granting of further *auxilia*, operative and cooperative, which account for the realization of the potential provided by habitual grace.

22. *Summa theologiae* 1–2.111.2.

23. See *Summa theologiae* 1–2.6–17. At 1–2.111.2, Thomas offers a much-simplified version of the complete human action, speaking of the 'stages' of the act in terms of 'interior' and 'exterior'. I have squared Thomas's present usage with the earlier analysis of the human act. Given Thomas's example of operative *auxilium* in this essay, there is no particular difficulty with equating the present 'interior' act with the earlier-mentioned intending of the good. Similarly, the 'exterior' act of 1–2.111.2 at the least must cover external performance. The real problem is whether the choice of means is to be ascribed to operative or to cooperative *auxilium*. Is choice of means 'interior' or 'exterior'? Now, elsewhere in the *Summa* (e.g., 1.83.3; 1–2.13.1), choice of means is said to be the act of the *liberum arbitrium*. And, later in the present article,

Any complete human act can be divided into three main parts: first, there is the intention or willing of a good; then, there is the choice of the means to attaining that good; and, finally, there is the actual performance of the act. In the present text, the willing of the good is ascribed to operative *auxilium*: here, God moves the will to the intention of a good, and the will is simply passive. The other two parts of the human act are ascribed to cooperative *auxilium*. In the choice of the means and the execution of the act, God is active, moving the will in such a way that it also moves itself.

To a large extent, the new dimensions of the *Summa*'s teaching on grace provide the distinctive shape of Thomas's mature teaching on merit. On the one hand, the insistence in question 114 about what cannot be merited reveals Thomas's desire to be faithful to his newly attained insights on operative *auxilium*. In 111.2, Thomas is content to mention but a single instance of operative *auxilium*, that of conversion. In conversion to God, God moves the will and it is simply moved.[24] There are other instances where the will intends good as moved by God, instances covered by other operative *auxilia*. Willing the good stands at the beginning of every good human action. The good that is realized through discrete actions both approximates the ultimate Good that is God and brings the person closer to the ultimate Good. Subsequent to the entry into grace, which is worked by the operative *auxilium* of conversion, every time a person wills a good that is subordinate to the ultimate Good that is God, it is similarly as moved by an operative *auxilium*. Operative *auxilium* both initiates and sustains the journey to God in heaven, accounting for the successful completion of the journey to God. In a word, Thomas has complemented his teaching on the operative *auxilium* of conversion with the affirmation of the operative *auxilium* of perseverance—and,

---

when speaking of cooperative habitual grace, Thomas ties *liberum arbitrium* closely to cooperative grace. The meritorious act proceeds from both (see also 1–2.114.1). Hence, in the present discussion of human activity, it is probable that choice of means comes under the 'exterior' act that is due to cooperative *auxilium*: in the choice of means, God moves us and we also move ourselves, and so merit. See also Lonergan, *Grace and Freedom*, pp. 135–136.

24. The point is repeated in *Summa theologiae* 1–2.112.2, where Thomas insists that there can be no preparation for the grace of *auxilium*. It is simply given by God, thus working the preparation required for the infusion of habitual grace.

indeed, he refers to the latter *auxilium* explicitly in the later articles of question 109.25 He has subsequently incorporated this teaching on the operative graces of conversion and perseverance into the later question on merit. Neither conversion in the first place nor perseverance in the grace that is granted in conversion can fall under merit; they are, Thomas repeats in the question on merit, the pure gift of God.

The earlier questions on grace also contribute to the treatment on merit, on the other hand, in what might be termed a 'more constructive' manner. Read in isolation, one might suppose that their is a rather perturbing gap in Thomas's analysis in question 114. While Thomas talks here of the 'ordination' that makes merit possible, and describes both what can and cannot be merited, he nowhere indicates in the question what constitutes the action that is meritorious. In 111.2, however, Thomas has already performed this task. As Thomas reminds us in the heading to question 114, merit is the "effect of cooperative grace." Thus, in the earlier article Thomas has already disclosed the locus of merit. Merit arises in the correct choice of means and in their actual performance, both of which are facilitated by cooperative grace.

Yet grace does not stand on its own in the *Summa*. Thomas's teaching on grace in the *prima secundae* itself presupposes and builds on the earlier analysis of predestination and indeed on the account of God's purpose in creating and redeeming. That by the time of the *Summa* Thomas had to link his teaching on grace explicitly and consistently to an understanding of predestination is suggested by the preceding. In the *Scriptum*, there is no particular problem in explaining how a person gets grace in the first place. God has made grace available to all; to get this grace, all one must do is take the first step to God. Hence, human initiative stands at the beginning of the journey to God and human decisions are sufficient to explain why

---

25. See *Summa theologiae* 1–2.109.9–10. I have examined Thomas's teaching about perseverance in greater detail—and argued for its distinctiveness in the context of thirteenth-century theology—in "'Perseverance' in 13th-Century Theology: The Augustinian Contribution," *Augustinian Studies* 22 (1991): 125–140. I show there how Thomas's sophisticated system of graces has allowed him to portray with greater nuance the different ways in which God provides for the successful completion of the journey to God.

some come to possess grace. In the *Summa*, on the other hand, this reading of the entry into grace has been excluded. Apart from grace, apart from God's preparation for grace, all we can do is sin, which, at least to the mind of the later Aquinas, is not a satisfying 'occasion' for the granting of grace.

Why, then, does one person receive grace in the first place, while others go without grace? One receives grace as the wholly unmerited gift of God, granted by God to some in accordance with God's will. God works conversion from sin to grace in those who have been predestined to convert; the grace of conversion is thus the effect of God's predestining will.[26] In the light of an increased pessimism about human beings, however, Thomas had to extend the scope of God's predestining and so add to the graces that accomplish God's will. The grace of conversion brings healing from sin, but healing is never

---

26. See in general *Summa theologiae* 1–2.112.2–4. In articles 2 and 3, Thomas offers his radical reinterpretation of the familiar scholastic saying, "facientibus quod in se est, Deus non denegat gratiam". In article 2, he asks whether a person must be prepared for the infusion of grace. The answer is no if one is thinking of (operative) *auxilium*: that is simply given by God. But if one is thinking of habitual grace, the answer is yes. The 'matter' of the soul must be prepared for the reception of this formal perfection. Yet, Thomas adds, preparation for habitual grace is itself worked by God, by God's (operative) *auxilium* that disposes the person for the infusion of habitual grace. In the third article of this question, Thomas asks in effect about the connection between the two parts of the scholastic saying. Does God 'have' to give habitual grace to one disposed for it? Thomas refers here to the two perspectives from which preparation for grace can be viewed. As worked in the human person, the granting of grace need not follow preparation for grace: God is not necessitated by any creature. But, as worked in the human creature by God, the infusion of habitual grace will in fact follow the preparation for grace: God does not act idly. Hence, if God has worked the preparation for habitual grace by operative *auxilium*, it is precisely because God has intended to infuse habitual grace in the one so prepared. As Thomas says there, "intentio Dei deficere non potest." What God has ordained (*ordinatur*) will come to pass. In 1–2.112.4, Thomas adds that one person can have more habitual grace than another, because that person will have been more fully prepared for habitual grace by God's *auxilium*. The greater preparation through *auxilium* is itself due to God's greater 'care' for that person, to God's decision to grant that person a more intense possession of habitual grace. Thomas's teaching in this article has an even greater resonance once we recall that predestination of people to salvation expresses God's causal love. Thomas also discusses the preparation for habitual grace and the role of God's *auxilium* inspiring a person to good purpose in 1–2.109.6.

complete in this life.[27] The person who is renewed by grace remains subject to temptation, both from within and from without, and apart from God's free decision to maintain a person in grace—and the execution of this decision by grace, the grace of perseverance—the person will fall prey to temptation, that is, will sin. In this way Thomas undergirds his mature teaching on grace by asserting a predestination by God of some people to salvation, a predestination that accounts for both conversion and continuance in the state of grace. One reaches God in heaven in accordance with God's will.

Thomas's teaching about predestination, however, is not *ad hoc*, as if advanced merely on account of an increased pessimism and the enumeration of a multiplicity of graces bestowed by God. This analysis of predestination is of a piece with Thomas's most basic convictions about God and in particular about God's motive in creating and redeeming. God creates in order to communicate God's goodness outside of God. Each creature displays the divine nature by its nature, acts, and end in the way appropriate to it. The totality of creatures brought into being by God and sustained in their movements by God reflects as best it can the goodness that is God.[28] In creating different kinds of creatures with their appropriate ends, God has not acted haphazardly. Rather, the communicaton of goodness outside of God is structured in accordance with a plan formulated in the divine wisdom.[29] In his comments about the sapiential communication of divine goodness, Thomas frequently employs the language of ordination. God has "ordained" creatures to their appropriate ends, and executes this "ordination" in the working-out of divine providence.[30] Thomas speaks in a similar vein when he turns to the part of providence that

---

27. The point is repeated in *Summa theologiae* 1–2.109.8- 10.

28. Thomas insists through the *prima pars* that God creates out of goodness and that what God creates reflects the divine goodness. See, for example, *Summa theologiae* 1.19.2.

29. See, for example, *Summa theologiae* 1.47.1–2; 1.44.3–4.

30. Thomas discusses providence in the *Summa* in 1.22. He defines providence as the *ratio* of the *ordo* in things to their ultimate end (the divine goodness) that exists in the divine mind (1.22.1,3). He uses the verb *ordinare* of divine providence in such texts as 1.22.4 (where it pertains to providence *ordinare res in finem*) and 1.23.1. Thomas draws a distinction between 'providence' and 'government'. Technically (as at 1.22.1 ad 2), 'providence' refers to the *ratio* established by God and that is in the divine mind; 'government' refers to the execution in the world of this plan. In

is 'predestination'.[31] In order to communicate the divine goodness in a special way, God has "ordained" human beings to come into the immediate presence of God and to share in God's own life and activity. God executes this ordination through the gifts of grace by which God brings the elect to their supernatural end.[32]

Just now, after this excursion into grace, predestination, and the sapiential communication of divine goodness, we are finally in position to return to the first difference noted between Thomas's early and later treatment of merit, namely, the later insistence on the 'divine ordination'. By his use of this term in explaining the possibility of merit, Thomas is, as it were, rewarding the attentive reader of the *Summa*. The first article of the question on merit cannot be read in isolation from what precedes it in the *Summa*. The consequence of such a disjointed reading would be the restriction of the 'ordination' to but a single meaning, and hence to miss Thomas's point. Once we recognize that this question is part of an integrated whole, and that it too assumes and builds on all that has come before, it is possible to see that the 'divine ordination' that grounds merit is rich in associations and in fact covers a wide range of meanings.

In a first approach to 1–2.114.1, all we were able to say of the divine ordination is that it included the promise of God to render reward for good action done in grace. Now we can say significantly more, and in the saying grasp the main purpose of the affirmation of merit in the *Summa*. 'Ordination' is a sapiential term. Its use in the present context brings us to the recognition that God has established the possibility of 'merit' precisely in order to display divine goodness through us and our salvation. What, then, does 'ordination' mean? It refers, in brief, to all the ways in which human existence, the call of human beings

---

practice, however, Thomas uses the term 'providence' to cover the *ratio* and the execution of the plan for creatures established in divine providence.

31. Thomas considers the relation of providence and predestination in *Summa theologiae* 1.23.1,3.

32. Thomas employs the language of 'ordination' when speaking of predestination throughout *Summa theologiae* 1.23. See, for example, the bodies of articles 1 and 3. On the relation between predestination and grace, see 1.23.2 ad 4. In 1.23.3, Thomas states that predestination includes the will to confer grace and glory, that is, both the end of the spiritual journey (glory) and the means to that end (transformational grace).

'MERIT' IN THE THEOLOGY OF THOMAS AQUINAS   111

to a higher destiny, and the movement of human beings to this end through their graced actions conspire to display the goodness of God outside of God. As voluntary agents, God has so constituted us that by our will and movements of will we imitate the willing of God in the way decided by God's wisdom.[33] In our salvation, people display in particular by the divine ordination the goods of both the divine mercy and the divine justice. As predestination, the divine ordination denotes God's loving call of people to share in God's own life.[34] As the promise that links our actions to God's reward, the ordination provides as well the possibility for the exercise of God's justice, of God rendering to us what we deserve for these acts.[35] Finally, again as

33. Recall *Summa theologiae* 1–2.114.1, where Thomas relates the *ordinatio* that grounds meriting to the "free choice" (*liberum arbitrium*) by which people move themselves to action. In 1–2.5.7, the fact that people are to come to heaven by their meritorious actions is expressly ascribed to the divine wisdom.

34. The teaching on predestination in *Summa theologiae* 1.23 assumes that on God's love in 1.20. In the earlier question, Thomas had differentiated God's love from human love. In both, 'love' means "to will good with respect to another." Yet our love is evoked by a good that is already present in another. God's love is causal, creative of good (1.20.2). God's love is responsible for the variety of goods in nature: God loves the better more in the sense that God has willed a greater good to some (1.20.4). Hence, that they both exist indicates that God loves both the nonrational animal and the human being. God has willed for each the good of being. That one exists as human indicates that God loves this being more, willing to it the greater good associated with being human. Thomas builds on this teaching on God's causal love in the discussion of predestination (1.23.4). All humans have been equal recipients of God's love to the extent that God's love creates them with the same nature and capacities by which they are capable of the good natural to their being. Yet those whom God loves more, those whom God has ordained to a greater destiny, have received an even greater good. God's special love for them infuses in them the grace, the effect of this love, that makes it possible to attain the special good that is life with God in heaven (1.23.4 corp. and ad 1).

35. See *Summa theologiae* 1.23.5. In this article, Thomas rejects the notion that 'foreknowledge of merits' is the equivalent of 'predestination'. God does not foresee that one will be good and so decide on that basis to reward that person with eternal life. Rather, our spiritual good is itself the result of God's predestination. Thomas insists that the entire salvific process—running from conversion through good works in grace and perseverance to eternal life itself—falls under God's predestining will. Still, he adds that one part of the salvific process—good works done in grace—is, by the divine ordination, the meritorious occasion of another part of the process, eternal life. Hence, by our merits, made possible by the grace granted to the elect, one can contribute to the attainment of the end set for the person by God.

predestination, the divine ordination furnishes the grace by which the movement to God through our voluntary actions is in fact achieved. Taken in its full range of meanings, the affirmation of the divine ordination as the ground of merit in the first article thus shapes our reading of the subsequent articles on the rewards of merit. Of course, at one level the discussion of merit ascribes great responsiblity and dignity to human beings. As aided by God's grace, and dependent on the divine will, we do merit our salvation. But with his talk of ordination Thomas has put the human achievement into its proper context; he shifts the focus to God, to what God has done and why God has provided for human salvation in this particular way. As Thomas states in the second response of the first article of 1–2.114: "What God seeks from our good works is not profit but glory, that is, the manifestation of God's own goodness; this is what God seeks from God's own works too. The reverence we show God is of advantage not to God but to us. And so we merit something from God, not as though God gained any advantage from our works, but inasmuch as we work with a view to God's glory."[36]

THOMAS'S ORIGINALITY

To this point, my examination of Thomas's teaching about merit has been confined to the Thomistic corpus. By comparing the two principal discussions of merit, it has been possible to discern the distinctive shape of the mature teaching on merit. Locating the question on merit in the *Summa* against the background of Thomas's thought on God's purpose in creating and redeeming, and, especially, on grace, has similarly proved beneficial. Reflection on these related concepts helps us not only to account for the developments in Thomas's teaching about merit but also to grasp the main purpose of Aquinas's affirmation of merit. I wish to conclude this examination by broadening the perspective of the inquiry, to include Thomas's contemporaries. Unable to engage in close readings of these other authors along the lines provided here for Thomas, my concluding

---

36. *Summa theologiae* 1–2.114.1 ad 2. The translation is by C. Ernst, from the Blackfriars edition of the *Summa* (London: Eyre and Spottiswoode, 1964–1980), vol. 30.

comments must by necessity remain wholly tentative. Yet, to complete this account of Thomas's teaching on merit, it will be worthwhile to offer some general comments about the distinctiveness of Thomas's approach. To what extent has Aquinas charted his own path in this use of the theological notion of merit to proclaim God?

Aspects of Thomas's mature teaching will, of course, be repeated in other authors. By Thomas's time, merit was a traditional topic in theological treatises, and a general consensus existed on some key points—for example, that by grace it is possible to merit eternal life, and that texts about reward provide the ultimate scriptural justification for affirming merit despite the difficulties associated with this affirmation.[37] But it would appear safe to say that in the *Summa*, Thomas has offered an analysis of merit that differs from all others in the thirteenth century. Although others will approximate discrete features of the Thomistic analysis of merit—I am thinking here, for example, of those who insist on the promise that grounds merit; or, again, of the general recognition of the need for grace for full merit—no one argues as insistently or consistently for the divine contribution in our meriting. The subtlety with which Thomas has approached the question of grace, detecting the need to show the various ways in which grace comes into contact with the human person, has facilitated the construction of what appears to be the most sophisticated treatment of merit in the thirteenth century, a treatment that grants to people their proper role in their salvation while making especially clear the divine role in merit and salvation.

The question of the genesis of this teaching on grace that provides the immediate context of the teaching on merit has proved vexing to students of Aquinas, in particular his introduction of the grace of *auxilium* and the division of it into operative and cooperative *auxilia*. Some have been inclined to ascribe Thomas's new insights on grace to a series of speculative endeavors, in which, for example, Thomas's reflections on the different movements of will led him eventually to distinguish more carefully between the two *auxilia*.[38] Others have explored Thomas's knowledge of the 'tradition', and have suggested

---

37. For an overview of some thirteenth-century approaches to merit, see Hamm, *Promissio*, pp. 135–312.

38. Lonergan, *Grace and Freedom*, concentrates on Thomas's speculative endeavors, casting only occasional glances at Thomas's work as an historian.

that the changes in Thomas's ideas on grace are due to a greater acquaintance with the tradition, or, to put it more fashionably, are due to the expansion of his repertoire of sources.[39]

For my part, there does not appear to be any good reason to make Thomas's speculative work compete with his historical research. The one complements the other. His speculative gains on will, for example, prepared the way for the fruitful reception of newly discovered theological sources, which in turn reinforced his speculative insights. In this light, the old thesis of Bouillard on the 'Augustinian' contribution to the mature teaching of Aquinas on grace takes on a new attractiveness.

As Bouillard notes, the most significant treatises of the later Augustine (that is, the works that date from after 426) had been lost to the Middle Ages after the Carolingian period. In order to account for Thomas's changed view on conversion—in particular, his different interpretation of the preparation for grace, so that God is responsible for not only the infusion but also the very preparation for grace—Bouillard suggested that Thomas in the early 1260s had rediscovered these late Augustinian works. In reading this Augustine, Thomas would have become sensitive to the 'Massilian' cast of his early account of conversion, and so he would have revised the teaching on conversion to bring it more fully in line with that of the late Augustine.

Bouillard, of course, had been most concerned with the first entry into grace, and so had concentrated on conversion. Yet the late Augustine shows an equal fascination with the grace of perseverance.[40]

---

39. Bouillard, *Conversion et grâce*, tends to overemphasize the role of Thomas's historical research in the construction of the mature teaching on grace. For Bouillard's discussion of the contribution of such late Augustinian writings as *De praedestinatione sanctorum* and *De dono perseverantiae* to the mature Thomistic doctrine of grace, see pp. 92ff.

40. For an excellent orientation to the main stages of Augustine's thinking about grace, see J. Patout Burns, *The Development of Augustine's Doctrine of Operative Grace* (Paris: Etudes Augustiniennes, 1980). According to Burns, Augustine had discovered by 418 an operative grace, tied to predestination, that is responsible for conversion. Only in the writings from 426 on (including *De praedestinatione sanctorum* and *De dono perseverantiae*) did Augustine complete his teaching about grace by insisting on a second operative grace, one responsible for perseverance, that is also tied to predestination.

'MERIT' IN THE THEOLOGY OF THOMAS AQUINAS   115

Once a person has entered the state of grace, why is it that he or she remains in grace despite the constant onslaught of temptation? Augustine replies that God has predestined not only conversion to grace, but perseverance in grace as well, accomplishing both by the transforming grace that is the effect of predestination. In reshaping his teaching on perseverance and on merits (recall what cannot be merited, according to the later Aquinas), Thomas would thus have learned much from Augustine.

Structurally, Thomas' and Augustine's accounts of salvation are remarkably similar. Both ground salvation in God's free decision to save some people, and insist that God works out this salvation through unmerited graces, the graces that Thomas will come to call the operative *auxilia* of conversion and perseverance. Verbal echoes of the late Augustine resonate in the *Summa*. Although the *Summa* possesses, in terms of Bouillard's original statement of his thesis, embarrassingly little that would disclose explicitly the Augustinian roots of the new teaching on conversion, Thomas does cite the late Augustine on the unmerited grace of perseverance.[41] Aquinas has learned from Augustine and made this teaching his own, although he has also been the beneficiary of post-Augustinian reflection on salvation, as with regard to the much fuller description of the possible rewards of merit.

I admit that Bouillard is likely to have been mistaken when he claimed that Thomas was the sole thirteenth-century reader of these late Augustinian treatises. It is in fact probable that Thomas's younger contemporary, the Franciscan Matthew of Aquasparta, read these treatises and read them in their integrity. In Matthew's disputed questions on grace, he quotes these late treatises at great length and clearly has learned from this Augustine to ascribe the beginning as well as the completion of the conversion process to God.[42] But, in

41. See *Summa theologiae* 1–2.109.10 sc. and ad 3.
42. See Bouillard, *Conversion et grâce*, p. 122, n. 126, referring to V. Doucet, editor of Matthew's *Quaestiones Disputatae de Gratia*, BFSMA 11 (Florence, 1935). For his part, Bouillard thinks that Matthew's knowledge of the late Augustine was mediated through Aquinas; given the extent of Matthew's explicit citation of this Augustine in the disputed questions on grace, the denial of a direct reading of Augustine by Matthew appears unfounded. Moreover, Richard H. Rouse has furnished evidence of the availability of Augustine's *De praedestinatione sanctorum* and *De*

comparison to Thomas's assimilation, Matthew's comprehension of the rediscovered Augustine has been only partial.

When it comes to the question of perseverance, Matthew's teaching is wholly traditional, wholly in keeping with those thirteenth-century theologians who had not been exposed to the late works of Augustine. Why does a person persevere? Because of an unmerited gift of God? No, Matthew tells us, perseverance is itself one of the rewards of merit. One stays in grace because one uses correctly the grace that has been received as a gift from God. In other words, probably because he remained more optimistic about human moral capacity, and, at least as is suggested by the disputed questions on grace, because he had not, as Thomas had, seen the need to distinguish carefully among the different movements of will, Matthew does not replicate Thomas's insistence on the prevenience and primacy of God throughout the salvific process. God may start the process, but it is up to the human person to continue the process, staying in grace by good actions and so becoming ever more worthy of God's reward.[43]

The claim with which I began these final observations still holds then. Without denying a human contribution to salvation, the principal focus of Thomas's mature teaching on merit is on God. In the forcefulness with which he makes God the main subject of this teaching, Thomas would seem to stand alone.

University of Notre Dame

---

dono perserverantiae in Paris in the last quarter of the thirteenth century. See his transcription of a fragment of a catalogue from the Sorbonne library, which he dates to c. 1275, in Mary A. Rouse and Richard H. Rouse, "The Early Library of the Sorbonne," in their *Authentic Witnesses: Approaches to Medieval Texts and Manuscripts* (Notre Dame, Ind.: University of Notre Dame Press, 1991), p. 401.

43. I have considered Matthew's teaching about grace and perseverance, and limned its continuity with most other thirteenth-century accounts, in my "'Perseverance' in 13th-Century Theology."

Another Look at the Plurality of the Literal Sense

MARK F. JOHNSON

There has been no unanimity among interpreters of St. Thomas Aquinas as to whether he held a doctrine of the plurality of the literal sense of Scripture, and the chief reason for this diversity of modern opinion lies in the few texts in which Thomas broaches the subject. While at first glance suggesting a doctrine of plurality, these texts have not been thought to state it with a clarity that puts the matter beyond all doubt; scholars who have denied that Thomas held the doctrine have felt free to interpret his texts by other means, such as by his doctrine of theology's basis in the literal sense, or of the inner and outer word.[1]

---

1. Those who have denied that Thomas held a doctrine of plurality include the following: Paul Synave, "La doctrine de s. Thomas d'Aquin sur le sens littéral des Ecritures," *Revue Biblique* 35 (1926): 40–65; Synave, note in *Bulletin Thomiste* 3 (1930–1933): 711–718; J.-M. Vosté, *Revue Biblique* 36 (1927): 112; Ceslao Spicq, note in *Revue des sciences philosophiques et théologiques* 20 (1931): 331; Spicq, *Esquisse d'une histoire de l'exégèse latine au moyen âge*, BT 26 (Paris: J. Vrin, 1944), pp. 276–279; N. Assouad, *France Franciscaine* 13 (1930): 409–504; G. Parella, "Il pensiero de s. Agostino e s. Tommaso circa il numero del senso letterale nella S. Scritture," *Biblica* 24 (1945): 279–302; P. Benoît, *La prophétie* (Paris: Desclée, 1947), appendix 2, pp. 356–359; Synave and Benoît, *Prophecy and Inspiration: A Commentary on the Summa Theologica II-II, Questions 171–178* (New York: Desclée, 1961), pp. 150–153;

I think, however, that the texts state clearly a doctrine of plurality, but have not been read with sufficient care even by those who maintain that Thomas did hold for the plurality of the literal sense.[2] My intention in this article, then, is to take another look at the disputed texts and to show that Thomas maintained the doctrine, with respect not only to Scripture's divine author, but also to its human authors as well. And in the course of the article I shall take a first look at a new text on the matter from Thomas's recently discovered Roman *Scriptum* on book 1 of the *Sentences*. When read in their context, the texts manifest a doctrine of plurality.

Steven Baldner, "The Use of Scripture for the Refutation of Error According to St. Thomas Aquinas," in *Hamartia: Essays in Honor of John M. Crosset* (Toronto: Cullen, 1984), pp. 149–169; Robert G. Kennedy, "Thomas Aquinas and the Literal Sense of Scripture" (Ph.D. diss., University of Notre Dame, 1985), pp. 212–229.

2. Among those who have maintained that Thomas held a doctrine of plurality, see the following: F. Albert Blanche, "Le sens littéral des Ecritures d'après saint Thomas d'Aquin: Contribution à l'histoire de l'exégèse catholique au moyen âge," *Revue Thomiste* 14 (1906): 192–212; F. Cueppens, "Quid S. Thomas de Multiplici Sensu Litterali in S. Scriptura Senserit?" *Divus Thomas* 33 (1930): 164–175; S. M. Zarb, "Utrum S. Thomas unitatem an Vero Pluralitatem Sensus Litteralis in Sacra Scriptura Docuerit?" *Divus Thomas* 33 (1930): 337–359; Zarb, "Unité ou multiplicité des sens littéraux dans la Bible," *Revue Thomiste* 15 (1932): 251–300; Zarb, "De Ubertate Sensus Litteralis in Sacra Scriptura Secundum Doctrinam Sancti Thomae Aquinatis," in *Problemi scelti di teologia contemporanea*, Analecta Gregoriana 68 (Rome: Pontifical University Gregoriana, 1954), pp. 251–273; Réginald Garrigou-Lagrange, *De Deo Uno* (Paris: Desclée, 1938), pp. 74–76; A. Colunga, "Dos palabras aun sobre los sentidos de la S. Escritura," *Ciencia Tomista* 64 (1943): 327–346; D. E. Nacar, "Sobre la unicidad o multiplicidad del sentido literal de las Sagras Escrituras," *Ciencia Tomista* 64 (1943): 193–210; Nacar, "Sobre la unicidad o la duplicidad del sentido literal en la Sagrada Escritura," *Ciencia Tomista* 68 (1945): 362–372; Henri du Lubac, *Exégèse médiévale: Les quatre sens de l'Ecriture* (Paris: Aubier, 1964), 2 / 2: 276–285; Maximin Arias Reyero, *Thomas von Aquin als Exeget: Die Prinzipien seiner Schriftdeutung und seine Lehre von den Schriftsinnen* (Einsiedeln: Johannes, 1971), pp. 143–144; Mark D. Jordan, *Ordering Wisdom: The Hierarchy of Philosophical Discourses in Aquinas*, Publications in Medieval Studies 24 (Notre Dame, Ind.: University of Notre Dame Press, 1986), pp. 27–28. The major Thomistic commentators, such as Cajetan, Bañez, and John of St. Thomas, all side with the view that Thomas did have a doctrine of multiplicity. See Cajetan, *In I Partem divi Thomae Aquinatis Summae Theologiae* 1.10, in *Sancti Thomae Aquinatis: Opera Omnia* (Rome: Propaganda Fidei, 1888), 4:26; Bañez, *Scholastica Commentaria in Primam Partem Summae Theologiae*, ed. L. Urbano (Madrid: Editorial FEDA, 1934), 1:90–99; John of St. Thomas, *Cursus Theologicus* 1.2.12 (Paris: Solemnes, 1931), p. 410, n. 19. Salamanca Thomists universally held

The whole issue is of some importance because it touches upon Thomas's general vision of scriptural interpretation, in which he of course was often engaged. And an understanding of his teaching on this matter is crucial if he is to be correctly understood in the broader context of the history of scriptural exegesis—in determining both his place among his contemporaries and, especially, his debt to the past.

Thomas's teaching on what the literal sense of Scripture is remains constant throughout his teaching career. He maintains consistently that the literal sense of Scripture is what the author of Scripture intends to be understood by the words that are written. The author is twofold, for Thomas maintains that the Holy Spirit is the principal author of Scripture, while a human author operating under the Spirit's inspiration has the role of an instrument. The medium of words makes the literal sense different from the spiritual senses, since in the spiritual senses the medium of meaning is through the things signified by the words of Scripture and is intended by the Holy Spirit alone, whereas in the literal sense the medium of meaning is the words alone, intended both by the human author and the Holy Spirit.[3] And because the spiritual senses of Scripture are based on the similitudes that are to be found among the things signified by the words of the text of Scripture, Thomas denies them any argumentative power, since the similitude at the basis of these senses can be employed in an indefinite

---

the interpretation. See the commentaries on *Summa* 1.1 edited by C. Pozo in *Fuentes para la historia del método teológico en la Escuela de Salamanca* 1, Biblioteca Teológica Granadina 6 (Granada: Facultad de Teología, 1962). Melchior Cano (p. 275) and Francisco de Vittoria (pp. 119–120) make the claim and investigate the matter somewhat, while Domingo de Soto (p. 214) makes the claim but only in the form of a conclusion, standard in that tradition of commentary. Ambrosio de Salazar (pp. 326–327) makes the same claim and, alone among the commentators, refers explicitly to the important text from the *De potentia*.

3. Thomas's main treatments of the literal and spiritual senses of Scripture are the following: *Super Sent.* 1.pro.5 and 2.12.1.2; *De quolibet 7* 6.1–3; *De potentia* 4.1; *Lectura super Sent.* [Rome] 1.pro.4; *Summa theol.* 1.1.9–10. For other texts in which Thomas mentions the senses of Scripture, see *Super ad Galatas* 4.7; *De quolibet 3* 14.1; *Super Psalmos* pro.; *Super Boethii De Trin.* 2.4; *Super Job* 1. Note also that for Thomas the literal sense includes the use of metaphor (as throughout *Super Job* and in *Summa theologiae* 1.1).

number of ways, and hence they lack certitude.[4] Only the literal sense can serve as a scriptural basis for argument in sacred doctrine.[5]

But in a few of Thomas's writings he appears to think that even the literal sense of Scripture can have many meanings; these texts raise difficulties, since a doctrine of plurality would seem to call into question the dependability of theology's argumentative basis in the literal sense of Scripture. I shall examine each text in turn, and, after establishing that Thomas does hold a doctrine of plurality, I shall suggest why his doctrine on this matter should not be considered troublesome.

Six texts touch on a plurality of the literal sense of Scripture. Chronologically ordered, they are the following passages:[6]

1. *Super Sent.* 2.12.1.2 (1252–1256)
2. *Super Sent.* 4.21.1.2.1 ad 3 (1252–1256)
3. *De quolibet 7* 6.1 ad 5 (1256)
4. *De potentia* 4.1 (1265–1266)
5. *Lectura super Sent.* 1.pro.4 (1265)
6. *Summa theol.* 1.1.10 (1266–1267)

I will consider now consider them in order.

SCRIPTUM ON THE SENTENCES

In his general treatment of the Christian doctrine of creation, in book 2, distinction 12, of his Parisian commentary on the *Libri sententiarum*, Thomas asks whether all things were created together. The question arises because of two differing interpretations

---

4. See *Super Sent.* 1.pro.5 and *De quolibet 7* 6.1 ad 4, where Thomas borrows the Augustinian example of the term "lion" being able to refer equally to Christ or the devil.

5. See *Summa theol.* 1.1.10 ad 1, as in *Summa theologiae*, ed. Ottawa Institute of Medieval Studies (Ottawa: Collège Dominicain, 1953), 1:10.

6. The dating is worked out in James A. Weisheipl, "A Brief Catalogue of Authentic Works," in his *Friar Thomas d'Aquino: His Life, Thought, and Work*, 2d ed. (Washington, D.C.: The Catholic University of America Press, 1983), pp. 355–405. For the dating of the Roman commentary see L. E. Boyle, "Alia Lectura Fratris Thome," *Mediaeval Studies* 45 (1983): 418–429, p. 424.

given by the Fathers to the text of Genesis 1:2, "and the earth was formless and void" ("terra autem erat inanis et vacua"). Thomas's main concern here, as in the parallel text from *De potentia*, is to show that the two different expositions do no violence to the context of the literal passage and that both interpretations can be sustained. The seventh difficulty at the outset of article 2 holds that, on the authority of Augustine, we should say that the world was, in fact, created in six days, for Augustine himself says that the authority of sacred Scripture on this matter surpasses the mind of any human being. To understand the text from Genesis in any other way, the argument implies, would be to derogate the authority of sacred Scripture. When Thomas replies, however, he does not appear even to address the argument, for he invokes the ability of the Holy Spirit to make the scriptures pregnant with more meaning than any human being can grasp. Hence no derogation of Scripture occurs, he claims, when it is given different interpretations that preserve the faith.[7] But the difficulty's whole point is that one should not expound Scripture "in many ways" (*diversimode*) at all. How can Thomas start with diverse expositions as a given? The answer to this question lies in his response in the body of the article.

Things pertain to the truth of faith in two ways, directly (*per se*) and indirectly (*per accidens*). That God is one and triune pertains to faith directly and cannot be denied by any believer; such teaching pertains to the substance of faith, without which further teaching cannot proceed. Other things, such as historical events narrated in Scripture, pertain indirectly to faith, insofar as denial of them is implicitly a denial of the truthfulness both of the Holy Spirit, who is the author of sacred Scripture, and, through Scripture, of faith. Now the two expositions of the Fathers—of Augustine, on the one hand; and of Basil and Gregory of Nyssa, on the other—do not deny in any way that God did indeed create the world, which pertains directly to faith. Their expositions differ, however, as to the order in which the creation of things took place, which Thomas thinks pertains indirectly to faith. For Augustine, the order expressed in the Genesis account of six days signifies the order of learning, the order of nature. For

---

7. *Super Sent.* 2.12.1.2 ad 7.

Basil and Gregory and Ambrose, however, the six days explain the temporal order of creation, an interpretation that Thomas notes is more common and more in accord with the letter of the text, at least on the surface.[8] The point here is that both expositions preserve the truthfulness of faith. Granted that they do differ, they nonetheless differ in the explanation of a secondary matter. In differing as to how creation came about, both accounts presuppose and safeguard the fact of creation, about which believers cannot disagree.[9] And even granted the truth of the various accounts, no account that at least preserves the substance of faith would seem able to exhaust the plenitude of truth virtually contained in the passage of Scripture: "quia majori veritate eam [scripturam] Spiritus Sanctus fecundavit quam aliquis homo adinvenire possit."[10] This passage is important for that very reason, for it indicates what would have to be the basis for a plurality of the literal sense of Scripture: the fullness of the Holy Spirit's knowledge and the Spirit's ability to impregnate a text with more meaning than any human being can discern. And the text from the *Scriptum* is also important because Thomas makes his claim in this particular doctrinal context, to which he returns in the important texts on the plurality of the literal sense of Scripture in the *De potentia*. He gives no further indications as to the exact way in which such a filling with more meaning comes about, but we shall encounter some of his ideas on this subject later in this survey.

The other highlighted text from the *Scriptum*, book 4, is important to us if only because it is the first place in Thomas's writings where he employs the notion of "adaptation" in the context of scriptural exposition.[11] The immediate doctrinal context here is that of the sacrament of penance, and in this passage, occasioned by Lombard's text, Thomas is speaking of the venial sins that are cleansed in purgatory. The tradition after Augustine, Lombard maintains, has understood that the words of Paul in 1 Cor. 3:12–13, "wood, straw and stubble" (*lignum, foenum et stipula*), refer to venial sins that are

---

8. *Super Sent.* 2.12.1.2 corp.
9. *Super Sent.* 2.12.1.2 corp.
10. *Super Sent.* 2.12.1.2 ad 7.
11. See the articles of Synave and Zarb, cited above in notes 1 and 2. Both authors get the terminology of "adaptation" from this text, as well as from the text from the *De potentia*.

destroyed by the fire of probation after this life.[12] The difficulty with which Thomas must contend is that no less an authority than Jerome uses these very words in discussing formal heresy, which is a mortal sin, not a venial sin. Apparently, then, *lignum*, *foenum*, and *stipula* are not venial sins. Thomas replies by pointing out that, beyond the principal sense of Scripture, which the author intends, other meanings can be not unfittingly adapted (*non incongrue aptari*), and this is what Jerome is really doing here.[13]

Some students of Thomas's thought see this text as an indication that Thomas did maintain a doctrine of the plurality of the literal sense of Scripture, and this for two reasons.[14] First, Thomas seems to use *principalis sensus* in an ordinal way, which would therefore allow for a posterior, second sense; at first glance, this seems tantamount to an admission of plurality. Second, he uses the verb *aptari* here and will use derivations of this verb in *De potentia* 4, where he seems to allow for a plurality of the literal sense.[15]

Despite some scholars' seizing on this as a prooftext for the plurality of the literal sense, a counsel of caution is in order here. The wording of the text may perhaps suggest a plurality of the literal sense, but those who cite this text do not mention that it lacks something that all later texts on a plurality of the literal sense propose: Thomas's claim that such an adaptation is a proper sense of Scripture.[16] As we shall see, when speaking of a plurality of the literal sense, Thomas customarily emphasizes that those meanings found in Scripture by its expositors that the Holy Spirit has already understood but that the

---

12. Peter Lombard *Sententiae* 4.21.2, ed. Ignatius Brady, (Grottaferrata: CSB, 1981), 2:380.

13. *Super Sent.* 4.21.1.1 ad 3.

14. I have Zarb particularly in mind here. See his "Utrum S. Thomas Unitatem," especially p. 339.

15. See *De potentia* 4.1, as in *Quaestiones Disputatae* 2, ed. P. Pession (Turin: Marietti, 1965), p. 105.

16. It might also be added that Thomas points out that Jerome's "certain kind of adaptation" is not Paul's intention. See *Super Sent.* 4.21.1.2.1 ad 3. Could this mean that Thomas took Jerome's use of the passage to be against the intention of Paul? The text does not say, but when Thomas later comments on the passage from the first letter to the Corinthians, he takes Paul's intention to be that "lignum, fenum et stipula" are venial sins. See *Super I Cor.* 3.2, as in *Super Epistolas S. Pauli Lectura* 1, ed. R. Cai (Turin: Marietti, 1953), p. 262, no. 155.

human author did not know are truly senses of Scripture. In fact, in one text he speaks of plurality in this sense as a property, a *proprium*, of sacred Scripture; he does not do so in this text. If for no other reason, it seems best not to cite this particular text as authoritative on the matter.

Furthermore, in all likelihood the verb *aptari* means something quite different here from what it means when Thomas employs it in describing plural senses of Scripture. We can gather this from the context of the argument to which Thomas is replying. The argument employs Jerome's comments on Isaiah 5:8, in which the prophet is foretelling the doom that will befall the land-grabbers who amass to themselves many houses and much property, for the Lord intends to destroy it all. Jerome sees a similarity between this amassing of property and the practice characteristic of heretics, who heap heretical teaching upon heretical teaching. Thus, they whose Christian house ought to be built with glorious and precious materials such as gold, silver, and precious stones, build them instead with the wood, straw, and stubble (*lignum, foenum et stipula*) of heresy.[17] Thomas presents the difficulty in this way:

> Praeterea, Isa. 5:8, super illud "vae qui coniungitis domum ad domum," dicit Hieronymus: "haeretici dogmata dogmatibus conjungunt, et qui super fundamentum aedificare debuerunt aurum, argentum, et lapides pretiosos, aedificant lignum, fenum et stipulam"; sed haeretici dogmata falsa confingentes non peccant venialiter. Ergo lignum, fenum et stipula non sunt peccata venalia.[18]

What Jerome did, then, was to take the words from the passage in the first letter to the Corinthians and use them in a different context, because the same words could be fitted (*non incongrue aptari*) to the new context. In any case, if perhaps Thomas does intend by this text to teach a real plurality of the literal sense of Scripture, he has left students of his thought many other texts that they can consult, and with greater profit. This text could not be used to prove absolutely that Thomas maintained a doctrine of plurality of the literal sense. Nor could it be used, as Zarb used it, to establish the terminology

---

17. For Jerome's text, see *In Esaiam* 2.5.8, ed. M. Adriaen, CCSL 73/1/2 (Turnholt: Brepols, 1963), p. 69, lines 21–27.

18. *Super Sent.* 4.21.1.2.1 ob.3.

that Thomas might use in explaining a doctrine of a plurality of the literal sense.

DE QUOLIBET 7

Our next text, De Quolibet 7 has escaped the notice of scholars but clearly has something to say about the plurality of the literal sense.[19] The text is from the disputed question *De sensibus sacrae scripturae*, Thomas's *De quolibet* 7 6. In the first article, Thomas asks whether other senses are to be found beyond the literal sense of Scripture, and he replies in the affirmative. The five preliminary difficulties raise different problems. Some argue that if there are other senses beyond the literal sense, then confusion and error will arise from sacred Scripture, and that is unfitting. Again, another points out, the spiritual senses cannot be used to make a sure point, and their presence would accordingly not befit sacred Scripture. The fifth argument, however, has a different approach. That argument holds that any meanings taken from the words of some passage that the author did not intend are not the proper meanings of that passage. But since, as Aristotle points out, one cannot understand many things at the same time, and perforce cannot understand many things in one Scripture, there cannot be many proper senses to sacred Scripture.[20]

For Thomas the answer to this difficulty is to be found in the principal author of Scripture, who is the Holy Spirit. The Spirit has already understood in one word of Scripture many more things than the expositors of Scripture can expound or discern: "Ad quintum dicendum quod auctor principalis sacrae scripturae est Spiritus sanctus, qui in uno verbo sacrae scripturae intellexit multo plura quam per expositores sacrae Scripturae exponantur, vel discernantur."[21] But Thomas continues. He denies the argument's claim that the human author cannot understand many things in one word. Invoking Jerome's

---

19. The import of this text was first suggested to me by Walter Principe.
20. The authority is Aristotle *Topics* 2.10.114b34–35, as in Boethius's version, versio Boethii, ed. Lorenzo Minio-Paluello, AL 5/1–3 (Leiden: Brill, 1969), p. 46.
21. *De quolibet* 7 6.1 ad 5, as in *Quaestiones Quolibetales*, ed. R. Spiazzi (Turin: Marietti, 1956), p. 146.

authority, Thomas points out that the prophets spoke about present events in such a way that they intended to signify future things as well. And so it is not impossible to understand many things at once, insofar as one thing is the figure of another.

> Nec est etiam inconveniens quod homo, qui fuit auctor instrumentalis sacrae Scripturae, in uno verbo plura intelligeret: quia Prophetae, ut Hieronymus dicit super Osee, ita loquebantur de factis presentibus, quod etiam intenderunt futura significare. Unde non est impossibile simul plura intelligere, in quantum unum est figura alterius.[22]

The point to be made here is that Thomas explicitly allows for the possibility ("nec est etiam inconveniens") that a human author, and not just the Holy Spirit, might have understood and intended more than one thing when writing a particular text—in this case intending both present and future events. Since Thomas emphasizes here the meaning of the words of the text ("in uno verbo plura intelligeret"), and not the signification by things signified by those words, which pertains to the spiritual sense and which human beings cannot accomplish, it seems clear that he is allowing here a plurality of the literal sense. This appears even more clearly when the passage is read alongside our next text, taken from *De potentia*.

DE POTENTIA 4.1

De potentia 4.1 contains what may safely be called Thomas's most thorough presentation of a doctrine of the plurality of the literal sense. In this article, Thomas is treating the question about the creation of matter and whether unformed matter was created prior in time to the creation of things. The treatment thus parallels that found in his Parisian *Scriptum* on the *Sentences* 2.2. Augustine, on the one hand, and Ambrose and the Greek Fathers, on the other, held different views on this question; but their explanations of the text from the first chapter of Genesis did no violence to the text and its context, and both interpretations preserved the truth that the world was created by God. For that reason Thomas felt compelled to respond

---

22. *De quolibet* 7 6.1 ad 5. For Jerome's text, see *In Osee* pro., ed. M. Adriaen, CCSL 76/1/6 (Turnholt: Brepols, 1969), p. 3, lines 83–88.

PLURALITY OF THE LITERAL SENSE   127

to both sides when he answered the arguments proposed by each view in his commentary on the *Sentences*, although he himself preferred the explanation of Augustine.[23] Before answering the immediate query of the article, Thomas provides a preface of sorts, concerning the discussion of the meaning of the text of Genesis, and he counsels caution on two matters. First, something clearly false should not be attributed to sacred Scripture, which is teaching the creation of things, because sacred Scripture is given to us by the Holy Spirit and cannot be subject to falsehood, just as the Holy Spirit is not subject to falsehood.

The second matter takes us almost to the other extreme. Whereas the first concerns the attribution of falsehood to Scripture, the second concerns an excessive limitation of the truthfulness of Scripture. We should not constrict the meaning of a text of Scripture in such a way as to preclude other truthful meanings that can, without destroying the context, be fitted to Scripture: "Aliud est ne aliquis ita Scripturam ad unum sensum cogere velit, quod alios sensus qui in se veritatem continent, et possunt, salva circumstantia litterae, Scripturae aptari, penitus excludantur."[24] The ability of Scripture to admit of many meanings is part of its dignity, Thomas continues, for because of these many meanings it can happen that the different minds of human beings can grasp a truth found in Scripture, and that those human beings will accordingly marvel in that grasping. These many senses seem to serve two purposes. The first purpose, is the edification of the faithful: the individual believer can read Scripture and delight in grasping some understanding of the text; the believer sees that an explanation he or she gives to a particular passage is both internally consistent, a prerequisite of anything true, and in accordance with the text and its context.

The second purpose is that defense of the truth of Scripture can more effectively be made. If an unbeliever were to give an interpretation of a passage of Scripture that is false, the believer has the option of turning to another sense that the unbeliever must acknowledge.

What does Thomas mean here by having recourse to "another sense of Scripture?" Is he speaking here of the spiritual senses of

23. See *Super Sent.* 2.12.1.2 corp. At the end of *De potentia* 4.1 corp., Thomas reiterates his intention to respond to both sides.
24. *Super Sent.* 2.12.1.2 corp.

Scripture and not at all about a plurality of the literal sense?[25] This seems unlikely for two reasons. First, Thomas consistently denies any argumentative power to the spiritual sense, because it is based upon similitude, which can be employed in an indefinite and hence uncertain number of ways.[26] Why would he suggest defending the faith against unbelievers by means of a type of theological argumentation the very efficacy of which he categorically denies?

Second, the context of the article precludes the spiritual sense. The creation of the world that Moses describes is intended neither to signify the New Covenant, since the Old Covenant had not yet been made, nor heavenly bliss, nor the moral actions of human beings. Moses is simply explaining the creation of the world.[27] If creation is understood as entailing total dependence in being on the part of all created things, then the possibility of creation's having been simultaneous or successive remains open, for both modes of creation presuppose total dependence in being.

Thomas does not provide us with an example of what "another meaning" (*alius sensus*) might be, but what he has said thus far may be of some help. He has cautioned against restricting the meaning of the text to one meaning because other meanings that are truthful and that fit the passage without disrupting its context may exist. If so, then one might be able to interpret a disputed passage of Scripture differently from how an unbeliever interprets the same passage. If the interpretation of the believer contains truth and is therefore not nonsense, and if it fits the letter of the passage and its surrounding context, then the believer can at least show that the unbeliever's interpretation is not necessarily the one intended by the passage, thereby preserving the inerrancy of Scripture.[28]

Having allowed for a plurality of meanings that preserve the surroundings or context of the passage, Thomas explains by whose agency

---

25. See Baldner, "Use of Scripture," p. 160.

26. *Super Sent.* 1.pro.5; *De quolibet* 7 6.1 ad 4.

27. *De potentia* 4.1. Note, however, that when Thomas presents the four senses of Scripture while expounding Galatians, he exemplifies them in the phrase, "Let there be light." See *Super ad Galatas* 4.7 (ed. Cai p. 621, no. 254).

28. This reading of Thomas's text is in accord with his standard apologetical norm that one cannot prove the teachings of faith to those who do not accept the principles; all one can do is solve their arguments and thereby spare the faith from the charge of falsehood. See *Summa theol.* 1.1.8.

such plurality might come about. He sees nothing incredible in thinking that Moses and other inspired writers could understand, by divine concession, the different truths that people might understand, and that they in turn could detail these truths in one passage, thus rendering each separate meaning a meaning of the author. "Unde non est incredibile, Moysi et aliis sacrae Scripturae auctoribus hoc divinitus esse concessum, ut diversa vera, quae homines possent intelligere, ipsi cognoscerent, et ea sub una serie litterae designarent, ut sic quilibet eorum sit sensus auctoris."[29] Who is the *auctor* here? Could the *auctor* be simply the Holy Spirit? While such a reading would help the interpretation of Synave and Zarb, who both deny a plurality of intended meaning on the part of the human author, the *auctor* here must nevertheless be the human author. To begin with, Thomas has just devoted a fairly complex sentence to explaining the possibility of the human writer's knowing and intending the many truths to be discovered by others. It would be very odd if Thomas were then without warning to attribute the intended communication of this knowledge to someone other than the human authors of whom he had been speaking. In addition, what follows this text precludes any interpretation other than that the *auctor* mentioned here is the human author; for, when he continues, Thomas distinguishes this author from the Holy Spirit, who would be the only other possible candidate for *auctor*. Even if it should happen, he says, that the author does not know some of the truths that expositors of Scripture fit to the text, there is no doubt that the Holy Spirit already knew these truths, and the Holy Spirit is the principal author of Scripture: "Unde si etiam aliqua vera ab expositoribus sacrae Scripturae litterae aptentur, quae auctor non intelligit, non est dubium quin Spiritus sanctus intellexerit, qui est principalis auctor divinae Scripturae."[30] Thomas finally brings this whole discussion to its end and concludes: every truth that can be adapted to divine Scripture, so long as it preserves the context of the passage, is its *sensus*, its meaning.[31]

The intelligibility of these passages depends on Thomas's conception of the authorship of sacred Scripture. He consistently maintains

29. *De potentia* 4.1.
30. *De potentia* 4.1.
31. *De potentia* 4.1.

that the author of Scripture is twofold: principal and instrumental.[32] The principal author of sacred Scripture is the Holy Spirit, and the instrumental author is the particular man who wrote the text. Now the Holy Spirit, it goes without saying, fully understands the message intended to be handed on to human beings. The human author, on the other hand, whom the Holy Spirit employs as an instrument, does not know what the Holy Spirit intends to hand on, except to the extent that he is moved by the inspiration of the Holy Spirit to know the truths to be handed on.[33]

The meaning, then, of the passage from the *De potentia* is this: Granted the possible deficiency of the human author's knowledge, it can still happen that the Holy Spirit should so inspire the human author that the human author would know the many true things that are contained virtually in his words, and thus intend to pass on any of those truths by the word or words he employed. And while it may or may not be the case that the human author understands the total virtuality of his words, it is clear that the Holy Spirit first understood the total virtuality that the words contain, and to that extent the Spirit wills all truthful predication by expositions of sacred Scripture that fits the words used.

---

32. See *De quolibet 7* 6.1 ad 5: "auctor principalis sacrae Scripturae est Spiritus sanctus...homo...fuit auctor instrumentalis sacrae Scripturae"; 6.3: "in ista Scriptura, cuius Spiritus sanctus est auctor, homo vero instrumentum; secundum illud Psalmi 44: 'Lingua mea calamus scribae velociter scribentis'"; *De potentia* 4.1: "non est dubium quin Spiritus sanctus intellexerit, qui est principalis auctor divinae Scripturae."

33. Kennedy uses Thomas's commentaries on the logical works of Aristotle as rule for interpreting Thomas's notion of biblical meaning and so feels compelled to deny the straightforward meaning of this text from the *De potentia*. Kennedy invokes instead Thomas's teaching from *Summa theol.* 2-2 on the imperfection of human knowledge in prophecy in order to diminish Thomas's claim here regarding the human author's ability to know and intend many meanings in the text that the author produces. See Kennedy, "Aquinas and the Literal Sense," pp. 228–229. Such a reading runs counter both to the flow of the text and to Thomas's own language. The use of *designarent* in this text is simply too strong in its meaning to suggest that the human author physically wrote some words that just happened to have many possible meanings, unbeknownst to the author. Of the 1405 occurrences of the verb *designo, -are* noted in the *Index Thomisticus*, fully one-third are found in Thomas's scriptural commentaries, and they overwhelmingly entail the notion of expressly pointing something out or detailing. See *designo, -are*, in *Index Thomisticus* sect.2 concord.1, pp. 843–858.

The main difficulty with these texts from the *De potentia* is seeing what might fit the literal sense of Scripture. Thomas is not specific here, but again perhaps the little he does say will be of some help. To start with, he seems to require two things: that the diverse truths be truthful in themselves and that their being fitted to the scriptural passage be consistent with the context.

What is it that contains truth within itself? Thomas gives us no immediate hint, but the context of the article does. The doctrinal question being considered here, again, is the creation of things and whether the creation was effected all at once or over time. Augustine's account of Genesis conceives the order of creation as the order of nature, and hence of learning. The Greek Fathers, on the other hand, see the order depicted by the text as referring to the temporal order of things, for they thought that the lack of form did not mean the lack of all form but, rather, the lack of the full, formal perfection of things. The point that Thomas makes in the middle of the determination of the present article is that neither of the two accounts is discordant with the Christian teaching that the existence of things depends totally on the creative activity of God.[34] If either account were discordant, then that account could not be said of Scripture, and for two reasons. The first reason is simply that such a predication would be false, for the subject could not admit of the predicate; to speak of the manner of the creation of things in a way that denied the very creative causality of God would be self-refuting. The second reason, which we have seen Thomas give before, is that God just does not tell untruths.[35]

What Thomas seems to have in mind by the phrase "continet in se veritatem" is simply that the subject of which the expositor of Scripture wishes to make a predication must be susceptible of that predication. Thus it may be said that the predications "Socrates is breathing," "Socrates is thinking," and "Socrates is running" require for their truth that Socrates be the sort of subject that is capable of breathing, thinking, or running.

But since Scripture is more specific, since its aim is not simply to provide a list of things of which possible predications can be made, Thomas stresses the importance of the context of the passage, the

34. *De potentia* 4.1.
35. *Super Sent.* 2.12.1.2; *De potentia* 4.1.

circumstantia litterae. The fact is that Scripture details certain events that did, in fact, occur. One consequence is that while what did occur can occur, two mutually exclusive attributes cannot have occured simultaneously. Although Moses could be at the foot of Mount Sinai or on its top, when he was on the top of Mount Sinai, he could not also have been at the foot. Similarly, the creation of things to which the text of Genesis bears witness could have occurred all at once or over time. Neither of these two modes of creation admits of the other, however, and unless the context of the text of Genesis, its *circumstantia litterae*, indicates to us clearly the modality of the creation of things, we shall not know that modality for certain. Thomas contends that the context allows for both accounts,[36] despite the fact that the text of Genesis seems to indicate a temporal succession,[37] in which case the account of the Greek Fathers and Ambrose would seem to have the upper hand; but Augustine's interpretation cannot absolutely be excluded. Therefore both accounts can be sustained, and both are in accordance with faith. The result is that, since the Holy Spirit knew that the words of Genesis would allow for either reading (which Moses would have known and intended, had the Holy Spirit so informed him) and since the accounts of Augustine and of the Greek Fathers and Ambrose do no violence to the text, then it can be said that at least the Holy Spirit, if not Moses himself, intended both accounts, and that they are, to that extent, senses of Scripture.

To my mind far too much emphasis has been placed on the notion of *adaptatio* by recent writers on this issue.[38] This is understandable in part, for the verb *aptari* and its related abstract noun *adaptatio* are mentioned here in this important text from the *De potentia* and the earlier text from book 4 of the Parisian commentary on the *Sentences* (discussed above). But because writers on both sides of this topic fix on

---

36. *Super Sent.* 2.12.1.2.

37. *De potentia* 4.1. The important biblical text for Augustine here, which led him to his position that the account in Genesis is an account of the order of nature and of doctrine, is Ecclesiasticus 18:1, "Qui vivit in aeternum creavit omnia simul." See *De genesi ad litteram* 6.6, ed. J. Zycha, CSEL 28/3/2 (Vienna: F. Tempsky, 1894), pp. 177- 178, lines 24–13.

38. Here again I have particularly in mind Synave and Zarb.

the notion of *adaptatio*, they do not concern themselves with the more crucial question at stake here. The crucial question is not about the so-called adapted senses, which expositors of Scripture discover without the human author's having intended so, but about the multiplicity of meanings known and intended by the human author of Scripture. It is precisely in the context of explaining why he accepts the equal scriptural fidelity of the accounts of Augustine and of Ambrose and the Greeks that Thomas goes so far as to say that Moses through the concession of God could have known and detailed the many diverse truths that would arise in the minds of later interpreters, and that, furthermore, each of these truths would be the meaning of the author.[39]

In sum, Thomas holds in this text that the human author of Scripture could know and intend a multiplicity of meanings that would arise from the letter of the text the author himself produces: a multiplicity of the literal sense. To be sure, Thomas points out that the human author can do this because of divine concession, but that does not change the fact that the resulting meaning on the part of the human author is restricted to the literal sense, since human beings can only signify by words. It is also true that this assertion on Thomas's part raises other questions, but that does not change the fact that this text from the *De potentia* explicitly allows for a multiplicity of meanings. And while Thomas never discusses his teaching on this matter in as much detail again, his subsequent discussions on the literal sense remain open to his teaching here, and none repudiates it.

THE ROMAN COMMENTARY ON THE *SENTENCES*

At this point we can turn to a text from Thomas's recently discovered Roman commentary on book 1 of the *Sentences*, a text that is contemporaneous with the *De potentia*. Although most

---

[39]. Note that in the passage from *De quolibet* 7 6.1 ad 5, Thomas says that the prophets "intended" to signify more than one thing: "quia Prophetae, ut Hieronymus dicit super Osee, ita loquebantur de factis presentibus, quod etiam intenderunt futura significare."

likely a student's *reportatio* of Thomas's classroom lectures at Santa Sabina in Rome, the text is authentic and solid enough to be used for studying Thomas's teaching.[40]

In the context of the general discussion of the nature and scope of sacred doctrine, Thomas includes an article that concerns the manner of procedure in *sacra doctrina*: "Videtur quod modus procedendi in hac scientia sit inconueniens." Among the four objected difficulties with which Thomas must contend, the third claims that sacred doctrine is handed on in an unfitting manner because a multiplicity of senses confuses the mind: "Multitudo sensuum confundit intellectum. Set hec habet multiplicem sensum. Ergo confundit intellectum, et sic inconuenienter traditur."[41]

Thomas begins his reply by acknowledging that there is a multiplicity in sacred Scripture that comes about because of its author, who is the Holy Spirit.[42] This multiplicity is the twofold sense of Scripture, the literal and mystical senses, and they differ because the literal sense is the one that the words convey while the mystical sense is the one whose meaning arises not from the words but from what is signified by the words. Thomas next gives the standard explanation of the spiritual or mystical sense of Scripture. The reason for the spiritual sense, he says, is that the Holy Spirit ordained things in such a way that the things signified by the words of Scripture should in turn signify something else. Thomas then adds that there are "many literal senses in Scripture" and that each of them is true.

> Item aliud proprium est quia in ista sunt plures sensus litterales et quilibet est uerus. In aliis autem unus solus sensus est uerus, ille scilicet quem auctor intendit. Cum enim sacra Scriptura tradita sit per Spiritum sanctum et nichil in ipsa possit excogitari quod non excogitaverit Spiritus sanctus,

---

40. For a brief account of the discovery and the authenticity of the Roman commentary, see my "*Alia Lectura Fratris Thome*: A List of the New Texts of St. Thomas Aquinas found in Lincoln College, Oxford, MS. Lat. 95," in *Recherches de théologie ancienne et médiévale* 57 (1990):34–61. See also L. E. Boyle, "Alia Lectura Fratris Thome," and Hyacinthe-F. Dondaine, "Alia lectura fratris Thome? (Super I Sent.)," *Mediaeval Studies* 42 (1980): 308–336. I shall be citing from my own transcriptions of the text. A critical edition is being prepared by John F. Boyle and L. E. Boyle.

41. *Lect. super Sent.* [Rome] 1.pro.4 ob.3, Oxford, Lincoln College lat. 95, f. 4v.
42. *Lect. super Sent.* [Rome] 1.pro.4 ob.3, Lincoln College lat. 95, f. 5r.

quicquid dicitur de sacra scriptura, dummodo non contradicat veritati fidei, est proprium sibi, sicut dicit Augustinus XII Conf.[43]

One sees here an unmistakable similarity to the text from the *De potentia*. As in the *De potentia*, the fullness of the Holy Spirit's knowledge is invoked to justify the claim of plurality. Anything one could think about sacred Scripture, the Holy Spirit has already understood. About this there is no doubt.[44] In the Roman *Sentences*-commentary Thomas provides as well the warning regarding the contradiction of the teaching of faith, although no mention is made here of the *circumstantia litterae* that figured in the *De potentia*. But then, perhaps, "dummodo non contradicat veritati fidei" subsumes into one phrase what Thomas said in two phrases in the *De potentia*. The attribution to Scripture of something that does not save the context of the passage would by that fact contradict the faith to the extent that such an attribution denies what Scripture really says to be true.[45]

The importance of this text rests in the use of the phrase "plures sensus litterales." Thomas does not use this exact phrase in any other work, and although it seems to be innocuous, some have been hesitant to use it in describing Thomas's teaching, because they fear that the attribution of plural senses to the literal sense renders the literal sense subject to equivocation and, consequently, renders suspect the faith that is revealed through Scripture.

Another point of interest in this text is Thomas's consideration of the plurality of the literal sense as a *proprium*. While precisely how he is using the word *proprium* is not definite—in the logic of Thomas's day the term usually admitted of four uses[46]—Thomas apparently means that this plurality is found only in sacred Scripture, as is the spiritual sense, though neither is to be found in every passage. But this can only be a guess.[47] At any rate it seems clear that, if this property

---

43. *Lect. super Sent.* [Rome] 1.pro.4 ad 3, Lincoln College lat. 95, f. 5r.
44. *De potentia* 4.1.
45. See *Super Sent.* 2.12.1.2 and *Summa theol.* 1.32.4.
46. See, for instance, Peter of Spain *Summule logicales* 2, ed. Lambertus M. de Rijk (Assen: Van Gorcum, 1972), p. 22.
47. Why not, say, in the fourth and most proper way listed by Peter of Spain? Might this not attest all the more to the dignity of Scripture? If this were Thomas's meaning, then it would seem that each and every literal passage of Scripture would

of many literal senses is found only in sacred Scripture, then this must be because of the breadth of its divine authorship, to which Thomas makes constant reference when he speaks of the all-encompassing grasp of the Holy Spirit's knowledge.

Thomas does not say here, as he did in the *De potentia*, that the Holy Spirit could have communicated its fuller knowledge to the human author, who could then have known and intended many meanings when writing the text. But Aquinas does not deny the *De potentia*'s teaching either. Either way, he repeats here the more important contention about the fullness of the Holy Spirit's knowledge, which makes possible the human author's knowing and intending many meanings. Given that the *De potentia* is a finished product of Thomas's public teaching, while this text is an unfinished report of elementary classroom teaching, the absence of one element from the present text need not be telling.

SUMMA THEOLOGIAE

Our survey of the texts in which Thomas speaks of a multiplicity of the literal sense comes to a close with a consideration of the text in the *prima pars* of the *Summa theologiae*. This text is found in the determination of 1.10, an article devoted to the senses of Scripture. Thomas does think, of course, that there are four senses to Scripture, one literal and the other three spiritual, and he begins his response with the now-standard answer that God is the author of sacred Scripture. God's power is such that God is able not only to make words signify things, as human beings can do, but also make the things signified through words further signify other things. Thomas follows all this with a description first of the literal sense and

---

be subject to this plurality, and so none would have an indubitable meaning. Perhaps there is an analogy here with Thomas's denial that scriptural exposition must always be done according to all four senses, the one literal and the three spiritual. See *De quolibet* 7 6.2 ad 4: "dicendum quod quatuor isti sensus [unus litteralis et tres spirituales] non attribuuntur sacrae Scripturae, ut in qualibet eius parte sit in istis quatuor sensibus exponenda; sed quandoque istis quatuor, quandoque tribus, quandoque duobus, quandoque uno tantum." Perhaps, for like reason, if Scripture does admit in some places of many literal senses, it need not be the case that each and every passage of Scripture be read according to many literal senses.

PLURALITY OF THE LITERAL SENSE 137

then of the three spiritual senses that depend on the literal sense. But after describing the manifold possibilities of the spiritual senses, Thomas returns to the literal sense and adds a clarification. "Quia vero sensus litteralis est, quem auctor intendit; auctor autem Sacrae Scripturae Deus est, qui omnia simul suo intellectu comprehendit; non est inconveniens, ut dicit Augustinus XII Confess., si etiam secundum litteralem sensum in una littera Scripturae plures sint sensus."[48] Here, as in both the Roman commentary and the *De potentia*, Thomas makes reference to the knowledge of God, who comprehends all things at once in God's understanding, when he stresses the divine authorship of Scripture. He does not point out here, as he did in both the *De potentia* and the Roman commentary, that the Holy Spirit has already understood whatever truth might be said about Scripture, but the phrase "qui omnia simul suo intellectu comprehendit" serves that function here. The phrase also seems to provide one of the terms for what seems to be a suppressed premise, namely, that whatever truth can be found in Scripture, God intends. Thomas invokes, for the second time, the authority of a passage from Augustine's *Confessions* that speaks explicitly of a plurality of the literal sense of Scripture.[49]

Some might be hesitant to say that Thomas is holding here for a multiplicity of the literal sense, but both his argument and his citation of Augustine seem to show that he does. His brief presentation of the literal sense at the outset of his response is not contradicted by this clarification, for that presentation did not claim that the literal sense must be one, and one only.[50] In addition, Thomas's placement of this

---

48. *Summa theol.* 1.1.10.
49. Thomas had invoked Augustine in the Roman commentary; see *Lectura super Sent.* [Rome] 1.pro.4 ad 3, f. 5r. The source is *Confessiones* 12.31.42, ed. L. Verheijen, CCSL 27/1/1 (Turnholt: Brepols, 1981), p. 240, lines 1–7. Note how Thomas's text from the *De potentia* recalls Augustine's "per quem deus unus sacras litteras vera et diversa visuris multorum sensibus temperavit." Compare *De potentia* 4.1, "hoc esse divinitus concessum, ut diversa vera, quae homines possent intelligere, ipsi cognoscerent."
50. Note, however, that shortly after his response Thomas does refer to the literal sense as "one." In responding to the article's first difficulty, which had argued that many senses in Scripture would breed falsehood, Thomas maintains that Scripture does not produce confusion when understood in his way, since all the other senses are based upon one, namely, the literal sense, from which alone argumentation can be taken (*Summa theol.* 1.1.10 ad 1). But Thomas's argument here simply seems to

clarification at the end of the response makes sense only if it is seen as taking the discussion of multiplicity found in the spiritual senses and applying it to the literal sense as well. When read in light of the two previous texts from the *De potentia* and the Roman Commentary on *Sentences* 1, with which it is roughly contemporary, this text from the *Summa theologiae* seems to bear witness to a teaching that is by now firmly rooted in Thomas's mind.

The straightforward reading of Thomas's texts indicates that he holds a doctrine of the possibility of there being a plurality of the literal sense of sacred Scripture, and, when his texts are read with sensitivity to the doctrinal issues under discussion, to the authorities he invoked, and to their context and purpose, this conclusion, while raising other questions, cannot be avoided. But while no problems arise by accepting this doctrine from a textual point of view, Thomas's teaching would seem, perhaps, to lead to other problems, problems that have prevented others of his interpreters from accepting the claims made here. Would not Thomas's teaching that it is possible that there be many literal senses lead to the very difficulty envisaged by Spicq, namely, that such an introduction of many literal senses would leave theology without a sure basis?[51] This ominous claim makes sense if one thinks that the only alternative to the universally negative proposition, "There is no scriptural passage subject to a multiplicity of the literal sense," is its contrary, "Every scriptural passage is subject to a multiplicity of the literal sense." If this were true, then indeed no scriptural passage would have an indubitable literal meaning, and thus the theologian, who can argue only from the literal sense, would have no sure basis on which to argue. But of course there is a middle ground.

The acceptance of the proposition "Some scriptural passage is subject to a multiplicity of the literal sense" does not commit one to the view that each and every scriptural passage is subject to a multiplicity of the literal sense. Thomas nowhere insists that such is the case. The very fact that the question of the multiplicity of the

---

be setting the literal sense off from the other three senses with regard to its doctrinal authority, contrasting the one literal sense with the three spiritual senses. The text is not claiming that within the literal sense there is only one sense. That is why Thomas closes his response to the difficulty with the claim that whatever pertains directly to faith is found according to the literal sense somewhere in Scripture explicitly.

51. Spicq, *Esquisse*, p. 279.

literal sense arises only in connection with Genesis 1:2 should serve to indicate that Thomas's use of the notion of multiplicity is for the purpose of explaining the question at hand; he is not out to make assertions that pertain to the entirety of sacred Scripture.[52]

Still, Spicq has a point. If a particular passage of Scripture is subject to many literal senses, then that passage's literal meaning will not be certain. Does this present a problem? I do not think so. Clearly not every passage in Scripture, however inspired it might be, is of equal importance to the substance of faith.[53] In the Gospel according to John (10:30) Jesus says, "The Father and I are One." Does this not have more to do with the substance of faith than the cause of Tobit's blindness (Tobit 2:10)? And yet both are communicated to the believer by the literal sense of inspired Scripture. Similarly, the importance of Genesis 1:1, "In the beginning God created the heaven and the earth," would seem, to Thomas's mind, to overshadow the importance of Genesis 1:2, "and the earth was without form and void." That God is the creator of all things is more important to the substance of faith than how God created—however interesting and beautiful that might be. Thomas's point in all of this is clear from his claim that "everything necessary to salvation is contained explicitly somewhere in the literal sense of Scripture."[54]

Given that Thomas does have a doctrine of a multiplicity of the literal sense, to what end would he see it ordered? He does not say what the end would be, but he has left us a clue. In the key text from the *De potentia*, he points out that an individual who discovers a truth in the words of Scripture would marvel at the discovery.[55] If someone should have cause for marvel in his or her investigations into certain obscure scriptural passages—and if through diligent study of those passages should come to study Scripture more and more, and

---

52. Note also that in the very last line of Thomas's text from *Summa theol.* 1.1.10, he says that there is nothing inappropriate in there being many senses of the literal sense "in one letter" (*in una littera*) of Scripture, which could possibly mean "in one text," or "in a passage," of sacred Scripture.

53. Thus Thomas makes a distinction between those things that pertain *per se* to faith, and those that pertain *per accidens*. See *Super Sent.* 2.12.1.2; and *Summa theol.* 1.32.4 and 2–2.1.6 ad 1.

54. *Summa theol.* 1.1.10 ad 1.

55. *De potentia* 4.1.

love God more and more—then is not God drawing that someone to God, which is the final cause of Scripture? Thomas does not say, but one doubts that he would quibble here.⁵⁶

But since Thomas does hold the doctrine of the plurality of the literal sense of Scripture it is important and perhaps perplexing to note that he does not seem to invoke the doctrine when he is actually engaged in scriptural exegesis. Having to date examined his expositions on Job, the Gospel of John, the letters of Paul, and the psalms, I have not encountered the doctrine. One will see Thomas on occasion suggest that one or another interpretation of a passage is better. But one does not find him saying, at least in these expositions, that one interpretation and another are both true and that both are the intended meanings of the Holy Spirit or of the human author, which was the significant claim made in the *De potentia*.

It may be, in the end, that Thomas holds the doctrine for reasons that arise largely from his intellectual context. Significant authorities in medieval theology, Ambrose, Augustine, Basil, and Gregory of Nyssa disagreed on Scripture's meaning with regard to the order of creation, though their various interpretations, to Thomas's mind, preserve both the truth of faith regarding the fact of creation and the text and context of Genesis 1:2. Augustine himself says explicitly that the divine author of Scripture can intend more than one meaning in a passage of Scripture. And Thomas's own presentation of scriptural inspiration is quite at home with the possibility of the human author's having known and intended, under the influence of the Holy Spirit, many diverse meanings in one text of the Scripture. Given such doctrinal circumstances, it is easy to see how Thomas can assert the doctrine of plurality.

All this is not to suggest that Thomas arrived at the doctrine in order to harmonize the cacophony of patristic voices regarding a particular passage in Scripture, for the authority of the Fathers, while significant, need not be saved at all costs.⁵⁷ It would be odd for Thomas to construct a new doctrine of biblical meaning in order

---

56. One finds the general tenor of this thinking in Thomas's defense of the use of metaphor and *verba obscura* in sacred Scripture. See, for example, *Super Boethii De Trin.* 2.4, ed. B. Decker, 2d ed. (Leiden: Brill, 1965), p. 100; and *Summa theol.* 1.1.9 ad 2.

57. *Summa theol.* 1.1.8 ad 2 and 2–2.10.12.

to save the authority of the Fathers in a matter that he consistently regards as being of secondary importance. I would, rather, suggest that Thomas's teaching of the possibility of the plurality of the literal sense of Scripture is to his mind a faithful application of the teaching of Augustine and even Jerome. In Thomas's own hands, it becomes an instrument used to explain that a legitimate diversity in theological understanding could well be the intention of the Holy Spirit and even of the Spirit's instrument, the human author of Scripture.

Duns Scotus on Autonomous Freedom and Divine Co-Causality

WILLIAM A. FRANK

John Duns Scotus teaches that God is an immediate, efficient cause of created volitions. He comes to this conclusion as an outcome of his logically prior commitments to the absolute contingency of God's relationship to the world and to the doctrine of God's certain, determinate foreknowledge of future, contingent events. On a first consideration, the doctrine of God's immediate causality would seem to imply determinism of the created will. If that were so, then this determinism would conflict with what is generally taken to be a hallmark of Scotistic thought, namely, the radically indeterminist freedom of the created will.

In what follows we shall first establish the fact and rationale of Scotus's teaching on God's immediate causality of created volitions. Second, we shall examine how Scotus understands this immediate causality so as to avoid the entailment of determinism, which he accomplishes through a remarkable application of his theory of partial, essentially ordered co-causes. In the third part we shall attend to two recent interpretations of Scotus that, contrary to our thesis, accept the entailment of determinism of created wills. Our engagement of these "revisionist" interpretations of Scotus's voluntarism will help to bring out something of the subtle and remarkable character of the cooperative unity of divine and created wills. Finally, we shall conclude with some observations on Scotus's regard for the element of mystery in our knowledge of God.

THE TEACHING OF IMMEDIATE DIVINE CAUSALITY

Duns Scotus introduces the thesis of God's immediate causality in *Ordinatio* 2.37.2[1] as an objection targeting the claim that a created will is the total, immediate cause of its volitions. The fundamental assumption supporting the targeted thesis is that freedom of will necessarily entails being the total, immediate cause of one's own volitional acts.[2] Under this assumption, the denial of the

---

1. John Duns Scotus, *Opera Omnia*, ed. by L. Wadding, 12 vols. (Lyons: Durand, 1639); as reprinted in 26 vols. (Paris: Vivès, 1891–1895), at 13:368–393. As yet there is no critical edition of this question. Subsequent citations to *Ordinatio* 2.37.2 will be taken from Allan B. Wolter's revision of the Wadding-Vivès texts on the basis of three manuscripts: Assisi, Bibl. comm. 137, ff. 136rb–137; Paris, Bibl. nat. lat. 15,360, ff. 197ra–198vb; and Vatican City, Bibl. Apost., Vat. lat. 883, ff. 143vb–145rb. These are the first three of the ten manuscripts being used by the Scotistic Commission in its edition of book 2 of the *Ordinatio*. See Wolter, "Scotus' Paris Lectures on God's Knowledge of Future Events," in *The Philosohical Theology of John Duns Scotus*, ed. Marilyn McCord Adams (Ithaca, N.Y.: Cornell University Press, 1990), 285–333, at p. 316, n. 82. For a description of the three manuscripts, see the "Introductio" to Scotus's *Opera Omnia*, ed. Commissio Scotistica (Vatican City: Typis Polyglottis, 1950), pp. 12*–28*, 32*–35*. In subsequent references, the commission's edition will be cited as the "Vatican" edition. In citing *Ordinatio* 2.37.2, I will refer both to Wolter's pagination and to that of the Vivès edition.

2. Two key terms in *Ordinatio* 2.37.2 are "total" and "immediate" cause. A cause is said to be immediate when the exercise of its causality is not the effect of its participating in the prior causal action of another agent. Take, for example, the theory of generation whereby a bull exercises his generative powers only by a participation in the generating power exercised by the celestial bodies. In this case, the bull exercises mediate efficient causality. To say that a cause is immediate is to deny any such hierarchial or vertical dependency. But this is not to deny dependency altogether. First of all, the immediate cause may be a dependent being in that it was created, and is continuously conserved in existence, by another—the main thing is that, now in existence, the exercise of its causality is not caused by another. And second, an

conditions of totality and immediacy amounts to a denial of freedom of will.[3] Accordingly, if the objection is sustained, it would count also as a denial of created, free will—unless, of course, either totality or immediacy is not a condition of freedom. This will be the key issue of the second part. The crucial thesis concerning divine causality is established with the following argument.

(1) God knows with certitude future contingents only because God knows the determinations of God's own (immutable and unimpedible) will with respect to these future contingents.[4] But (2) if the created will were the total, immediate cause of its own volition bearing itself contingently toward that volition, then the created will would be able to will otherwise than what the divine will has determined in its immediate volition. (That is, the created will might will *b* rather than *a* when the divine will has already willed *a* rather than *b*.) Consequently, (3) God's determinate foreknowledge could never be certain. However, given that (4) God has certain foreknowledge of future contingents, it follows that (5) the created will cannot be the total, immediate, efficient cause of its volitions.

---

immediate cause in order to be effective may depend laterally upon another cause causing. In other words, an immediate cause need not be a total cause. Take, for instance, the case of two mules pulling a barge. Let us say that neither is sufficient by itself to move the barge, though with each pulling its own weight, they can do the job together. Each is a partial cause. Note, however, that the dependency is lateral in the sense that each mule pulls its own load and in doing so does not derive that causal power from the other. Hence it is possible to have a partial, immediate cause: In order for one cause (C_1) to bring about an effect (E) it depends upon another cause (C_2) bringing about the same effect (E), but C_2 does not cause C_1's causing. These concepts will be developed later in reference to Scotus's texts, especially in the second section below.

3. Scotus marshals six arguments on the basis of reason to this effect (*Ordinatio* 2.37.2. nos.1–4 [Vivès 13:368–370]) and five arguments from authority (no. 5 [Vivès 13:370–371]). See Wolter, "Scotus' Paris Lectures," pp. 316–321, for a précis of the rational arguments.

4. One must not read too much into this proposition. It should be understood to imply only that the divine volition of future contingents is a necessary condition for the certain knowledge of the event. It does not imply that the divine volition suffices for the causal efficacy of such events, nor does it suggest any explanation of how God knows future contingents. The fourth section below develops the significance of properly understanding the nature of the knowledge Scotus claims we have of God's knowledge of future contingents.

AUTONOMOUS FREEDOM AND DIVINE CO-CAUSALITY 145

Therefore, (6) God must be an immediate, efficient cause of the created volition.[5]

The voluntarist account of divine foreknowledge expressed in premises (1) and (4) is simply invoked in the argument in *Ordinatio* 2.37.2. The position itself Scotus develops in conjunction with *Sentences* 1.38–40.[6] There Scotus first argues to the fact of divine foreknowledge and then explains how such a fact could be true of a God whose relationship to the world is radically contingent.

We can approach the first part of the doctrine[7]—the fact of divine foreknowledge—by concretely imagining that either tomorrow Adam

---

5. Statements (1)–(6) are my reconstruction of one of the arguments Scotus deploys to defeat the proposition that the created will is the total and immediate cause of its own volition (as in Wolter p. 394, no. 96; Vivès 13:373–374).

6. There are four versions of Scotus's opinion on the issue of divine foreknowledge of future contingents as it is taken up in Peter Lombard's *Sentences* 1.38–40. None of them represents the final determination of the question. When it came time to treat the topic in his *Ordinatio*, Scotus left blank a section corresponding to the second part of distinction 38 and all of distinction 39. Presumably he intended to return to it after determining other issues. The three extant versions are: (1) his early lectures (*Lectura* 1.39.1–5 [Vatican 17:481–510]); (2) an "examined report" of Scotus's Paris lectures on the *Sentences* (*Reportatio examinata* 1A.38–40 [as in Vienna, Österreichische Nationalbibliothek lat. 1453, ff. 113rb–117vb]); (3) a text probably put together by disciples or associates from (1) and (2) and some other source(s) in order to fill the lacuna Scotus left in the *Ordinatio* (as in Vatican 6:401–444); (4) what appears to be an abridgement of (2) by Scotus's secretary, William Alnwick, now known as the *Additiones magnae*. On the nature and authenticity of (3), see the editors' "Adnotationes," Vatican 6:26*–30*, and Wolter, "Scotus' Paris Lectures," pp. 285–287. An edition of (4) was mistakenly offered by Wadding as a Parisian report (Vivès 22:468–478); on its correct attribution, see Vatican 7:4*, and Wolter, *John Duns Scotus: Philosophical Writings, A Selection*, 2d ed. (Indianapolis: Hackett, 1987), pp. xxv–xxvi. Comparative studies of the different versions are available in Hermann Schwamm, *Das göttliche Vorherwissen bei Duns Scotus und seinem Anhängern* (Innsbruck: F. Rauch, 1934), pp. 5–60; and Wolter, "Scotus' Paris Lectures." See also William Lane Craig, "John Duns Scotus on God's Foreknowledge and Future Contingents," *Franciscan Studies* 47 (1987): 98–112, which focuses on (3). Since (2) appears to represent Scotus's latest teaching on the matter, it will be the chief source for this study.

7. Scotus *Reportatio examinata* 1A.38, f. 114ra: "Respondeo ergo ad quaestionem quod Deus novit determinate et infallibiliter eventum omnem contingentem, non solum in generali quod futura evenient, sed in speciali quod hoc futurum eveniet. Quare autem ita sit hoc potest sic declarari: Deus potest scire alteram partem contradictionis determinate, quam etiam hoc possum certo scire cum altera pars evenit. Sed

will consent to eat the forbidden fruit or he will refuse it. But today the fact of the matter is undetermined, and we cannot say with any certitude what will be so. Yet by the end of tomorrow we could know certainly one of the contradictory parts to be true. This knowledge we could have tomorrow of the determinate, contingent event will come as something new. Now if a finite person were to have certain, determinate knowledge of this fact, then so also must God know this. But in contrast to the finite knowers, God does not come to the knowledge as something new. Indeed, God must always already have known this contingent reality. In other words, God has certain foreknowledge of the future contingent, "Adam will consent to eat the forbidden fruit." In the next step, in fathoming the rationale of such knowledge, Scotus introduces divine voluntarism.

Indeed, Scotus posits at the source of the contingent act to be known an act of the divine will.[8] When God knows anything not coeval with the uncreated Godhead, God knows it either by seeing the determination of God's own will or through knowing God's own essence inasmuch as it includes God's free and contingent volition of created realities.[9] To put it concretely, both Adam consents and

---

Deus non potest scire hoc de novo, quia nihil est in eo novum; alias mutaretur; ergo ab aeterno novit vel alteram partem contradictionis vel utrumque. Non utrumque, quia hoc nihil est noscere, quia tunc nosceretur idem esse hoc et non esse hoc, quae formaliter repugnant; ergo determinate novit alteram partem contradictionis cuiuslibet, et per consequens infallibiliter."

8. Scotus *Reportatio examinata* 1A.38, f. 114rb: "ita quaelibet talis contingens est vera, quia veritas eius est primo causata per actum voluntatis divinae, et non quia vera, ideo voluntas vult eam esse veram, sed econtra; et ideo veritate causata in complexione talium terminorum determinata per actum voluntatis, intellectus divinus tunc primo novit unam partem contradictionem contingentium esse veram."

9. Scotus entertains two possible ways that the prior divine volition is known posteriorly in an act of the divine intellect. An actual determination of the issue, however, is irrelevant to the immediate issue. Thus *Reportatio examinata* 1A.38, f. 114rb: "Sive ergo dicatur primo modo vel secundo, quod scilicet intellectus determinetur ad unam partem contradictionis ex essentia sola sicut ex ratione cognoscendi, sive ex determinatione voluntatis acceptantis unam partem et non aliam et omnipotentia eius non impedibili, sequitur statim ex his duobus quod intellectus divinus habet notitiam certam determinatam et infallibilem unius partis contradictionis futuri contingentiae." In fact, Scotus seems to favor the second account (i.e., the divine essence as the basis for knowing); see Wolter, "Scotus' Paris Lectures," pp. 289–292. The first account, which Scotus sees as less probable, represents the position

God immediately wills Adam's consent, and by knowing God's own immutable and unimpedible volition God knows the created reality. More generally, the idea here is that God knows these things through knowing God's own creative volition of *a* rather than not-*a*. In other words, what God knows is what God freely determines by an act of will. Within the larger scheme of Scotus's thought, of course, the reason for this voluntaristic account is that only thus does he think it possible to avoid some vilification of divine freedom.

Yet a deterministic understanding of the created will may seem an inevitable outcome of such a theory. Under these terms, can a created will be the originative, efficient source for its volition of *a* rather than not-*a*? When Adam consented to eat the forbidden fruit, could he have not consented or even refused? By the argument of *Reportatio* 1A.38, Scotus has come to think that God has immutably and unimpedibly willed, by a volition coeval with God's original, creative act, Adam's consent to eat the fruit. So when in the course of time Adam consents to the deed, what sense would it make to say that Adam could have done otherwise?

Scotus could not have been unaware of the deterministic implication. First of all, the doctrine of divine foreknowledge is called upon by Scotus as a premise in an argument deployed in refutation of a thesis that makes freedom of the created will co-implicant with the created will's being a total, immediate cause of its volition. And so, one might argue, to take away the created will's total domination over its acts is to take away its freedom.

Second, the doctrine of God's immediate causality occurs in a question situated within a set of distinctions devoted to the issue of sin.[10] At *Ordinatio* 2.37.2 the development is brought to the point

---

of Henry of Ghent; see John F. Wippel, "Divine Knowledge, Divine Power, and Human Freedom in Thomas Aquinas and Henry of Ghent," in *Metaphysical Themes in Thomas Aquinas* (Washington: The Catholic University of America Press, 1984), pp. 243–270, especially p. 263 and following.

10. Most immediately, with the unit comprising *Ordinatio* 2.34. (whether sin originates from something good as from a cause), 2.35 (whether sin is essentially the privation of the good), 2.36 (whether sin is a punishment for sin), 2.37.1 (whether sin can be from God), and 2.37.2 (whether the created will is the total and immediate cause of its own volition in such a way that God has no immediate, but only mediate, efficiency with respect to that volition). For these, see Vivès 13:335–392. The broader context is the last half of book 2, distinctions 21–44 (Vivès 13:132–498).

of explaining what responsibility God bears for the evil of God's creatures' sin. In the first part of *Ordinatio* 2.37.2 Scotus has explained how God would be exempt from culpability if created wills were total and immediate causes for their own volitions.[11] But, as we have just seen, Scotus thinks the antecedent cannot be true. In the next phase of the question,[12] then, Scotus is constrained to explain how God is not culpable for the evil of an act that God immediately causes. Since evil acts are morally imputable and since an act is morally imputable only to a free agent, it follows that if the created will acts deterministically then it would seem that God is responsible for the evil of sin. Scotus goes to some length to avoid this consequence, and, as we shall see, his strategy entails a denial of any determinism of the created will.

IMMEDIATE DIVINE CAUSALITY AND DETERMINISM

Scotus's account of sin in *Ordinatio* 2.37.2 presupposes an indeterminist freedom of the created will.[13] The basic idea goes like this: (1) There are two distinct factors in the composition of a sinful act, namely, its matter and its form. (2) The specific evil of sin lies in the formal factor. (3) The formal factor must necessarily be the effect of a free agent. (4) Only created wills are immediately responsible for the formal aspect of sin. Therefore, (5) if there is sin, then there must be freedom of the will on the part of the created will.[14] What this means, then, is not only does the created will

---

11. Section 5 (Wolter, pp. 321–322, n. 91–92; Vivès 13:372).

12. Sections 9–18 (Vivès 13:374–381).

13. Scotus's most sustained account of free will is in *Quaestiones in Metaphysicam* 9.15, as in *Duns Scotus on the Will and Morality*, ed. Allan B. Wolter (Washington: The Catholic University of America Press, 1986), pp. 145–172. Compare B. M. Bonansea, "Duns Scotus' Voluntarism," in *John Duns Scotus, 1265–1965*, Studies in Philosophy and the History of Philosophy 3 (Washington: The Catholic University of America Press, 1965), pp. 83–121; William Frank, "Duns Scotus' Concept of Willing Freely: What Divine Freedom beyond Choice Teaches Us," *Franciscan Studies* 42 (1982): 68–89; and Allan B. Wolter, "Duns Scotus on the Will as a Rational Potency," in *The Philosophical Theology of John Duns Scotus*, pp. 163–180.

14. *Ordinatio* 2.37.2.9–13 (Vivès 13:374–377).

exercise an indeterminist free will in its act of sinning, but the created will is an immediate, efficient cause of this act; yet God also is an immediate, efficient cause for the same act, which raises the question: How can there be two immediate, efficient causes for the same act and in such a way that one is not responsible for the evil of the act whereas the other is? In what follows we shall first of all elaborate Scotus's concept of sin and then, second, answer the question through an explication of his theory of partial, essentially ordered co-causes.

ON SIN

Scotus explains that sin has both a material and a formal cause.[15] The "matter" of sin is the material performance, the positive act (or omission) that we could describe in nonevaluative terms. For instance, in the case of a lie, the material performance consists of a person's saying something untrue to a neighbor under particular circumstances of motivation, manner, place, and time. The "form" of sin is the privation of justice due to such a concrete, material performance. In other words, in the act of will resulting in the material performance, the agent was aware that the intended act was not in conformity with the dictate of the agent's right reason. Accordingly, when the will thus wills, its act is deprived of due justice.

Notice here that a person sins by performing an act whose very generation and meaning includes a rejection of an alternative act projected in the face of the same material elements but in which the alternative act possesses a form as dictated by the agent's right reason. This is to say, then, that sin is always a case of an act that could have been otherwise. The "other" not willed is possessed of a becoming harmony reflective of due justice. By contrast, the sin appears as sin precisely in the privation of such moral beauty.

---

15. *Ordinatio* 2.37.2.9 (Wolter, pp. 325–337, sect. 100, 102–104; Vivès 13:375). See the selected texts on sin in *Duns Scotus on the Will and Morality*, pp. 459–534. On the notion of "due justice" as the form of a morally good act, the privation of which is the form of moral evil, see *Ordinatio* 1.17.62–67 (Vatican 5:163–169) and *Quaestiones quodlibetales* 18.8–23, in *Cuestiones cuodlibetales*, trans. Felix Alluntis (Madrid: Biblioteca de Autores Cristianos, 1963); and *John Duns Scotus: God and Creatures, the Quodlibetal Questions*, trans. by F. Alluntis and A. B. Wolter (Princeton: Princeton University Press, 1975).

As regards this privation, Scotus invokes a traditional, Augustinian account in explaining that there is no efficient cause, but rather a "de-ficient" cause.[16] Because Scotus considers the will-as-such a pure perfection, univocally predicable of God and creature, he takes pains to insist that it is the will-as-somehow-deficient that causes sin. In and of itself, apart from accidental deficiencies, the will possesses no innate limitations or imperfections. Indeed the infinite will necessarily acts perfectly, and finite wills can act perfectly or not.[17] Only finite wills are liable to cause efficiently an entity deprived of due justice.

But if God must be an immediate co-cause of the sin, how does one explain God's lack of responsibility? In reply, Scotus explains that where essentially ordered causes concur to produce a common deficient effect, the defect can result wholly from the failure on the part of one cause.[18] He cites as an example his doctrine of the intellect and will's co-causality of a volition.[19] In this case, the intellect may operate perfectly within the limits of its nature, but because its co-cause, the will, functions deficiently, their common effect is imperfect. Similarly, Scotus thinks God's contribution to the common effect is a perfect instance of divine volition, but the outcome is still a sin, due, however, to the failure of the creaturely partner.[20]

If God never acts unjustly, where is the justice in the sinful acts God co-causes? Perhaps Scotus could answer: There is no justice, for the creature's deficiency deprived God of an opportunity to be the co-cause of some just volition. Yet in this there is no culpable injustice either, for God is not bound in justice to God's creatures, and so there can never be on God's part the privation of a justice due a creature by God.[21]

---

16. *Ordinatio* 2.37.2.9 (Wolter, p. 326, no. 103; Vivès 13:375).

17. *Ordinatio* 2.37.2.9–10 (Wolter, p. 327, nos. 104–105; Vivès 13:375). See also *Ordinatio* 2.44, in *Duns Scotus on the Will and Morality*, ed. Wolter, pp. 460–463. Compare Frank, "Duns Scotus' Concept," pp. 86–87; and W. Höres, *Der Wille als reine Volkommenheit nach Duns Scotus* (Munich: Anton Pustet, 1962).

18. *Ordinatio* 2.37.2.14 (Wolter, p. 328, no. 107; Vivès 13:378).

19. *Ordinatio* 2.37.2.14. On the doctrine of the will/intellect co-causality and its development within Scotus's works see Bonansea, "Duns Scotus' Voluntarism."

20. *Ordinatio* 2.37.2.14 (Wolter, pp. 327–329, no. 107; Vivès 13:378–379).

21. *Ordinatio* 4.46, in *Duns Scotus on the Will and Morality*, ed. Wolter, pp. 244–255. See Marilyn McCord Adams, "Duns Scotus on the Goodness of God," *Faith and Philosophy* 4 (1987): 486–505; B. M. Bonansea, "The Divine Will and Its Bearing on

Nevertheless, there is a great loss, for out of sheer generosity God would unfailingly give rectitude if the created will were, for its part, to will justly. For its part the created will can and is bound to do this. In sinning, the creature does not do what it is bound to do, thereby depriving God of the opportunity to do what God would do but is not bound to do. As Scotus puts it in scholastic terms: by God's antecedent will God gives rectitude to every created volition God co-causes. God does this in making the original gift of free will to the creature, for as part of the gift God gives the created will the invitable power and obligation to act in rectitude. Furthermore, by God's consequent will God will give rectitude to each actual volition unless some impediment rooted in the co-cause precludes this.[22]

Scotus offers a helpful clarification when he warns against a false conceit concerning the interrelationship between God's antecedent will and the creature's cooperation. He says it is not a case of the creature obliterating or canceling what God had posited in a prior act.[23] This false conceit envisions two distinct effects, somewhat after the fashion of a contract originally struck and subsequently broken, or a word originally written and in a second moment erased, or a rod first wrought straight and later bent. In reality there is ever only one effect. The privation appears as the absence of a counterfactual, of what God would have co-caused had the creature done otherwise. God's antecedent will is evident not as a prior act subsequently eliminated, but more subtly as the background of what would have been (namely, God's consequent cooperation if God had been given the opportunity) and what could have been (since God endowed created wills with the power of liberty).

This account of sin makes two things evident. First, Scotus clearly holds the created will fully responsible for the absence of due justice—the evil—of sin. The created will by its very nature has the ability

---

the Moral Law and Man's Predestination," in his *Man and His Approach to God in John Duns Scotus* (Lanham, Md.: University Press of America, 1983), pp. 187–224; and Allan B. Wolter, "Native Freedom of the Will as a Key to the Ethics of Scotus," in *Deus et Homo ad Mentem I. Duns Scoti* (Rome: Soc. Intern. Scotistici, 1972), pp. 359–370; reprinted in Wolter, *Philosophical Theology*, pp. 148–162.

22. See note 20, above; and Bonansea, "Divine Will," pp. 194–198.
23. *Ordinatio* 2.37.2.14 (Wolter, p. 328, no. 107; Vivès 13:378–379).

to act in accordance with the dictates of its right reason. It sins only because it exercises an option for the less perfect of opposite acts: at the instant of its act it could have done otherwise. The sin is therefore a contingent act, and the created will is an originative source of its contingency. In short, the will acts out of an indeterminist freedom. Second, Scotus evidently presumes God and the created will to be immediate, but partial, co-efficient causes of the created volition. The next step is to examine the nature of this co-causality.

ON CO-CAUSALITY

The doctrine of partial, efficient causes employed in the solution of *Ordinatio* 2.37.2 had been worked out by Scotus in other contexts.[24] We find it chiefly in his account of the origin of intellection through the co-causality of both intellect and object.[25] This original doctrine then served as a model for his account of volition as the effect of the co-causality of both intellect and will.[26] As a third application, Scotus now invokes the theory in *Ordinatio* 2.37.2 to explain the form of God's causal partnership with created wills.

The basic idea is that two causes concur in the causation of a single effect. Each cause's contribution is necessary, but not sufficient, for the effect. Furthermore, the two cohere in such a way as to constitute a total cause. Scotus then refines this broad description by means of a classification. He first divides co-causes into those that exercise natures or powers of the same sort and those of a different sort. As an example of the first dividing part we can imagine two mules pulling

---

24. *Ordinatio* 2.37.2.14–15 (Wolter, pp. 328–329, no. 107–108; Vivès 13:378–379). To my knowledge there has been little critical analysis of this idea in Scotus. There is a good description in Roy R. Effler, *John Duns Scotus and the Principle "Omne Quod Movetur ab Alio Movetur"* (St. Bonaventure, N.Y.: Franciscan Institute, 1962), pp. 156–159. See also Isidoro Guzmán Manzano, "El principio de causalidad parcial de Escoto," *Antonianum* 65 (1990): 290–311.

25. *Quodlibet* 15.26–39; *Ordinatio* 1.3. nos.427–429, 463–470, 486–494, and 559–562 (Vatican 3: 260–261, 279–282, 289–297, and 333–334). See, for instance, Effler, *Scotus and the Principle*, 147–158; Reinhold Messner, *Schauendes und begrifflicher Erkennen nach Duns Skotus* (Freiburg: Herder, 1942); and Etienne Gilson, *Jean Duns Scot: Introduction à ses positions fondamentales* (Paris: Vrin, 1952), pp. 523–543.

26. Scotus's development on this issue is evident in the various versions of his commentary on *Sentences* 2.25. See Bonansea, "Duns Scotus' Voluntarism"; and the editors' "Praefatio" to Scotus's Lectura 2 (Vatican 18:xi–xii).

a load.[27] There is nothing qualitatively different about the power that each mule exercises in pulling its load: each contributes to the effect in virtue of the same generic power. Although neither mule is sufficient on its own to pull the common load, it is conceivable that an intensification of the power already present in one mule would enable it to pull the whole load by itself. The distinction between the two mules combined in their union as a team expresses accidental differences of quantity. Accordingly, Scotus calls such ordered causes accidental.[28]

Opposed to such accidentally ordered causes are essentially ordered causes. In this, the concurrent causes unite in virtue of a distinction expressive of different natures. Although neither cause in fact suffices to bring about the effect, no increase in accidental features of either cause suffices to overcome the limitation of essence that is overcome only by the holistic integration of the two natures. The concurrence of male and female in begetting offspring is an example Scotus frequently uses. Neither mother nor father suffice independently of the other, and, further, the necessary contribution of each is rooted in an essential difference between their generative powers.

Scotus also holds that where there are two different essences or natures they can be ranked or ordered as prior and posterior. The idea here is that one nature is greater or more perfect than the other relative to some hierarchial scheme. When united with another in a co-causal relationship, the greater manifests its superiority by "giving more" to the effect, even if it gives only mediately through

---

27. *Quodlibet* 15.33: "Dico quod causae concurrentes quandoque sunt eiusdem rationis et ordinis, ut plures trahentes navem"; parallel idea at *Ordinatio* 1.3.3.2.495–496 (Vatican 3:293), and at *Lectura* 2.25, published by Charles Balić as *secundae additiones* in "Une question inédite de J. Duns Scot sur la volonté," RTAM 3 (1931): 191–208.

28. The distinction between essentially and accidentally ordered causes pervades Scotus's thought. It is clarified at *Ordinatio* I.2.1.1–2.47–51 (Vatican 2:153–155) and *De primo principio* 1 and 3.10–11, as in John Duns Scotus, *A Treatise on God as First Principle*, ed. Allan B. Wolter, 2d ed. (Chicago: Franciscan Herald, 1984), pp. 2–11 and 44–47. See the commentaries on *De primo* by Robert Prentice, *The Basic Quidditative Metaphysics of Duns Scotus as Seen in His De Primo Principio* (Rome: Antonianum, 1970), especially chapters 4–5; Wolfgang Kluxen, *Johannes Duns Scotus: Abhandlung über das erste Prinzip* (Darmstadt: Wissenschaftlicher Buchgesellschaft, 1974); and Wolter, *A Treatise on God*.

the instrumentality of another. Indeed, Scotus insists that the lesser, posterior co-cause can be the total, immediate cause of its effect without contradicting its inferior status. For example, in the case of God and the created will, Scotus thinks that even if God were only a mediate, efficient cause of the created volition, the divine will would be the superior efficient cause because it "gives more"—it exercises greater influence insofar as God creates and conserves the created will with its power for independent action.[29] What is important to observe here is that Scotus separates this issue of causal immediacy and independence from excellence of causal nature.

Essentially ordered co-causes are subsequently divided into what I shall call "participative" and "autonomous."[30] In the case of participative, essentially ordered causes, the superior cause moves the inferior. More precisely, the inferior only exercises its causality by participating in the causality being exercised simultaneously by the superior. In one example, Scotus speaks of the hand moving the stick to move the ball. In a second example, he refers to the father's exercise of his generative powers by participating in the universal, generative powers of the sun moving along its celestial path, thereby perpetuating the cycle of generation and corruption among animate things.[31] The definitive feature of such participative, concurrent causes is that the inferior exercises its proper causality only by sharing in the fuller possession of causal power being exercised by the superior.

Opposed to participative, essentially ordered causes are autonomous, partial co-causes. Although the two causes are ordered as superior to inferior according to their essential natures as active powers, the inferior's dependence on the superior in its act of causing is not a matter of participating in the other's fuller causality, nor does the superior otherwise move the inferior to exercise its causality. Rather,

---

29. Against the claim that an essentially inferior cause could not be a more immediate cause of an effect than the relevant superior cause of the same effect, see Scotus's reply at *Ordinatio* 2.37.2.7 (Wolter, p. 323, no. 95; Vivès 13:373). On the distinction of the order of dependence from the order of eminence, see *De primo* 1.6–9 and 2.44–49.

30. Compare Effler's division of the same into "dependent" and "independent" in *Scotus and the Principle*, p. 157.

31. *Quodlibet* 15.33, *Ordinatio* 1.3.3.2.496 (Vatican 3:293–294), *Lectura* 2.25 (Balić, p. 203).

both superior and inferior causes act on behalf of the common effect with an independent, self-moving exercise of causality. To be sure, neither on its own effort suffices to cause the effect: neither is the total cause. In short, each cause independently exercises its own causality, but only in cooperation do they bring about the effect.

To illustrate autonomous co-causes Scotus cites the examples of mother and father with respect to their common offspring, the interdependence of nib and quill in the act of writing, and the cooperation of husband and wife in the regulation of a household. He develops the first example somewhat: although the mother in her capacity as generative cause is inferior to the father, she nevertheless contributes to the total, generative act a necessary, positive aspect absent from the father's contribution. In order to make her contribution, to exercise her essential, generative efficiency, the mother is dependent on the father's simultaneous exercise of his generative efficacy. Yet this dependence is not a case of the mother receiving her causality from the more perfect father, nor does the more perfect father in any way possess the total causality in an eminent fashion. Each cause provides the other the opportunity for the exercise of their separate, but coordinated and complementary, lines of efficient causality.[32]

Such then is the general form of autonomous, essentially ordered causality. It combines aspects of the other two kinds of concurrent causality. Like the participative, one cause is superior in nature to the other; yet unlike it, the superior does not cause the inferior's causing. In this latter respect, the autonomous is like accidentally ordered concurrent causes, where each cause independently pulls its own load, so to speak. But unlike the accidental, each autonomous co-cause has something distinctive from the other and proper to its own essence from which it derives its causal efficacy.[33]

As mentioned before, Scotus exploits the possibilities of this form of concurrent causality in three important philosophical issues: how the intellect and the intelligible object cause intellection; how the will and the intellect cause volition; and how God and the created will cause created volitions. In each case Scotus argues that the two

32. Ibid.
33. To arrive at this notion of a distinctive operative difference in essentially ordered co-causes I have extrapolated from Scotus's examples, emphasizing that the order of the two must respond to qualitative differences in the causes compared.

cooperate as autonomous, essentially ordered, partial causes.[34] The first two topics are well considered in Scotus studies; the third is the subject of this study.

Now let us bring the doctrine to bear on the issue of determinism raised at the end of the first part. Recall the determinist argument: If God from all eternity is an immediate, efficient cause of Adam's volition, then at the time Adam willed he could not have done otherwise, and hence Adam exercises his will deterministically. In line with the above account, Scotus's reply would be that Adam also is an immediate, efficient cause. Indeed, both God and Adam are autonomous, essentially ordered, partial co-causes of the single effect, namely, Adam's consent. Both agents operate independently, yet simultaneously, with respect to the same intentional object. Each gives the other the opportunity to act without either causing the other's causing. With respect to the common effect, each is a necessary, but not sufficient, condition. Furthermore, each acts in accordance with its own nature, which means freely and contingently. In the order of eminence, God's will, identical with God's essence, is a nature superior to Adam's created will. Because of their independent lines of causality, deficiency on the part of one co-cause suffices to explain imperfection in the effect without entailing deficiency on the part of the other co-cause.

One might wonder, however, whether this account does not imply some imperfection in God by the fact that in order to be an efficient cause of a created volition God must depend on the contingent exercise of a created will. Perhaps the objection could be sustained either if the created will were to cause the divine volition or if God were somehow needful of the effect. But the first is not so, for the whole idea of autonomous, partial co-causes avoids such caused causing. Nor is the second so, for the prior demonstration of God's infinite perfection[35] makes it clear that God is not needful.

---

34. If one were to systematize these three doctrines, a simple human volition would have as its total cause the integration of four essentially ordered partial co-causes: (1) divine will and (2) human will, which in turn operates only as a co-cause with (3) human intellect, which in its turn co-causes intellection with (4) the intellect's object.

35. On Scotus's concept of the infinite see *Quodlibet* 5.5–11; for his treatment of God's infinity see *Ordinatio* 1.2.1.1–2.74–146 (Vatican 2:174–214) and parallel

A second objection might start from the requirement of the simultaneity of God and Adam's co-causality. Did not this issue arise in the first place by the requirement of God's foreknowledge of Adam's consent, a knowledge God could have, so the theory insisted, only because God immediately willed this consent in a moment coeval with the original, creative act? Scotus would reply that God's willing of Adam's consent takes place in the eternal now, whereas Adam's willing takes place in a temporal now. Granting that the eternal now is prior to the temporal now, Scotus nevertheless carefully explains that the precedence is not similar to the way some earlier temporal now precedes a later temporal now.[36] Therefore it can be true: (1) that the divine will's immediate causing of Adam's volition is in the eternal now, and (2) that the eternal now is coincident with a temporal now temporally prior to the temporal now in which Adam is the immediate cause of his volition. But it does not follow (3) that God's volition is temporally prior to Adam's act.

Scotus's idea is that the eternal now is coincident with every temporal now. But to think of the eternal now as coincident with a sequence of time misleads, for a sequence of time has no temporal now. Indeed, Scotus observes that such a mis-thought derives from a false imagination. Because God's act is in the eternal now we incline

---

treatment in *Lectura* 1.2.1.1–2.64–86 (Vatican 16:134–142); *Reportatio* 1A.2.1 (281–307); and *De primo* 4.46–70. Also see the corresponding commentaries on *De primo* by Kluxen, Prentice, and Wolter, as well as the latter's "Oxford Dialogue on Language and Metaphysics," *Review of Metaphysics* 32 (1978): 323–348.

36. *Ordinatio* 1.40.9 (Vatican 6:311–312). The parallel in *Reportatio* 1A.39–40, fol.117va, says: "quod actus iste divinus secundum causalitatem suam non transiit in praeteritum, sed solum secundum modum suum significandi. Actus enim huius verbi 'praedestinavit' est ita praesens modo sicut fuit ab aeterno, sed dicitur 'praesens' inquantum nunc aeternitatis in quo Deus cuncta facit, coexistit nostro presenti et praeteritum inquantum coexistit nostro praeterito et ita de futuro quae non differunt in Deo nisi tantum secundum nostrum modum significandi, quia secundum Augustinum super Ioannem, quaere de Christo idem est in Deo, audiet, audit et audivit. Actus tamen qui, secundum realitatem suam transiit in praeteritum, est necessarius et propositio scita de eo vera est necessaria absque praeteritione reali actus vel obiecti. Iste igitur imaginatur Deum dormissive usque hucusque et Deum praeconsiliari et tunc potest determinare se ad actum praedestinationis. Dico ergo quod quodlibet est sibi ita novum hodie sicut ab aeterno, quia numquam fuit aliquid sibi novum. Unde si voluntas mea haberet actum suum in instanti, non magis accipit necessitatem ex illo. Sic nec actus divinus nihil necessitatis accipit ex instanti aeternitatis."

to think of it as past, no doubt because the eternal now was coincident with any past now.

> But this imagined situation is false. For that now of eternity in which this act exists is always present. And concerning the divine will or his volition, one ought to understand it... just as if, *per impossibile*, God were now to begin to have the volition in this temporal now. (*Ordinatio* 1.40.8)

Regarding the argument for determinism, then, Scotus would deny that determinism follows from the fact of God's immediate causality. His theory of partial, essentially ordered co-causes exposes a more flexible logical space. There are sound reasons for insisting on the immediate and free causality of both Adam and God. And Scotus's causal theory allows him to integrate both.

RECENT DETERMINISTIC INTERPRETATIONS

Recently two scholars have challenged the received view of Scotus's concept of freedom of the created will.[37] In their own fashion each takes Scotus's account of divine foreknowledge to imply that God is the sole source of the contingency of any created volition. But according to the received interpretation, a necessary condition of the will's freedom is its power to operate contingently out of self-determination. More precisely, this means (1) at the instant in which the created will acts it could have acted otherwise; (2) prior to its action the effect to be brought about is ontologically undetermined; and (3) the responsibility for the effect being or not being such as it becomes is nonreductively rooted in the will's exercise of its power to act for either of opposite effects.[38] In accord with contemporary usage we might call this sort of freedom "indeterminist," or we might say

---

37. See Marilyn McCord Adams, 2 vols. *William Ockham* (Notre Dame, Ind.: University of Notre Dame Press, 1987), 2:1715–1750, and her introduction, with Norman Kretzmann, to *William Ockham: Predestination, God's Foreknowledge, and Future Contingents* (New York: Appleton, Century, Crofts, 1969), pp. 1–33; and Douglas Langston, *God's Willing Knowledge: The Influence of Scotus' Analysis of Omniscience* (University Park, Penn.: Pennsylvania State University Press, 1986).

38. See note 13, above.

Scotus has a "libertarian" concept of free will.[39] The main basis for the challenge to this view is the inference that if God is necessarily an immediate cause of any created volition, then God is its sufficient cause. Therefore, if a volition is contingent or could have been otherwise, the total cause of its being one thing rather than its opposite lies in the operation of the divine will.

Let us first consider Douglas Langston's interpretation. In light of a reading of *Ordinatio* 1.38–39,[40] Langston observes that "the price paid for this knowledge" of future contingents "seems to be a loss of freedom: Human beings cannot do other than God wills and hence seem not to be free."[41] The idea, of course, is that God has determined in advance what shall be. On the basis of this conviction, the burden of Langston's subsequent interpretation is to deny the apparent contradiction between divine foreknowledge and human freedom. He does this by imputing to Scotus a "nonlibertarian" account of the will's freedom.[42] To put it simply, the libertarian thinks it inconsistent for the same effect to be the immediate effect of a free agent and simultaneously determined by an agent other than that free agent. A nonlibertarian, then, is either a "pure determinist" who denies any truth to freedom of the will or a "compatibilist" who maintains that the same event can be the result simultaneously of both deterministic and free factors.

It serves the purposes of our study simply to observe how Langston adapts the terms of the modern debate over free will and determinism

---

39. These terms, taken from modern and contemporary philosophic tradition, are adapted to the discussion of Scotus's doctrine by Langston, *God's Willing Knowledge*; Lawrence D. Roberts, "John Duns Scotus and the Concept of Human Freedom," in *Deus et Homo*, pp. 317–325; and Roberts, "Indeterminism in Duns Scotus' Doctrine of Human Freedom," *Modern Schoolman* 51 (1973): 1–16; and Roberts, "The Contemporary Relevance of Duns Scotus' Doctrine of Human Freedom," in *Regnum Hominis et Regnum Dei* (Rome: Soc. Inter. Scotistici, 1978), pp. 535–544; and John Martin Fischer, "Scotism," *Mind* 94 (1985): 231–243. For broader discussion of free will in the contemporary idiom in a way that engages the ancient, medieval, and modern traditions, see Anthony Kenny, *Will, Freedom, and Power* (Oxford: Basil Blackwell, 1975); and Robert Kane, *Free Will and Values* (Albany: SUNY Press, 1985).

40. Langston consistently refers to Scotus's *Ordinatio* treatment of 1.38–39, but as indicated in note 6, above, we most probably do not have any determination in the *Ordinatio* of these questions.

41. Langston, *God's Willing Knowledge*, pp. 26, 50, 121.

42. Langston, *God's Willing Knowledge*, pp. 24–52.

to a reading of Scotus's text. Langston argues that if Scotus were a libertarian, then he would hold that the created will satisfies three conditions: (1) it always possesses the ability to cause x rather than non-x, (2) it can always exercise this ability, and (3) when it acts it acts in accordance with its nature. However, for reasons of divine foreknowledge, condition (2) cannot be met: prior to the exercise of its ability, the option between x and non-x is predetermined by a higher power who makes the action on behalf of one opposite a part of the created person's nature. This means then that the creature's life of freedom is a matter of unfolding predetermined, contingent events through its life of action.[43]

In passing, I should mention that Langston thinks his conditions (1), ability, and (3), acting out of one's nature, suffice for a legitimate, though nonlibertarian, concept of freedom. He accordingly argues that Scotus's fuller voluntaristic teaching is consistent insofar as he employs such an "abbreviated" concept of free will.[44]

Our reading of *Ordinatio* 2.37.2 makes it evident that Langston concedes too much to divine causality and too little to the created will, making it rather like an instrument. To use our terms, he seems to treat the created will as a participative, partial cause, whereas Scotus considers it autonomous. For Langston, the reality of x rather than non-x is totally determined by God, and the created will is set to the work of unfolding in time what has already been determined.[45] This interpretation does not do justice to the subtlety of the God/creature co-causal union that Scotus proposes. Even though they do not have a sufficient, efficient cause, Scotus does not think of created actions as the active unfolding of another's exclusive decision. Rather, by its action the created will shares more fully in responsibility for the contingent reality, the freshness, of things.

Marilyn McCord Adams also draws the deterministic conclusion from Scotus's doctrine on divine foreknowledge. As she puts it: Scotus "has given the impression in distinctions 38–39 that such divine

---

43. Langston, *God's Willing Knowledge*, pp. 24–52.
44. Langston, *God's Willing Knowledge*, pp. 51–52.
45. For example, Langston, *God's Willing Knowledge*, p.46: "Scotus assumes that the divine will does determine human wills, but that they are only contingently determined by the divine will"; p. 48: "the higher agent determines the [created] will by determining the will to act according to its nature."

choice is logically sufficient for the creatures' choices."[46] And "Scotus does not make it unambiguously clear whether or not he believes that divine choice is logically sufficient for creature's choices; but there is substantial evidence in that direction."[47] Similarly, she claims that for Scotus, God is the "sufficient and unobstructible cause" of the contingent features of creation that are not ontologically determinate.[48] And finally, in her earlier work, Adams wrote that Scotus's voluntaristic account of divine foreknowledge in *Ordinatio* 1.38–39 means "that God can have such foreknowledge because He wills one part to be true and the other part to be false and His willing in some way settles it that one part rather than the other is determinately true."[49] Of course the crucial issue is the phrase "in some way." If it is open to our *Ordinatio* 2.37.2 autonomous, partial, essential order, we have no quarrel with this reading. If, however, God's "settling it" means that creatures do not exercise autonomous responsibility for contingent volitions, then this reading essentially conforms to a deterministic account of the creaturely exercise of volitional power. The drift of all this is that God's choice determines creatures' volitions; Adams is careful, however, to shy away from any apodictic assertion that this is Scotus's teaching, for she holds sufficient respect for Scotus's other commitments to the radically free will. But she does consider it probable that Scotus is simply inconsistent.[50]

The critical formulation in Adams's reading is that God's creative volition is logically sufficient for determining that the created will wills x rather than non-x. Does this mean that if God wills x, x will be, and we know this? If so, this leaves us to wonder about the basis for God's willing. In other words, it is perfectly possible to think of God's will as a partial cause. Such a nondeterministic reading seems wholly consistent with *Ordinatio* 2.37.2. But if it means that God's will makes it so in such a way that the created will shall never have exercised any determinate, contingent causality, then the proposition is not harmless and needs to be confronted with the teaching of *Ordinatio* 2.37.2.

46. Adams, *William Ockham*, 2:1135.
47. Adams, *William Ockham*, 2:1135.
48. Adams, *William Ockham*, 2:1127.
49. Adams with Kretzmann, *Predestination*, "Introduction," p. 21.
50. Adams, *William Ockham*, 2:1322 and 1135, n. 43.

MYSTERY IN THE KNOWLEDGE OF GOD

Consideration of Adams and Langston suggests that it is helpful to distinguish two meanings of "created will's contingent acts." As common ground, both meanings acknowledge that the created will exercises its own causal power. Furthermore, both meanings acknowledge that the effect or the will's elicited act is contingent, which is to say, at the time it became it could have not become or could have become otherwise. The difference between the two meanings lies in the origin of contingency. (1) Does the contingency derive from the created will itself, from the inner nature of the will's causal power, such that all things being equal, the created will is necessarily a reason for its being x rather than non-x? Is it perfectly possible that all things remaining equal and up to the very exercise of the created will's causal power, it could have not willed x, and the basis for the difference lies in the created will's own mode of exercising its self-determining power? If so, then the created will is an originative source of the contingency of its contingent acts. Or, on the other hand, (2) Is the created will only a "carrier" or "transmitter" of the contingency originating exclusively in the divine will? In accordance with this second meaning, the created will is truly an efficient cause of x, and x contingently exists in opposition to non-x, but the created will's exercise of its efficiency on behalf of x rather than non-x is determined by divine freedom.

What does Scotus mean when he speaks of the contingent acts of created wills? Langston and Adams seem to endorse the second meaning, for it coheres with their deterministic understanding of divine efficacy. Yet on behalf of the first understanding we have the dialectic of *Ordinatio* 2.37.2 and the clear text of Scotus's *Reportatio* 1A.39–40:

> In us, that is, in the will, there is contingency that stems both from ourselves and from God. In some other things, however, there is necessity of themselves but contingency on the part of God.... But in every effect or thing willed by us as such there is no necessity but only contingency.[51]

---

51. *Reportatio* 1A.39–40, fol. 116ra: "in nobis, i.e., in voluntate, a se et a Deo est contingentia. In aliquibus autem <aliis> necessitas est a se, sed contingentia ex parte Dei.... sed in omnibus in effectibus vel rebus a nobis volitis in quantum huiusmodi, nulla est necessitas sed tantum contingentia." We note that the outright identification

The text clearly affirms a double source of the contingency of effects of created will: the freedom of God and the freedom of the created will. For Scotus, immediate experience teaches us that our will is an immediate source of contingent effects.[52] Theological argument on the issue of divine foreknowledge convinces Scotus that God is an immediate cause of the same effects. And the argument of *Ordinatio* 2.37.2 provides the causal theory to integrate both doctrines without losing anything of the radical truths about freedom of the will, be it the divine will or the created will.

Hence, when Scotus insists in 1.38–40 that God knows created volitions with certain and determined knowledge because God is an immediate, efficient cause of such entities, we must understand that God's causality is sufficient for God's knowledge in an extensional rather than in an intentional sense. This is to say, although God is not its total, immediate cause of the volition (i.e., God's causality does not suffice *de facto* for the existence of the entity), nevertheless, God's causal act is so integrated with the creature's co-causal act that God's knowledge of God's own act suffices for knowledge of the effect.

In its logical structure, Scotus has proffered a *quia* rather than a *propter quid* demonstration. This is to say that he argues that a created volition is the effect of a total cause comprising divine and created wills as partial, essentially ordered, autonomous co-causes; he does not explain how this can be. In a parallel case, Scotus argues that God has certain knowledge for God's own immediate volition of created contingent volitions; he does not explain how this works within the divine psychology.

Yet we might think to look for more light on these issues. For instance, regarding the God/creature co-causality of *Ordinatio* 2.37.2 we might well wonder: How can two agents simultaneously intend the same object? If God is going to will what Adam wills must God not have Adam's volition as an intentional object? But then, if we are

---

of the two autonomous sources of the contingency in human volitions is not present in the text of Appendix 6 used by both Adams and Langston. Although nothing it says precludes the human will from being an autonomous source of contingency, the text of Appendix 6 seems almost exclusively ordered to affirming the freedom of the divine, first cause at the source of any contingency.

52. *Questiones in Metaphysicam* 9.15; *Duns Scotus on the Will and Morality*, ed. Wolter p. 153.

going to consider that Adam wills something, must we not presume that God has in some sense, however subtle, already moved Adam? These queries probe how God's causality cooperates with Adam's; they look to define the relevant explanatory factors. But Scotus does not attempt any such explanations. He seems content to leave in silence what must have appeared to him the mystery of God's inner life.

As has been observed already by others, much of the subsequent history of considerations of the issues of freedom and foreknowledge takes it point of departure from Scotus's doctrine.[53] Indeed, at least as it comes to a crescendo in the Molina, Suarez, Bañez controversy of the sixteenth and seventeenth centuries, a portion of this history tries to demystify God's epistemological and causal role in regards to future contingents.[54] For Scotus, it seems to have sufficed to have established the mere fact of those roles consistent with God's radically contingent relationship to the world, God's omniscience, immutability, and omnipotence, and rational creatures' indeterminist freedom of the will. The burden of this study has been to show that a good portion of the project rests on the remarkable doctrine of divine and creaturely co-causality in *Ordinatio* 2.37.2.

University of Dallas

---

53. Schwamm, *Das göttliche Vorherwissen*; Langston, *God's Willing Knowledge*; and Wolter, "Scotus' Paris Lectures." See also Calvin Normore's survey, "Future Contingents," in CHLMP, pp. 358–382.

54. Normore, "Future Contingents," pp. 378–381.

Pico, Plato, and Albert the Great: The Testimony and Evaluation of Agostino Nifo

EDWARD P. MAHONEY

Giovanni Pico della Mirandola (1463–1494) is without doubt one of the most intriguing figures of the Italian Renaissance. It is thus no surprise that he has attracted the attention of many modern scholars. By reason of the varied interests that are reflected in his writings, contrasting interpretations of Pico have been proposed.[1] Our purpose here is not to present a new and different picture of Pico but, rather, to offer a contribution to one fruitful area of research pursued by some recent historians of philosophy, namely, Pico's debt to, and

---

1. For general presentations of Pico's life and thought, see the classic study of Eugenio Garin, *Giovanni Pico della Mirandola: Vita e dottrina* (Florence: F. Le Monnier, 1937); Garin's magisterial *Storia della filosofia italiana*, 2d ed. (Turin: G. Einaudi 1966), 1:458–495. Among more recent general accounts are Pierre-Marie Cordier, *Jean Pic de la Mirandole* (Paris: Debresse, 1958); Engelbert Monnerjahn, *Giovanni Pico della Mirandola* (Wiesbaden: F. Steiner, 1960); Paul Oskar Kristeller, *Eight Philosophers of the Italian Renaissance* (Stanford: Stanford University Press, 1964), pp. 54–71; Giovanni di Napoli, *Giovanni Pico della Mirandola e la problematica dottrinale del suo tempo* (Rome: Desclée, 1965); Charles Trinkaus, *In Our Image and Likeness* (Chicago: University of Chicago Press, 1970), 2:505-526; and Henri de Lubac, *Pic de la Mirandole: Etudes et discussions* (Paris: Aubier Montaigne, 1974).

use of, medieval philosophy in his overall philosophical enterprise.[2] Of particular concern will be the influence of Albert the Great on Pico, which can be established by a connection that has apparently not been noticed by Pico's historians. A rather unusual interpretation that Pico offered of Plato's notion of the soul will be shown to have already been set forth by Albert the Great, one of Pico's favorite medieval sources.[3] It will be argued that Pico drew this interpretation from Albert, possibly having forgotten its source. The plausibility of this thesis obviously rests in part on the ground of Pico's general interest in Albert.[4] This use of Albert by Pico is but further evidence of a tradition of "Albertism" to be found in Italy during the late Middle Ages and the Renaissance.[5]

---

2. See in particular the pioneering study of Avery Dulles, *Princeps Concordiae* (Cambridge, Mass.: Harvard University Press, 1941), and also the more recent study of Paul Oskar Kristeller, "Giovanni Pico della Mirandola and His Sources," in *L'opera e il pensiero di Giovanni Pico della Mirandola nella storia dell'umanesimo* (Florence: Ist. naz. di studi sul Rinascimento, 1965), 1:35-133. See also Innocenzo Colosio, "Pico della Mirandola e la scolastica," in *Studi Pichiani* (Modena, 1965), pp. 41-57.

3. Albert is listed by Pico in his celebrated *Oration on the Dignity of Man* among the medieval Christians who engaged in philosophy. The others mentioned are Thomas Aquinas, Duns Scotus, Giles of Rome, Henry of Ghent, and Francis Meyronnes. Albert is distinguished in that his works contain something that is "ancient, copious, and great" (*priscum, amplum et grande*). See *De hominis dignitate, Heptaplus, De ente et uno*, ed. Eugenio Garin, (Florence: Vallecchi, 1942), p. 140. It should also be noted that Albert is placed first among the Latins represented in Pico's *Conclusiones sive theses DCCCC*, ed. Bohdan Kieszkowski (Geneva: Droz, 1973), pp. 27-28.

4. This interest is indicated by the works of Albert that were found in Pico's library: see Pearl Kibre, *The Library of Pico della Mirandola* (New York: Columbia University Press, 1936), pp. 61-62, 70, and 113. Albert's commentaries on Aristotle and other works like the *De homine* appear in the inventory published by Kibre (pp. 119-297). Especially significant is the presence of Albert's *Metaphysica* (pp. 147-148, entry no. 196).

5. For discussions regarding Albert's influence in Italy in the late Middle Ages and the Renaissance, see Martin Grabmann, *Mittelalterliches Geistesleben* 2 (Munich: Max Hüber, 1936), pp. 396-400 and 407-408; Edward P. Mahoney, "Albert the Great and the *Studio Patavino* in the Late Fifteenth and Early Sixteenth Centuries," in *Albertus Magnus and the Sciences*, ed. James A. Weisheipl (Toronto: PIMS, 1980), pp. 537-563; Graziella Federici Vescovini, "Su alcune testimonianze dell'influenza di Alberto Magno come 'metaphysico', scienziato e 'astrologo' nella filosofia padovana del cadere del secolo XV: Angelo di Fossombrone e Biagio Pelacani da Parma," in *Albert der Grosse: Seine Zeit, sein Werk, seine Wirkung*, ed. Albert Zimmermann, Miscellanea Mediaevalia 14 (Berlin and New York: W. de Gruyter, 1981), pp. 155-176; Gregorio

In his commentary on Calo ben Calonymus's fourteenth-century Latin translation of Averroës's *Tahafut al-Tahafut*, known as the *Destructio destructionum*,[6] Agostino Nifo (c. 1470–1538)[7] sketches out three basic positions on the soul, namely, (*a*) the position that was attributed to Plato by Giovanni Pico della Mirandola in a conversation that he had with Nifo, (*b*) the position of Aristotle and Averroës, and (*c*) the position that is held by Christian faith and that Nifo believes to be Plato's real position.

The first two positions (*a* and *b*) maintain that the soul is one in number for all humans both before its entry into the human body and also after it departs from the body, but it is multiplied while it is in the body. These two positions differ inasmuch as position *a*, attributed to Plato, states that a *real* multiplication of souls is brought about (*multiplicatio fiat secundum rem*) as long as the soul is in the body, whereas position *b*, of Aristotle and Averroës, maintains that the single intellect is "multiplied" according to the many relationships (*secundum respectus et habitudines multas*) which exist only in human bodies and not in the single intellect itself. That is to say, there is no real multiplication of the separate intellect or intellective soul for Aristotle and Averroës. Nifo makes clear that however one understands position *b*, it is false and not to be believed.

Position *b*, that is, that of Aristotle and Averroës as he understands them, Nifo rejects. But he does not do so on the basis of

---

Piaia, "La genèse de l'interprétation historique et philosophique d'Albert le Grand (XVe-XVIIIe siècles)," in *Albert der Grosse*, ed. Zimmermann, pp. 237–255; Luigi Olivieri, *Pietro d'Abano e il pensiero neolatino* (Padua: Antenore, 1988).

6. On this translation and Nifo's edition, see Moritz Steinschneider, *Die hebräischen Übersetzungen des Mittelalters und die Jüden als Dolmetscher* (Berlin: Bibliographische Bureau, 1893), pp. 330–333; Maurice Bouyges, ed., *Averroès: Tahafot al-Tahafot*, Bibliotheca Arabica Scholasticorum, serie arabe 3 (Beirut: Imprimerie Catholique, 1930), pp. xxiii–xxvi. The work was translated again in the sixteenth century by another Calo Calonymos, namely, Calonymos ben David of Naples. See Beatrice A. Zedler, ed., *Averroes' "Destructio Destructionum Philosophiae Algazelis" in the Latin Version of Calo Calonymos* (Milwaukee: Marquette University Press, 1961), pp. 24–31.

7. On Nifo's life and works, see Edward P. Mahoney, "Agostino Nifo," *Dictionary of Scientific Biography* 10:122–124; Pietro Borraro, "Agostino Nifo, umanista e filosofo," *Archivio storico di terra di lavoro* 5 (1977): 169–192. For his years at Padua, see Bruno Nardi, *Saggi sull'aristotelismo padovano dal secolo XIV al XVI* (Florence: Olschki, 1958); Edward P. Mahoney, "A Note on Agostino Nifo," *Philological Quarterly* 50 (1971): 125–132.

any philosophical refutation, for at this point in his philosophical development he believed that reason was incapable of finding such a refutation. Instead he invokes the authority of the "Christian law" (*lex nostra*), that is, the doctrinal teaching of the church, which maintains that human souls remain after death as individual souls— those souls which did good are glorified while some are damned, namely, those which sinned. Nifo adds that he thinks that this view, namely, that individual souls survive death, is also the opinion of Plato and Avicebron. Nonetheless, Nifo is careful to add that the famed opinion of Plato can still be explained according to the first interpretation (*a*). Indeed Nifo reveals that one of his contemporaries believed that the first position (*a*) was Plato's own mind.[8]

Earlier in his commentary Nifo had in fact indicated that in a conversation with him Giovanni Pico della Mirandola (*comes Mirandulus*) had attributed just such a theory to Plato. The conversation apparently took place in late May 1494, while the two young philosophers were traveling from Ferrara, where the young Thomas de Vio (1468–1534), later to become Cardinal Cajetan,[9] had given a public

---

8. Agostino Nifo *Expositio*, in *Destructiones destructionum Averroys cum Augustini Niphi de Suessa expositione* 4 doubt 7 (Venice, 1497), fol. 65ra: "Debes scire quod illa prima opinio de anima, dicens quod anima est una ante adventum ad corpus et post, et dum est in corpore multiplicatur, potest intelligi duobus modis. Uno modo quod ista multiplicatio fiat secundum rem ipsi animae ita quod ipsa anima dum corpori unitur est multa secundum rem, dum separatur uniatur secundum rem et fiant omnes una. Et haec videtur opinio attribuita Platoni, ut fuit visum in prima disputatione. Alio modo potest intelligi quod anima prout est intellectus est unus numero, prout intelligitur in corpore efficitur multa secundum respectus et habitudines multas, non quidem respectibus et habitudinibus inhaerentibus ipsi intellectui, sed corporibus in quibus unitur. Et haec est opinio Aristotelis et Averrois ut recitatum fuit in prima disputatione in solutione 23. Sed quomodocumque intelligitur est falsa et non est credibilis. Immo lex nostra ponit quod animae mortuorum remanent post et quaedam in gloria, ut illae quae fecerunt bene, aliquae damnatae, ut illae quae peccaverunt. Et haec est opinio Avicebronis et Platonis, ut puto. Potest tamen illa opinio famosa secundum primum intellectum adhuc exponi, quoniam unus vir coetaneus meus volebat illam esse mentem Platonis." This volume formed a unit with Nifo's edition of Aristotle and Averroës published in 1495–1496. See *Gesamtkatalog der Wiegendrücken* 2 (Leipzig: Hiersemann, 1926), no. 2340, cols. 572–574; 3 (1928), no. 3106, cols. 216–217.

9. Cajetan's years at Padua remain to be studied in greater depth. On his life and works, see M.-J. Congar, "Bio-bibliographie de Cajetan," *Revue thomiste* 39 (1934–1935): 3–49.

disputation at the general chapter of the Dominicans, in the direction of Bologna, where they were to attend the general chapter of the Franciscans and a public disputation by Alessandro Achillini (1463–1512).[10] The text that served as the occasion of Nifo's recounting his conversation with Pico is a passage in al-Ghazzali's *Tahafut al Falasafah*, that is, the *Incoherence of the Philosophers*.

Al-Ghazzali presents as Plato's view—which he himself rejects as erroneous—that the one and eternal (*una et antiqua*) soul is divisible (*divisibilis*) according to the division of bodies but returns (*redit*) to its source (*radix*) and is made one (*unitur*) when it separates itself from individual human bodies.[11] In his commentary, Nifo confesses that he considered this passage for a long time but always remained in doubt as to its meaning. He then goes on to relate the explication of Plato that Pico had offered while they were traveling together to Bologna. Plato's position is supposedly that there is one Idea of souls (*una idea animarum*), which is related to those souls like the pieces of wood in the arches and vaults of houses. According to Pico, just as these pieces of wood that are placed beneath (*subterposita*) the stones strung together (*incalcinatis*) in the manner of an arch leave their "trace" (*vestigium*) when they are removed after the stones have dried—this trace is called the "vault" (*volta*) or "arch" (*arcus*)—so too does the single Idea of all souls (*una idea numero omnium animarum*) leave its "shadow" (*umbra*) or "trace" (*vestigium*), which is called "soul." This occurs when bodies have been formed by the soul's generative power (*virtus genitiva*) and it withdraws from them. Pico takes Isaac Israeli's statement that the soul is produced in the shadow

---

10. For an account and dating of this incident, see Nardi, *Saggi*, p. 319 and also pp. 227–228. However, di Napoli (*Giovanni Pico*, pp. 49–50) has argued that the incident must have occurred in the academic year 1485–1486; he does not note that Nifo would have been sixteen years old at the time. It is noteworthy that Nifo relates that he himself disputed a particular point at Bologna. See *Expositio Destructio destructionum* 1 doubt 11, fol. 13vb.

11. Text of al-Ghazzali in *Destructiones destructionum* 1 doubt 8, fol. 9ra: "Ait Algazel. Et si forte aliquis diceret quod opinio Platonis est vera, videlicet quod anima est una et antiqua et dividitur divisione corporum et in corporea separatione redit ad suam radicem et unitur, nos vero respondemus quod haec opinio est absurdior opinionibus animae et contra intellectus sententiam." For the English translation of the Arabic text, see *Averroes' Tahafut al-Tahafut*, trans. Simon Van Den Bergh (London: Trustees of the E. J. W. Gibb Memorial, 1969), 1:15.

(*umbra*) of the Intelligence to mean that the soul is produced in the shadow of the one Idea (*in umbra ideae*) of souls. The soul itself, that is, the individual human soul, is thus for Plato the "reverberation" (*resultatio*) or "trace" (*vestigium*) of that Idea, just as the Idea itself is the "nursery" (*seminarium*) or "root" (*radix*) of souls. Pico apparently understood Plato to be referring to this single Idea of souls when he said that souls return to their nursery (*seminarium*) at the time that they abandon their bodies. The explanation is that souls are no longer "traces" (*vestigia*) after they flow into their nursery. Nifo sums up Pico's interpretation of Plato by saying that Plato thus maintained that all souls are one in their source (*radix*), although they are also somehow many in their "beginnings" (*originaliter*). This interpretation of Plato's position Nifo considers to be very much in agreement with what al-Ghazzali and Averroës are saying here. Indeed, Nifo takes al-Ghazzali's attempt to prove the multiplicity of souls in the lines that follow to be a sign that Plato thought the soul to be one in number.[12]

Nifo's own reaction to Pico's interpretation of Plato appears to be twofold. First of all, he attempts to find some similarity between the notion of a single Idea of all souls and what Themistius, a "solemn

---

12. Nifo *Expositio Destructio destructionum* 1 doubt 8, fol. 9rb: "Ego diu consideravi verbum istud, et cum inspexi hoc semper steti in dubio et petii declarationem illius. Dixit comes Mirandulanus corona nostrae aetatis in corbula me petente Bononiam quod opinio Platonis ponit unam ideam animarum quae se habet respectu animarum sicut ligna in voltis et arcubus domorum. Dicebat enim quod, sicut ligna illa subterposita lapidibus incalcinatis ad modum arcus post exsiccationem illorum remota dimittunt vestigium eorum, quod vocatur volta seu arcus, sic est una idea numero omnium animarum, quae cum corpora formantur a virtute genitiva egreditur illa et recedit dimittitque eius umbram seu vestigium eius, quod anima vocatur. Et sic dixit dictum Isaac Israelitae intelligi, scilicet quando dicit animam esse productam in umbra, intelligitur idest ideae. Ista ergo resultatio seu vestigium apud Platonem anima erat, et ideo illa ideam seminarium seu radicem dicebat. Et tunc dixit Plato quod quando animae desinunt corpora, tunc redeunt ad earum seminarium in tantum quod vestigia illa, quae animae erant, amplius non sunt post redundant in suum seminarium, ut dicit. Et hanc opinionem dixit esse Platonis ille vir. Et ita Plato posuit omnes animas esse unam in radice, plures autem originaliter. Et sic huic multum consonat series verborum Algazelis et Averrois, quoniam nititur Algazel probare multitudinem animarum in verbis sequentibus, propter quod signum est quod Plato opinabatur unam esse tantum." This passage is reproduced in Garin's edition of Pico's *De hominis dignitate*, pp. 84–85. On Pico's villa at Corbola, see di Napoli, *Giovanni Pico*, pp. 227 and 253.

Platonist" (*solemnis Platonicus*), supposedly says about Plato according to Averroës. Paraphrasing a crucial passage from book 12 text 18 of Averroës's long commentary on the *Metaphysics*, Nifo presents Themistius as stating that Plato postulated an Idea of the earth (*idea terrae*) made from the secondary gods, where Aristotle speaks of the same as composed of the sun and the inclined orb. Nifo adds that it is apparent from the passage and also from his own exposition on that passage that Themistius is talking about an Idea.[13] And in his early commentary on book 12 of the *Metaphysics*, Nifo does indeed relate that Themistius proved on behalf of Plato that there had to be Ideas in order to save the notion that animals are generated from putrefaction.[14] On Nifo's reading, Themistius argued that since such animals are not brought into being by parents, and in particular from a father, they must be produced by their "like" (*simile*), namely, an Idea. Nifo then connects this "Idea" with the world-soul (*anima mundi*) that Plato puts forth in the *Timaeus*, though Nifo admits another interpretation is possible. What is noteworthy is that Nifo considers Themistius himself to agree with Avicenna and Plato that substantial forms come from a being separated from matter.[15]

There are in fact passages in the commentary on the *Destructio destructionum* in which Nifo groups Themistius together with Avicenna and Plato. In one of these passages, Nifo reviews Plato's conception of the world-soul in the *Timaeus*, noting that it is simultaneously the soul and the mover of the orbs, an Intelligence placed in that soul by God, and a seed-bearing and vital power infused in matter. He then finds a similar doctrine in the conception of the agent intellect put forth by Themistius in his paraphrases on the *De anima*. Also supposedly similar is Avicenna's notion of a "giver of forms" (*dator formarum*)—called *colcodea* in Arabic according to Nifo—which is

---

13. Nifo *Expositio Destructio destructionum* 1 doubt 8, fol. 9rb: "Huic etiam Themistius solemnis Platonicus, ut narrat Averroes 12 *Metaphysicae*, commento 18, concordat dicens quod Plato posuit ideam terrae factam ex diis secundis; Aristoteles autem a sole et orbe declini, ubi loquitur de illa idea, ut apparet ibidem et in expositione mea." Compare Averroës, *Commentaria in libros metaphysicorum Aristotelis*, in *Aristotelis Opera* 8 (Venice, 1562), 12 text 18, fol. 304rb. Nifo himself would come to view Themistius as considering the world-soul, not an Idea, to be the source of animation for all souls.

14. Nifo *In duodecim metà tà physikà seu metaphysices Aristotelis et Averrois* text 13 (Venice, 1505), fol. 8va.

15. Nifo *In metaph.* text 18, fols. 11rb–12va.

the source of substantial forms in things.[16] It should be underscored that the assimilation of Plato, Themistius, and Avicenna was inspired to some extent by Averroës himself and also by Albert the Great, and that this assimilation had already been anticipated by Nifo's teacher, Nicoletto Vernia (d. 1499), who also was an acquaintance of Pico's.[17] Nifo promises to take up in his *De intellectu* Avicenna's conception of the *dator formarum*, or *colcodea*, and Plato's and Themistius's notion of a single soul of all forms and souls.[18] At this point, Nifo does not seem to distinguish sharply the position of Themistius from that of Plato.

The second aspect of Nifo's reaction to Pico's interpretation was to tell Pico that it was not Plato's own doctrine, as was obvious from the *Phaedo*. Nifo claims that when he showed Pico the text of the *Phaedo*, Pico did not contradict it. However, what Nifo himself then presents as Plato's thought surely goes beyond the text of that dialogue. Nifo takes Plato to have held that souls are created by God in a set number and abide in glory in the heavens or the nursery orb

---

16. Nifo *In metaph.* 9 doubt 2, fol. 97va-b. See also 11 doubt 1, fol. 107va. On Themistius making the agent intellect to be the cause of all sensible forms in book 1 of his *abbreviatio* of the *De anima*, see 7 doubt 3, fol. 86rb. This reference appears to be inspired by Averroës, *In metaph.* 7 text 31, fol. 181ra. Nifo does not quote Ermolao Barbaro's translation of Themistius. On the term *colcodea*, see Carlo A. Nallino, *Raccolta di scritti editi e inediti* (Rome: Insitituto per l'Oriente 1948), 6:261; Bruno Nardi, *Studi su Pietro Pomponazzi* (Florence: F. Le Monnier, 1965), pp. 234–235, n. 1; Harry A. Wolfson, *Studies in the History of Philosophy and Religion*, ed. Isadore Twersky and George H. Williams (Cambridge, Mass.: Harvard University Press, 1977), 2:573–576.

17. See Averroës *In metaph.* 7 text 31, fols. 180vb–181vb; 12 text 18, fols. 393rb–305rb; and Albert the Great *Metaphysica* 11.1.8, ed. Bernhard Geyer in *Opera Omnia* 16/2 (Münster: Aschendorff, 1964), pp. 468b–470a; Nicoletto Vernia, *Quaestio an dentur universalia realia*, in *Urbanus Averroista philosophus summus . . . Commentorum omnium Averrois super librum Aristotelis De physico auditu expositor clarissimus* (Venice, 1492), unnumbered folio 3rab. On Averroës's interpretation of Themistius here, see Charles Touati, "Les problèmes de la génération et le rôle de l'intellect agent chez Averroès," in *Multiple Averroès*, ed. Jean Jolivet (Paris: CNRS, 1978), pp. 157–164.

18. Nifo *Expositio Destructio destructionum* 9 doubt 2, fols. 97vb and 98ra. Albert is cited (fol. 98va) on the manner in which forms are contained in matter. On Vernia's and Nifo's acceptance of Albert's doctrine of *inchoatio formae*, see my articles, "Nicoletto Vernia's Question on Seminal Reasons," *Franciscan Studies* 38 (1978): 299–309, and "Philosophy and Science in Nicoletto Vernia and Agostino Nifo," in *Scienza e filosofia all'Università di Padova nel quattrocento*, ed. Antonino Poppi (Padua: LINT, 1983), pp. 135–202, at pp. 160–163 and 189–190.

(*in signifero seu orbe seminario*). The souls then descend into bodies. When their descent (*descensus*) is completed, they are individual in their respective bodies. Subsequently, there will be the "great year" (*annus magnus*), that is, a great circuit, in which all things will return (*redibunt*) to the way they had been originally. This circuit or cycle will take place an infinite number of times and souls will often come back again (*reiterabuntur*). Nifo presumes that al-Ghazzali's problems regarding Plato's doctrine of the soul can be solved with this reading. The "root" (*radix*) to which souls return is not a single soul or Idea of a soul but rather the orb in which they abide and which Plato calls the "first nursery" (*seminarium primum*).[19] What must be noted in particular is that the interpretation that Nifo has set forth here closely resembles the overall interpretation to be found in Albert the Great, an interpretation whose general outlines were also adopted by Nifo's teacher, Nicoletto Vernia.[20]

The lines that follow contain further remarks that may provide a key to Pico's interest in such an interpretation of Plato and also throw light on the general intellectual milieu of the period. Nifo relates that al-Ghazzali rejected the supposed doctrine of Plato that there is only one soul, since it would then follow that the soul of one human being is also the soul of another human, whereas in fact the soul of an individual human, say that of Peter, knows that it differs from another soul, say that of William. If all the souls of human beings were one, then their knowledge would also be one or identical, since

19. Nifo *Expositio Destructio destructionum* 1 doubt 8, fol. 9rb: "Sed licet haec opinio sit solennis ut vides, dixi sibi quod opinio Platonis non est ista, ut apparet in *Phaedone*. Et ei monstravi textum, cui non contradixit. Videbatur enim mihi Platonem velle animas esse creatas a deo in quodam numero certo et eas stare in signifero seu orbe seminario in gloria. Et tunc ponit quod illae descendunt ad corpora et cum completur eorum descensus sic quod singula in corpore fuerint, tunc erit annus magnus in quo iterum omnia ut prius redibunt. Et hoc fiet infinities, et reiterabuntur saepe. Et tunc vult ipse per radicem orbem signorum, quem appellat seminarium primum in quo stant. Et si ista est opinio Platonis, tam soluta est quaestio Algazelis."

20. See Albert the Great *Summa de creaturis* 2: *De homine* 5.2, ed. Borgnet, *Opera Omnia* 35 (Paris: Vivès, 1896), p. 67; and 5.3, 35:75 and 79–80. Compare Albert *Liber de natura et origine animae* 2.7–8, ed. Bernhard Geyer, *Opera Omnia* 12 (Münster: Aschendorff, 1955), pp. 30–32. On Vernia's interpretation of Plato's psychology, see Mahoney, "Nicoletto Vernia on the Soul and Immortality," in *Philosophy and Humanism: Renaissance Essays in Honor of Paul Oskar Kristeller*, ed. Mahoney (New York: Columbia University Press, 1976), pp. 144–163, at pp. 150–151.

knowledge is an essential property of the soul. Nifo appears to consider al-Ghazzali's insistence that knowledge is a substantial property to rule out the possibility that souls were created in a set number and presumably would enter, depart, and reenter various human bodies over the course of time.[21] But what is still more interesting is that Nifo also considers al-Ghazzali's subsequent remarks to touch on Averroës's doctrine of the unity of the intellect.

Al-Ghazzali himself—that is, the Latin al-Ghazzali as Nifo reads him—examines the proposal that there is but one soul which is divided according to its "dependence" (*dependentia*) on different bodies, but he rejects such a view on the ground that something lacking the magnitude of measurable quantity cannot be so divided. On the other hand, Nifo glosses the "dependence" in question as an "ordering" (*ordo*) to bodies. He notes, moreover, that the position seems to be that of the Peripatetics, since Averroës, himself a peripatetic (*Averroes peripateticus*), thinks that the intellect of all humans is numerically one in itself, though it can be multiplied extrinsically (*extrinsece*) according as it signifies an "ordering" to the different bodies of which it is the first perfection (*perfectio prima*). In a word, Nifo has placed al-Ghazzali's and Pico's supposedly similar readings of Plato's concept of the soul in the context of interpreting Averroës's doctrine of the unity of the intellect, a doctrine that Nifo believed at this point in his career to be the position of Aristotle himself.[22] Indeed, Nifo even states that al-Ghazzali's arguments in the text under consideration preclude that one intellect (*unus intellectus*) could be many.[23]

---

21. Nifo *Expositio Destructio destructionum* 1 doubt 8, fol. 9rb. Nifo will return to this passage in his *De intellectu*.

22. On the shift in Nifo's evaluation of Averroës as an accurate interpreter of Aristotle, see Mahoney, "Agostino Nifo's Early View on Immortality," *Journal of the History of Philosophy* 8 (1970): 387–409.

23. Text of al-Ghazzali in *Destructiones destructionum* 1 doubt 8, fol. 9ra, and Nifo, *Expositio Destructio destructionum* 1 doubt 8, fol. 9rb: "'Et si forte aliquis arguat, dicens quod sint unum animae,' id est, quod omnes animae sint unum, 'sed dividuntur secundum dependentiam,' id est ordinem ad corpus, sicut videtur opinio peripateticorum, vult enim Averroes peripateticus, ut dixi, quod intellectus omnium est unus numero in specie, potest tamen multiplicari extrinsice prout est dicens ordinem ad diversa corpora quorum est perfectio prima. Contra hoc arguit Algazel dicens: 'Nos dicimus quod dividi id quod magnitudinem quantitatis mensurabilium non habet est falsum.' Ergo supra impossibile est unicum intellectum esse multos respectu corporum." For the English translation of al-Ghazzali, see *Averroes' Tahafut al-Tahafut*, ed. Van Den Bergh 1:15.

In his own rejoinder to these remarks of al-Ghazzali, Averroës takes up the possibility that Peter differs from William numerically but is one with him in form, namely, in their soul. In this case, if the soul does not cease at the cessation of the body, then, when it is separated from the body, it will of necessity be one in number. Although this might seem at first glance to be a concession to al-Ghazzali's interpretation of Plato, it is not. Averroës considers al-Ghazzali's argumentation against Plato to be sophistical. First of all, there is an equivocation at work regarding the terms "same" and "different," since they can have different meanings. The soul of William and the soul of Peter can be called "one" as regards their form and yet "many" as regards their substrata (*ratione subiectorum*)—that is, the different underlying "subjects" in which they exist, namely, human bodies. Furthermore, al-Ghazzali errs in saying that what lacks quantity cannot be divided, for it can be divided at least accidentally through its substrata. Indeed, Averroës insists that it is precisely in this way that form and soul are divisible, that is, by the division of their substrata (*divisione subiectorum*). He adds that the soul thus closely resembles light insofar as light is divided by the division of illuminating lights, whereas it again becomes one on the removal of these other illuminating lights. It is the same with the soul and bodies.[24]

In his commentary on this text, Nifo draws on his own understanding of Averroës's doctrine of the unity of the intellect. He explains that the "form of the human being" (*forma hominis*)—which is in fact the lowest of the Intelligences[25]—can be considered in two different ways, namely, as it is "soul" and as it is "intellect," that is,

---

24. Averroës *Destructiones destructionum* 1 doubt 8, fol. 9va. In his translation from the Arabic text, Van Den Bergh reads "illuminated" and not "illuminating." See Averroës *Tahafut al-Tahafut*, ed. Van Den Bergh 1:16.11. This passage influenced Moses Narboni (c. 1300–1366) in a commentary that he wrote on one of Averroës's treatises on conjunction. Indeed, he appears to have fashioned a Plato "quotation" from Averroës's remarks. Moreover, he connects what he attributes to Plato with Averroës's doctrine of the unity of the intellect. See *The Epistle on the Possibility of Conjunction with the Active Intellect by Ibn Rushd with the Commentary of Moses Narboni*, ed. and trans. Kalman P. Bland, Moreshet Series, Studies in Jewish History, Literature, and Thought 7 (New York: Jewish Theological Seminary of America/KTAV, 1982), Introduction, p. 22. Bland (p. 113, n. 4) recognizes Averroës as Narboni's source and correctly excludes any genuine source in Plato or Plotinus.

25. On the lowest Intelligence as the *forma hominis*, see Nifo *Expositio Destructio destructionum* 1 doubt 8, fol. 9rb; 1 doubt 23, fol. 23rb; and 6 doubt 2, fol. 74vb.

a separate substance. Going beyond the text—but in fact borrowing from Averroës's *Physics* and perhaps also from Walter Burley's commentary on that work[26]—Nifo argues that just as a column is "left" or "right" not of itself but from its "ordering" to different human beings (*ex ordine ad diversos homines*) standing near it in such fashion that there is no newness (*novitas*) or modification in the column, so too is the intellect "many souls" without any real multiplication occurring in it, for all multiplication comes about on the part of human bodies. Accordingly, the intellect can be called "many" *per accidens* and extrinsically—that is, without any modification in its very substance—just as the column is called "right" only *per accidens* by reason of the thing that is "right" *simpliciter*, that is, the objects near the column. The intellect can be considered "many" *per accidens* and extrinsically (*extrinsece*), that is, many "souls", as it regards (*prout respicit*) the bodies of different human beings.[27]

Nifo thus considers Averroës to have reduced Plato to his own position insofar as he takes Plato to hold that the soul is in some way one and in some way many, since it is *one* simply and absolutely in its substance and yet *many* by its relationships to different substrata.

---

26. See Averroës *In phys.* 7 text 20; *Aristotelis Opera* 4, fol. 322va; and Walter Burley *Expositio in libros octo De physico auditu* 7 text 20, ed. Nicoletto Vernia (Venice, 1482), sig. K1va-K3ra.

27. Nifo *Expositio destructio destructionum* 1 doubt 8, fol. 9rb: "Debes scire quod forma hominis potest dupliciter considerari, videlicet inquantum anima et inquantum intellectus, substantia existens separata. Si primo modo, dico quod sicut columna est dextra et sinistra non per se sed ex ordine ad diversos homines sic quod nulla est novitas in ea sic intellectus prout respicit homines diversos est anima multa, non multiplicatione accidenta ei sed multiplicatione se tenente ex parte corporum. Et sic potest dici multus per accidens extrinsece sicut columna dicitur dextra per accidens ratione rei dextrae simpliciter. Si autem consideratur ut intellectus est, sic est unus per se et per accidens, quoniam ut sic separatur ab omni respectu ad quodcumque extrinsecum. Et sic anima est una quodammodo et plures quodammodo, una quidem per se et simpliciter, multae autem extrinsece et per accidens." A like interpretation of Averroes is given by Nicoletto Vernia, Nifo's teacher, in his *Contra perversam Averrois opinionem de unitate intellectus et de animae felicitate quaestiones divinae* (Venice 1505), fol. 6vb. This interpretation was vehemently attacked by the Franciscan theologian at Padua, Antonio Trombetta. See Mahoney, "Antonio Trombetta and Agostino Nifo on Averroes and Intelligible Species: A Philosophical Dispute at the University of Padua," in *Storia e cultura al Santo*, ed. Antonino Poppi (Vicenza: N. Pozza, 1976), pp. 289-301.

Nifo himself attempts to aid Averroës's reading of Plato by suggesting that when Plato says man is nothing but his soul, insofar as he uses the body as its instrument, what is meant is that the soul remains *one* simply and absolutely like an individual artisan and yet becomes *many* in the way that the single artisan becomes many by using different instruments. Oddly enough, despite his having earlier challenged Pico's interpretation by citing the *Phaedo* and his having presented as Plato's position that God created a fixed number of *individual souls*, Nifo now states that the notion of *a single soul for all* does seem to be Plato's own opinion as he himself has written in his own *De intellectu*.[28] This seeming discrepancy in Nifo's interpretation of Plato may be explained in various ways. Nifo may have offered the *Phaedo* passage and maintained that Plato held to a plurality of souls before he had read much Plato. Or again he might have simply been engaging in a dialectical joust with Pico and was not committing himself absolutely to the view that for Plato there was a fixed number of individual souls that had been created by God. In any case, throughout his career Nifo would continue to worry the question whether the soul was one or many for Plato.[29]

Although Pico is mentioned again in Nifo's early commentary on the *De anima*, which was published in 1503, he is now cited not for his interpretation of Plato's psychology but for his views on whether we can believe a proposition to be true or false as we please.[30] In this

---

28. Nifo *Expositio Destructio destructionum* 1 doubt 8, fol. 9rb: "Circa dicta primo debes scire quod opinionem Platonis Averroes reduxit ad opinionem eius intantum quod Plato ut Averroes innuit nihil aliud nisi sit quodammodo una et quodammodo plures. Est enim una simpliciter et absolute in substantia et plures respective et in habitudine ad diversa subiecta, ut dixi iam. Et hanc opinionem Averroes ascribit Platoni. Et addo quod Plato videtur dicere quod homo non est aliud nisi anima prout utitur corpore tanquam instrumento. Et ideo sicut navis est nauta tantum utens instrumento, sic homo est anima utens corpore tanquam instrumento et sicut artifex est quodammodo unus simpliciter et absolute, sic et anima. Et haec videtur opinio Platonis, ut scripsi in libro *De intellectu*."

29. For a more detailed discussion, see Mahoney, "Plato and Aristotle in the Thought of Agostino Nifo (ca. 1470–1538)," in *Platonismo ed aristotelismo nel mezzogiorno d'Italia (secc. XIV–XVI)*, Biblioteca dell'Officina di Studi Medievali 1, ed. Giuseppe Roccaro (Palermo: Officina di Studi Medievali, 1989), pp. 79–102.

30. Agostino Nifo *Collectanea ac commentaria in libros De anima* (Venice, 1522) 2 coll. 153, fol. 146rb–va. I cite this edition for the sake of convenience. For the first edition, see *Augustini Niphi super tres libros De anima* (Venice, 1503).

commentary, Nifo considers Averroës to be so true an interpreter of Aristotle that he calls him the "Arab Aristotle" (*arabs Aristoteles*).[31] Aristotle and Averroës are agreed on the doctrine of the unity of the intellect.[32] On the other hand, Nifo shows strong interest in the possibility of conciliating Plato and Aristotle, and he explicitly mentions Ammonius, Themistius, and Simplicius along these lines.[33] Nifo makes constant use both of Ermolao's translation of Themistius's paraphrases on the *De anima* and also of a now-lost translation of the *De anima* that has traditionally been attributed to Simplicius, and he prefers on occasion their explanations of the text to those of the Latins, namely, Albert the Great, Thomas Aquinas and Giles of Rome.[34]

Nifo reveals remarkable sensitivity to the Platonic orientation of the *De anima* attributed to Simplicius, listing Simplicius among other *platonici* like Plotinus and Origen and stating at one point that Simplicius's exposition seems to be more in accord with Plato than with Aristotle.[35] Indeed he attempts to assimilate Themistius, Simplicius, and the Plotinus who emerges from Ficino's commentary on the *Enneads*, in a manner that bears on our topic of Pico's interpretation of Plato. Basing himself on Ermolao's translation of Themistius's paraphrases on the *De anima*, Nifo attributes to Themistius a theory of a rational soul which extends into each individual living body an "animation" (*animatio*) or "life" (*vita*), adding however that Themistius leaves in doubt whether this first soul, that is, the rational soul,

---

31. Nifo *Collectanea* 2 coll. 97, fol. 122vb.

32. Nifo *Collectanea* 1 coll. 12, fol. 20rb–21va; compare 3 coll. 1, fol. 2ra–b; 3 coll. 5, fol. 11rb–va.

33. Nifo *Collectanea* 1 coll. 36, fol. 65va. For Nifo's "conciliation" of Plato and Aristotle on divine knowledge and on whether unity is above being and the other transcendentals, see 2 coll. 5, fol. 16rb–va. Garin thinks that on the latter question Nifo has rejected Pico for Ficino. See Eugenio Garin, *La cultura filosofica del Rinascimento italiano* (Florence: Sansoni, 1961), p. 117.

34. In *Collectanea* 3 coll. 5 (fol. 16vb), Nifo also cites Simplicius's *De coelo* and *Physics*. In the commentary on the *Destructio*, Nifo cited both these works but not the *De anima* that is attributed to Simplicius. His use of this latter work in his own early commentary on the *De anima* has been noted by Nardi, *Saggi*, pp. 377–382. The Greek Commentators would come to have an ever greater importance in Nifo's philosophical works.

35. Nifo *Collectanea* 3 coll. 23–24, fols. 47va and 48rb.

is one or many—in the later *De intellectu* he will take Themistius to hold it to be one. What is significant for our purposes here is that Nifo takes Themistius to attribute this same theory to Plato and Aristotle, and he himself goes on to see it present in Plotinus's *Enneads* 1.³⁶ This explication of Themistius is clearly inspired by remarks of Marsilio Ficino who, in his own commentary on the *Enneads*, takes the rational soul, the "first soul," to pour forth into the body a "life" (*vita*), which is properly called an "animation" (*animatio*) and "vivification" (*vivificatio*), whereas the rational soul alone is properly called "soul." Ficino appears to believe that Themistius adopted from Plato and Plotinus a conception of a single intellect informing the many rational souls which he then attributed to Aristotle.³⁷ Moreover, Nifo uses almost the same passages from Ficino to explicate the psychology that emerges from the commentary on the *De anima* attributed to Simplicius.³⁸ He even cites Themistius's supposed notion of "animation" when explicating how one intellect provides the soul

---

36. Nifo *Collectanea* 2 coll. 37, fols. 93vb–94ra. For the source in Themistius, see Themistius *In libros Aristotelis De anima paraphrasis*, ed. R. Heinze, Commentaria in Aristotelem Graeca 5/2 (Berlin: G. Reimer, 1899), pp. 25–27. Compare Themistius *Libri paraphraseos . . . in libros De anima* 1.23, in *Libri paraphraseos Themistii in Posteriora Aristotelis, in Physica, in libros De anima . . . interprete Hermolao Barbaro* (Treviso, 1481), sig. bb2r–bb2v. See Plotinus *Enneads* 1.1.7, 1.1.10, and 1.1.12.

37. Marsilio Ficino, *argumenta* to *Enneads* 1.1.1 and 1.1.7, in *Opera Omnia* (Basel, 1576), pp. 1548–1549 and 1551–1552. For a presentation of the relevant passages in Themistius's paraphrases on the *De anima* and their impact on earlier medieval philosophers, see Mahoney, "Themistius and the Agent Intellect in James of Viterbo and Other Thirteenth-Century Philosophers (Saint Thomas, Siger of Brabant, and Henry Bate)," *Augustiniana* 23 (1973): 422–467, especially pp. 424–431. See also Mahoney, "Neoplatonism, the Greek Commentators, and Renaissance Aristotelianism," in *Neoplatonism and Christian Thought*, ed. Dominic J. O'Meara (Albany: SUNY Press, 1982), pp. 169–177 and 264–282, especially pp. 171–172 and 264–266. There are detailed surveys of the scholarly literature in the notes of these two studies.

38. Nifo *In De anima* 3 coll. 1, fol. 1rb. Compare Nardi, *Saggi*, pp. 378–379, who identifies some of the passages that Nifo quotes from Simplicius, but who does not notice Nifo's clear dependence on Ficino. For a more general discussion, see Mahoney, "Marsilio Ficino's Influence on Nicoletto Vernia, Agostino Nifo, and Marcantonio Zimara," in *Marsilio Ficino e il ritorno di Platone: Studi e documenti*, ed. Gian Carlo Garfagnini (Florence: Olschki, 1986), 2:509–531, at pp. 517–524. Eckhard Kessler does not bring out Ficino's influence on Aristotelians of the Renaissance in his study, "The Intellective Soul," in *The Cambridge History of Renaissance Philosophy*, ed. Charles B. Schmitt, Quentin Skinner, and Eckhard Kessler (Cambridge: Cambridge

for many individual human beings.[39] Whether or not Nifo has interpreted Themistius and Simplicius in a wholly accurate fashion, he has correctly seen that the problem of the one and the many was central for them and related to a like worry in Plotinus.[40]

The *De intellectu* is of course Nifo's major early work touching on questions of philosophical psychology. It is also one of the works in which he shows strong interest in delineating the similarities as well as the differences among various philosophers of antiquity and the medieval period. He appears to be the first Aristotelian commentator of the Renaissance to compare in detail the *platonici*, especially Plotinus, both with Themistius and Simplicius and also with Averroës. This interest in Simplicius and Themistius he shared with his own teacher, Nicoletto Vernia, as well as with Pico himself.[41] But it must be added

---

University Press, 1988), pp. 484–534. Some of his remarks on Vernia, Nifo, and Pomponazzi are imprecise.

39. Nifo *De anima* 3 coll. 20, fol. 44rb. Nifo's reading of Simplicius is not wholly accurate here.

40. It should be noted that in *De anima* 3 coll. 5 (fol. 10va), Nifo does seem to believe that the intellect is one in number for Themistius. For further discussion on Nifo's relating Plotinus to the two Greek Commentators, see Mahoney, "Neoplatonism, the Greek Commentators, and Renaissance Aristotelianism," pp. 171–173 and 272–274. What gives Nifo's approach to Simplicius an unusual twist is that he takes Simplicius to have held that the single intellect together with the individual "life" in each human being forms the "whole soul" (*tota anima*) or the "whole rational soul" (*tota anima rationalis*), that is, a certain essential unity (*quoddam unum essentiale*). Nifo has thus applied to Simplicius a terminology that he took from an interpretation of Averroës found in Siger of Brabant's now lost *De intellectu*. Although Nifo accepted Siger's explication of Averroës as correct when he wrote his early commentary on the *De anima*, he would abandon it soon thereafter in the *De intellectu* and attack Pico for having adopted it. On Siger's theory, see Bruno Nardi, *Sigieri di Brabante nel pensiero del Rinascimento italiano* (Rome: Edizione Italiane, 1944); and Mahoney, "Saint Thomas and Siger of Brabant Revisited," *Review of Metaphysics* 27 (1974): 531–553; and Mahoney, "Sense, Intellect, and Imagination in Albert, Thomas, and Siger," in *The Cambridge History of Later Medieval Philosophy*, ed. Norman Kretzmann, Anthony Kenny, and Jan Pinborg (Cambridge: Cambridge University Press, 1982), pp. 602–622.

41. On Pico's interest in Simplicius and Themistius, see Nardi, *Saggi*, pp. 373–375; Garin, *Storia della filosofia italiana*, pp. 460–462; and Kristeller, "Giovanni Pico della Mirandola and His Sources," pp. 54–55 and 62. There are *conclusiones* for Themistius and Simplicius in Pico's *Conclusiones*, ed. B. Kieszkowski, pp. 39–41. In an earlier study, Kieszkowski had argued that Pico's entire knowledge of Themistius and Alexander was based on questions and commentaries prepared for him by Elia del Medigo. Supposedly only after Pico had composed the *Conclusiones* did he study the

that the remarks made about the *platonici* and even about Plato are at times inspired by statements to be found in the writings of Albert the Great.[42] We might thus characterize Nifo as under the joint influence of Renaissance Platonism (through the works, the translations, and the commentaries of Ficino) and of medieval Platonism (through the writings of Albert). As we shall see, Pico, too, borrows from a work of Albert in his approach to Plato's psychology.[43]

On occasion in the *De intellectu*, Nifo appears to attribute to Plato himself belief in personal immortality.[44] And while *platonici* like Plotinus and Iamblichus are presented, on the one hand, as holding that in

---

Greek Commentators directly. See Bohdan Kieszkowski, "Les rapports entre Elie del Médigo et Pic de la Mirandole (d'après le ms. lat. 6508 de la Bibliothèque Nationale)," *Rinascimento* 4 (1964): 41–91, at p. 53. The author's remarks on Pico, Themistius, and Simplicius are questionable. For recent valuable discussions on Elia, see Herbert Davidson, "Medieval Jewish Philosophy in the Sixteenth Century," in *Jewish Thought in the Sixteenth Century*, ed. B. D. Cooperman (Cambridge: Cambridge University Press, 1983), pp. 106–145, at pp. 110–111; and Alfred L. Ivry, "Remnants of Jewish Averroism in the Renaissance," in the same volume, pp. 243–265, at pp. 250–261. Of special relevance here is Kalman P. Bland's important new study, "Elijah del Medigo's Averroist Response to the Kabbalahs of Fifteenth-Century Jewry and Pico della Mirandola," *Journal of Jewish Thought and Philosophy* 1 (1991): 23–53.

42. The mixture is strikingly apparent in Nifo *Liber de intellectu* 1.1.8 (Venice, 1503), fol. 5va, where he presents "Platonic arguments" (*demonstrationes platonicae*) from Plotinus that are borrowed to the word from Ficino's *argumentum* to Enneads 4.7.epilogue, in *Opera Omnia*, 1754. His "other argument of Plato" (*alia Platonis ratio*) and the argument cited from the Phaedrus (*De intellectu* 1.1.8, fol. 6rab) are taken from Albert *De natura et origine animae* 2.1 (12:18–19), and 2.6 (12:26–27). For discussion, see my "Agostino Nifo's Early Views," pp. 451 and 456–457.

43. On Nifo's "Albertism," see my "Albert the Great and the *Studio Patavino*," pp. 551–554. Because he does combine what he learns about Plato's teachings both from reading Plato himself in Ficino's newly available translations and also from reading what Albert and Ficino attribute to Plato and the *platonici*, Nifo would come to express in his later writings his own puzzlement as to Plato's position. It is no surprise then that in his *De immortalitate animae* and his second, Pisan commentary on the *De anima* he should take up Eusebius's charge that Plato was inconsistent in his remarks about the soul. For details and discussion, see Mahoney, "Plato and Aristotle in the Thought of Agostino Nifo," pp. 91–96. For a major contribution to our knowledge of Plato's impact on the Renaissance, see James Hankins, *Plato in the Italian Renaissance*, Columbia Studies in the Classical Tradition 17 (Leiden: E. J. Brill, 1990).

44. Nifo *De intellectu* 1.1.9, fol. 6va. See *Opera Platonis*, trans. Marsilio Ficino (Venice, 1491), fol. 262vb, for the *Timaeus* passage; fol. 180rb–va, for the *Phaedo* passage.

the preexistent state there are many distinct rational souls, Theophrastus, Themistius, and Averroës are presented, on the other hand, as holding that the rational soul is a single Intelligence.[45] When Nifo does turn to Themistius and Theophrastus in particular, he explains that they hold that there is one soul for all living things, called the world-soul (*mundi anima*), that sends forth an "animation" (*animatio*), "life" (*vita*), or "soul" (*anima*) into all living things, just as the sun sends forth illuminations into all bright things. This same world-soul is also called "the intellect of the human being" (*intellectus hominis*) insofar as it sends forth the power of thinking to the soul. What is important for our purposes is that Nifo quotes passages from Ficino's translation of *Timaeus* 34B and 41C which appear to show that Plato, too, held to a world-soul that universally vivifies all living things by extending to them an animation (*animatio*) or life (*vita*) and that is like a seed (*semen*) and principle (*principium*) containing within its own power (*continens in sua virtute*) all the forms and all the activities of all the forms. He adds that Themistius himself takes Aristotle to be speaking of such an animation or "second soul" (*anima secunda*)— and not the soul which is one for all—when he calls the soul the first act. According to Nifo's reading of Themistius, there is, then, no conflict between Plato and Aristotle on the distinction between the one single rational soul and the individual "animation" (*animatio*) or "second soul" (*anima secunda*) that is found in the individual living thing.[46] On several occasions in the *De intellectu*, Nifo returns to this theory of the world-soul that he has attributed to Themistius and that

---

45. Nifo *De intellectu* 1.1.17, fols. 9vb–10ra.
46. Nifo *De intellectu* 1.1.17, fol. 10rb–va. Nifo is closely following here Ermolao's translation. See Themistius *Libri paraphraseos . . . in libros De anima . . . interprete Hermolao Barbaro* 1.23, sig. bb2r–v, cited above in note 32. Nifo returns to Themistius's interpretation of Plato as upholding a single soul and also individual souls in 1.2.18, fol. 24rb, where he quotes from Ermolao's translation about Plato in *Libri paraphraseos . . . in libros De anima* 3.38, sig. ff4r–v. Compare Themistius *In libros Aristotelis De anima paraphrasis*, ed. R. Heinze, p. 107, lines 23–29. Nifo challenges Themistius's conciliation of Plato, Aristotle, and Theophrastus. See Nifo *De intellectu* 1.5.21, fol. 52rb–va. In doing so, he may also intend to criticize Vernia. On the latter's conciliation of Plato and Aristotle, see Mahoney, "Nicoletto Vernia on the Soul and Immortality," pp. 153, 155, and 158–162; "Neoplatonism, the Greek Commentators, and Renaissance Aristotelianism," pp. 170–171 and 268–269; and "Philosophy and Science in Nicoletto Vernia and Agostino Nifo," pp. 167–168 and 171–172.

he had already discussed in his earlier commentaries on the *Destructio destructionum* and the *De anima*.⁴⁷

In one discussion regarding Themistius and the *platonici*, Nifo begins by noting that "outstanding men of Plato's sect" (*praestantissimi viri ex Platonis secta*) hold that the rational souls (*rationales animae*) flow from the world-soul (*anima mundi*) and that these souls give human beings their existence and put them in their species. Some of the followers of Plato say that the rational souls are parts of the world-soul, a position that Plato sometimes appears to maintain. Nifo cites the *Philebus, Phaedrus, Timaeus,* and the *Republic* to justify this statement about Plato. However, he is careful to distinguish Plato from those who identify the world-soul with God, noting that Plato would perhaps say, as is obvious from the *Timaeus*, that God and the world-soul differ and that the world-soul is located in the middle of the world.⁴⁸

Nifo then turns from the *platonici* to later philosophers (*posteriores philosophantes*), such as Themistius, Theophrastus, al-Ghazzali, and Avicenna, who thought that all the souls of living things flowed from the world-soul just as illuminations (*illuminationes*) flow from the sun. They do not hold that the numerically one rational soul, called "the world-soul" (*anima mundi*), directly animates within living things (*intus viva*) but that it provides all living things with individual souls that are also called rational souls. Nifo explains how it is necessary according to Themistius to postulate two such rational souls (*duae rationales animae*). The one rational soul is individual, inseparable from the body, and destructible at the death of the body. This is the

---

47. Nifo *De intellectu* 1.1.24, fol. 13rb. Nifo again cites what he takes to be Themistius's account of the phenomenon of spontaneous generation. See Themistius *Libri paraphraseos . . . in libros De anima* 1.23, sig. bb2r–v. Compare Themistius, *In libros Aristotelis De anima paraphrasis* (Heinze 25–26). For other relevant passages in Nifo *De intellectu*, see 1.1.7 (fol. 19ra1), 1.1.18 (24rb), 1.3.9 (31ra), 1.3.20 (33rb–34ra), 1.4.14 (41va), 1.5.10 (48va–b), 1.5.11 (49ra), 1.5.13 (49vb), and 1.5.22 (52vb). For the *colcodea* language, see 1.4.9 (40ra) and 1.4.11 (40va), as well as Nifo *De demonibus* 2.15, in *De intellectu*, fol. 80rb. On Nifo's adoption of this terminology for Avicenna's *dator formarum*, see Harry A. Wolfson, *Studies in the History of Philosophy and Religion*, 2:574–576.

48. Nifo *De intellectu* 1.1.24, fol. 13ra–b. The citations presented in behalf of the view that God is the world-soul are borrowed from Albert the Great *De homine* 5.2 (Borgnet 35:68a and 71a).

soul that Themistius calls "the rational soul" and that Aristotle says he is defining in book 2 of the *De anima*. The other rational soul is separate and one in number for all living things and all animals. This is the soul that Themistius calls both "the intellect of the human being" (*intellectus hominis*), since it provides the power of thinking, and also "the world-soul" (*mundi anima*). Avicenna, on the other hand, calls it the "giver of forms" (*dator formarum*), while Averroës calls it an Intelligence (*intelligentia*). However, Nifo appears puzzled as to the precise nature of the individual rational soul or "animation" for Themistius and seems to suggest several lines later that it was a "creation" for the ancient commentator. Nifo contrasts those who speak of "animations" (*animationes*), "lives" (*vitae*), or "second lives" (*animae secundae*) coming forth from the world-soul—presumably the "outstanding men of Plato's sect" mentioned earlier—with Themistius and others of his sect (*alii suae sectae*) who say that the animation comes from the world-soul as a creation (*creatio*).[49]

To make clearer the nature of the animations that flow from the world-soul according to these *platonici*, Nifo turns to the very same comparison that Pico had used to represent his own account of how there was for Plato one Idea of souls and yet many souls. Nifo first explains that for these *platonici* the animation comes forth from the world-soul neither by "creation" (*creatio*), as with Themistius and his followers, nor by the division of the world-soul, but rather through an "impression" (*impressio*) left by the world-soul from its entering (*ingressus*) into the body. He then offers an example of such a process that he says is given by John Saracene (*Joannes Saracenus*), and he expressly points out that this example or comparison is narrated by Albert the Great. Just as in vaults and arches of walls (*in testudinibus ac parietum arcubus*) a wooden arch is first set up on which the vault is completed, and after that arch has been removed there remains both its "trace" (*vestigium*) in the vault and also the separate arch (*separatus arcus*) itself, so too the world-soul (*anima mundi*) animates living substances by means of a "trace" (*vestigium*) in that living substance.[50]

---

49. Nifo *De intellectu* 1.1.24, fol. 13rb–va. Nifo's interpretation of Themistius on "animation" owes much to Averroës. For the latter's presentation of Themistius on generation, see Touati, "Les problèmes de la génération."

50. Nifo *De intellectu* 1.1.24, fol. 13vb: "Post hos adhuc animationes ac vitas, quae animae secundae nuncupantur, dicunt ab anima mundi provenire, non quidem per creationem ut Themistius et alii suae sectae, nec per divisionem animae mundi,

In a word, Nifo appears to have discovered in Albert the source of the analogy that Pico had related to him during their journey together to Ferrara some years earlier.

It should be carefully noted that Nifo has somewhat bent the passage from Albert to his own purposes. Although the passage does concern Plato's remarks in *Timaeus* 41 A–D, the supposed quote from John Saracene that is found in Albert refers not to the world-soul (*anima mundi*) but rather to "Idea-Forms" (*formae ideales*) which inform sensible substances.[51] In the same chapter, Albert himself appears to take Plato to be saying that all forms are induced in matter by a giver of forms (*dator formarum*) that is an Idea (*idea*) separated from matter. The form induced in matter is called an "image" (*imago*), since it imitates the forming form that is outside matter. Albert points out that some people have called such an image a "reverberation" (*resultatio*), while others have called it a "shadow" (*umbra*) inasmuch as it darkens on entering matter.[52] And elsewhere in his *Metaphysics* Albert refers to such an image as a "life" (*vita*).[53] It would thus appear that Pico borrowed not only the comparison of the arch from Albert but also his interpretation of Plato according to which there is a single Idea which leaves its "reverberation" (*resultatio*) or "trace" (*vestigium*) in individual human beings. Indeed, the interpretation of Plato that Pico offers seems closer, as we shall now see, to that of Albert than does that of Nifo.

Whatever be the accuracy of Nifo's presentation of this passage from Albert regarding Plato, it is striking that Nifo himself makes

---

sed per impressionem relictam ex ingressu eius in corpus. Cuius exemplum Joannes Sarracenus dedit Alberto narrente dicens quod quemadmodum in testudinibus ac parietum arcubus primo ligneus supponitur arcus super quem testudo concluditur et postea remoto arcu remanet vestigium in testudine ac separatus arcus remanet, ita est in mundi anima animante substantias vivas, quae non nisi per vestigium est in viva substantia. Et hoc iuramentum erat deorum, quod Appollo reddit sacramento."

51. See Albert *Metaphysica* 11.1.8 (16:469.13–24).

52. Albert *Metaphysica* 11.1.8 (16:468.68–85 and 470.31–32/68–76). Albert himself rejects this view of Plato that forms are not educed from (*educitur*), but are rather induced (*inducitur*) in, the potency of matter (16:471.5–7). See also Albert *Metaphysica* 1.4.9 (16:60.33–36). It has been suggested that Albert here has borrowed his interpretation of Plato from Boethius. See Georg Wieland, *Untersuchungen zum Seinsbegriff im Metaphysikkommentar Alberts des Grossen*, BGPTM NS 7 (Münster: Aschendorff, 1972), p. 73, n. 33.

53. Albert *Metaphysica* 1.1.2 (16:4.20).

heavy use of Albert to claim that the position he has ascribed to Plato was maintained by various *platonici*.[54] A few chapters later, when presenting the "true position" on the origin of the soul, which is borrowed word for word from Albert's *De natura et origine animae*, Nifo himself turns to *Timaeus* 41CD. While Albert had used this passage just after ascribing to Plato the view that there are Ideal Forms in the divine mind, Nifo reads it to mean that Plato understood by the seed (*semen*) a light from which all things flow and which Plato took to be the soul situated in the middle of things, vivifying them all. Nifo adds that if Plato did think this then his view can be reduced to what Nifo is defending—and borrowing from Albert—namely, that God produced all things from God's own light.[55] However, it should not be thought that Nifo eliminates the notion of Divine Ideas or exemplars from his own presentation of Plato. When he takes up the question whether there can be more than one world, he suggests that Plato allowed this possibility insofar as he says in the *Timaeus* that the sensible world is made in accord with the exemplar (*exemplar*) of the intelligible world (*mundus intelligiblis*), that is, the Idea of the world (*idea mundi*). And just as there can be many houses of the same nature and yet only one Idea of a house, so there could be many worlds (*plures mundi*) from God's one sole Idea (*una dei sola idea*).[56]

When Nifo returns yet again to contrast Themistius and Theophrastus to the *platonici*, he draws both on Albert's *De natura et origine animae* and also on Ficino's commentary on his translation of the *Enneads* of Plotinus. What is both striking and of special importance here is that Nifo now uses a comparison very similar to that of the wooden arch and the impression it leaves in the resulting stone arch when it is removed. The comparison that he offers is of the impression left in wax when a ring that has been pressed against it is removed. This comparison, too, is drawn from one of Albert's discussions regarding Plato. Following Albert closely, Nifo points out

---

54. Nifo *De intellectu* 1.1.24, fol. 13va. See Albert *De homine* 5.3 (Borgnet 35:79b), 27.3 (152ab), 21.1 (176a), 61.2 (523b). For Isaac, see also Albert *De anima* 2.1.8, ed. C. Stroick, *Opera Omnia* 7 (Münster: Aschendorff, 1968), p. 76ab.

55. Nifo *De intellectu* 1.1.28, fols. 15vb–16ra. See Albert *Metaphysica* 1.5.12 (16:64), and 1.5.15 (16:89). Albert combines the notions of the Divine Ideas, "seed," and light in his own discussion of Plato.

56. Nifo *De intellectu* 1.3.5, fol. 30ra. Pico and Henry of Ghent are mentioned later in the chapter.

that Plato distinguished two kinds of form. The first kind is that of forms *ante rem*, that is, an exemplar and model (*exemplar et paradigma*) existing universally, immaterially, and simply in the intellect moving in nature, that is, God. These forms are called "first forms" (*formae primae*) because they have the power of forming things.[57] The second kind of form is that which the *platonici* call "images" (*imagines*) of the first sort of form. They are as it were like the "imprint" in wax from a ring (*sigillum ab annulo in cera*), since the forms in matter, as Plato says, come from separate intelligible forms (*separata intelligibilia formalia*) as if from a certain "imprint" (*ethermagrum*).[58] Oddly enough, Nifo now borrows this comparison from Albert in order to explicate the doctrine of the world-soul that he had ascribed to Themistius, despite the fact that he had earlier contrasted Themistius with the *platonici*—Themistius supposedly held that the animation was "created" by the world-soul, whereas the *platonici* held that it was an "impression" from the world-soul. Needless to say, the present-day reader may justifiably question whether the same sort of comparison can helpfully illuminate different conceptions of the vivifying process. It is possible, of course, that Nifo's dependence on this comparison reveals his own puzzlement as to what Themistius actually meant by the "creation" of an animation—if we concede to Nifo his interpretation of Themistius.

Nifo recounts that according to Plato the mind of the First Intellect is the form *ante rem* containing in itself all possible images (*imagines*); this form can be likened to the figure of a ring which contains all living things. The similarity between Plato and Themistius that Nifo goes on to delineate is that the many "souls" that Themistius sees flowing from the one world- soul and which different people variously call "lives" (*vitae*), "animations" (*animationes*), "reverberations" (*resultationes*), "images" (*imagines*), "traces" (*vestigia*), and "impressions" (*impressiones*) are comparable to the figures or shapes left in wax by a ring. Nifo discerns a resemblance between the view of the soul that he attributes to Themistius and Theophrastus and the view of such

---

57. See also Albert *Metaphysica* 1.4.9 (16:60).
58. Nifo *De intellectu* 1.2.7, fols. 18vb–19ra. See Albert *De natura et origine animae* 1.2 (12:4–5), and Ficino, *argumentum* to *Enneads* 1.1.7–8 (pp. 1551–1552). The comparison to a figure or image impressed in wax also appears in Albert's *Metaphysica* at 1.4.13 (16:66.73–75), and at 11.1.8 (16:471.3–4), and in his *De intellectu et intelligibili* 1.2.5 (Borgnet *Opera Omnia* 9 [Paris: Vivès, 1890], p. 496). The term *ekmageion* occurs in the *Timaeus* 50C.

platonici as Porphry, Iamblicus and Plotinus. None of them thinks that the one and single soul directly animates living things; their position is rather that its animating power (*virtus animativa*) extends a "life" into the living thing. In Nifo's judgment, Themistius and these *platonici* thus stand opposed to Aristotle's conception of the soul.[59]

By this point it should be abundantly clear that Pico's account of Plato's theory of the soul as narrated by Nifo was indebted to Albert the Great, especially to the passage in his *Metaphysics* containing the comparison from "John Saracene." Oddly enough, this connection between Pico and Albert has not been noted by scholars interested in Pico. What has been detected by Bruno Nardi and others is a supposed connection between Pico and both Simplicius and Siger of Brabant: it is Nifo himself who provides the most significant clues relating Pico to these two philosophers. A detailed examination of Nifo and Pico, on the one hand, and Simplicius and Siger, on the other, would take us beyond the bounds of the present study, but surely enough should be set forth to bring out the connection of Pico's views on Siger to his views on Plato that we have just now examined.

Nifo sets forth as the true interpretation of Simplicius's account of the unity and the multiplicity of rational souls that from the single intellect that is one for all humans, on the one hand, and the sensitive or cogitative souls, on the other hand, there results a certain whole (*quoddam totum*), namely, the "rational soul," which is individual with each human being and numbered according to the number of existing bodies. This rather distorted reading of Simplicius enables Nifo to claim that for that commentator the intellect is one and yet the

---

59. Nifo *De intellectu* 1.2.8, fol. 19rb. On the other hand, Nifo pits the *platonici* and Themistius against one another in 1.3.12–13, fol. 31rb–vb, on the grounds that the former, especially Plotinus, hold there to be a plurality of intellects that are immortal by reason of a plurality of rational souls or "first lives" which extend "second lives" into individual human bodies. Basing himself on texts from Averroës and from Ermolao's translation of Themistius, he takes Themistius to have been unable to explain how there could be rational souls which were both separate from matter and also numerically many. See especially Themistius *Libri paraphraseos . . . in libros De anima* 3.32–33, sig. ff2v–ff3r, and *In De anima paraphrasis* (Heinze 103.20–104.23). Themistius is identified with Averroës and Theophrastus as holding an erroneous position (*error purus*) on the unity of the intellect in *De intellectu* 1.3.30, fol. 37va. At 1.5.21 (52rb–va), Nifo also rejects Themistius's attempt to reconcile Plato and Aristotle.

multiplicity of rational souls, each of which gives existence to an individual human, can be saved. Adding that many believe this to be the mind of Plato himself, Nifo quotes from al-Ghazzali's statement in the *Destructio* that the opinion of Plato is that the one and eternal (*una et antiqua*) soul is divided according to the division of bodies but returns (*redit*) to its source (*radix*) when it is separated from the body. He then quotes Averroës's comment on this text from al-Ghazzali, namely, that the soul of Peter and the soul of William can in some way be said to be one and the same (*una et eadem*) on the part of the form but in another way be many by reason of their substrata (*ratione subiectorum*). He also quotes Averroës's later remark in the *Destructio* that all the wise commonly think that the newness (*innovatio*) of the soul is wholly relative, since it results from its ability to be joined to different bodies, as well as Averroës's remark in his long commentary on the *Metaphysics* that for Aristotle the form of humans as they are humans results from their union (*continuatio*) with the intellect. Nifo then notes that some take from these passages that Averroës, like Simplicius, holds the intellect to be one for all human beings though it is multiplied and numbered in human beings as their individual "rational soul" (*rationalis anima*).[60] Since these passages that Nifo has quoted from al-Ghazzali's *Destructio* and Averroës's own *Destructio* are the very ones that occasioned his discussion of Pico in his commentary on those works, it seems safe to infer that Pico himself presented the reconciliation of Simplicius and Averroës that Nifo has presented here. Nonetheless, it is instructive to note that in the very next chapter of the *De intellectu*, Nifo presents texts and arguments from Averroës to show the falsity of such an interpretation of the latter's psychology.[61]

Pursuing his ideal of exhaustive coverage of all possible positions, Nifo next sets out Siger of Brabant's attempt to mediate between Averroës and medieval Latins so as to assert the unity of the intellect with Averroës and yet assert that the intellect constitutes each human being in his or her individual existence as this individual human

---

60. Nifo *De intellectu* 1.3.16, fol. 32ra–b. See the text of al-Ghazzali in *Destructiones destructionum* for 1 doubt 8 (fol. 9ra), quoted above in note 11. See also Averroës *Destructiones destructionum* 1 doubt 8 (fol. 9va) and doubt 23 (23ra), as well as Averroës *In metaph.* 12 text 38, fol. 321rb.

61. Nifo *De intellectu* 1.3.17, fol. 32rb–va. Nifo would later reverse his position in the Pisan commentary on the *De anima*.

being.⁶² Nifo now reveals that Giovanni Pico (*Joannes Picus*), in order to show that he could sustain any position howsoever false, attempted in discussion with Nifo to justify this position as being in accord with Aristotle, Averroës, Themistius, and all the ancient commentators on Aristotle—presumably Simplicius would be one of the latter. Evidently Nifo and Pico had engaged in debate regarding Siger's thesis, for while marshaling some twenty-seven passages and arguments culled from Averroës himself against that thesis, Nifo notes Pico's attempts to blunt the force of two of these passages.⁶³

Having demonstrated that Siger's position does not square with the mind of Averroës himself, Nifo now sets out to show that the others whom Pico had claimed could be reconciled with Siger's view actually held opposed positions. Turning to Themistius, he cites passages from Ermolao's translation of the paraphrases on the *De anima* in order to show that for the ancient commentator the "whole rational soul" (*tota rationalis anima*) is composed only of the agent intellect and the potential intellect.⁶⁴ Furthermore, Averroës sees the single rational soul united to individual humans operationally through the cogitative power whereas Themistius sees the one rational soul united to humans by the animation that it extends to each individual human being.⁶⁵ Nifo also denies that Themistius and Simplicius agree on the nature of the soul and intellect.⁶⁶

Nonetheless, Nifo does go on to suggest that Averroës, Themistius, and all philosophers—Plato included—take as a self-evident proposition that there can be a multiplicity of individuals within the same species only through the division of matter. Basing himself on remarks

---

62. Nifo *De intellectu* 1.3.18, fols. 32vb–33ra. Nifo relates Siger's position as found in the latter's now lost *De intellectu*, which was written in reply to Aquinas's *De unitate intellectus contra Averroistas*. For discussion, see Nardi, *Sigieri di Brabante*, pp. 11–38; Mahoney, "Saint Thomas and Siger of Brabant Revisited," pp. 537–540; Mahoney, "Sense, Intellect, and Imagination in Albert, Thomas, and Siger," pp. 613–616; Fernand Van Steenberghen, *Maître Siger de Brabant*, PM 21 (Louvain: Publications universitaires, 1977), pp. 360–363. See note 41, above.

63. Nifo *De intellectu* 1.3.19, fol. 33ra–vb. Garin reproduces key excerpts from this chapter in his edition of Pico, *De hominis dignitate*, pp. 85–86. See the first and seventeenth arguments of Nifo for Pico's counterinterpretations.

64. Nifo *De intellectu* 1.3.20, fol. 34ra.

65. Nifo *De intellectu* 1.3.23, fol. 34va. See also 1.3.20, fols. 33vb–34ra.

66. Nifo *De intellectu* 1.3.22, fol. 34rb.

of Aristotle and Thomas Aquinas, Nifo argues that Plato did not hold a multiplicity of Ideas that were similar in species, since the very cause of their being individuals, namely, matter, was lacking.[67] Nifo thus appears to see a parallel between Averroës's postulating only one intellect for all human beings (since it is separated from matter and therefore from whatever would cause it to be multiple) and Plato's postulating an Idea of the human being that is by essence (*per essentiam*) numerically one (because he holds that by its very essence that Idea is separated from individuals and exists without matter). Nifo again appeals to Siger's *De intellectu* for an account of how the intellect can be one for Averroës and yet be the form of the many human beings who actually exist. Noteworthy for the development of the "Albert connection" is that Nifo here presents Siger as a serious man who belonged to the Averroist sect during the time of the "Expositor," that is, Thomas Aquinas, and who was a disciple of Albert the Great (*Suggerius vir gravis, sectae Averroisticae fautor aetate expositoris, discipulus Alberti*).[68]

What surely merits attention is that in this same chapter Nifo has seen a parallel between Averroës's one intellect for all human beings and Plato's single Idea for all human beings, based on their acceptance of matter as the principle of individuation, and has again recounted from Siger's *De intellectu* a way to reconcile Averroës's doctrine of the unity of the intellect with the plurality of humans—a solution that Nifo had told us Pico himself had adopted. But even more significant

---

67. Nifo *De intellectu* 1.3.24, fol. 34vb. See Themistius *Libri paraphraseos . . . in libros De anima* 3.32, sig. ff2v; compare his *In De anima paraphrasis* (Heinze 103.26–30). The relevant passage in Aristotle is *Metaphysics* 1.6.987b14–18. Nifo quotes from Thomas Aquinas *Super Metaphysicam* 1.10, ed. M. R. Cathala and R. M. Spiazzi (Turin: Marietti, 1971), no. 157. He follows Thomas's use of the concept of matter as the principle of individuation in order to analyze Plato's theory of ideas. See Thomas *Super Metaphysicam* 1.10, nos. 154–155, but also 1.14, no. 209. On the problem of individuation in medieval philosophy, see Johannes Assenmacher, *Die Geschichte der Individuationsprinzips in der Scholastik* (Leipzig: F. Meiner, 1926); Jorge J. E. Gracia, *Introduction to the Problem of Individuation in the Early Middle Ages* (Munich: Philosophia, 1984); and Joseph Owens, "Thomas Aquinas: Dimensive Quantity as Individuating Principle," *Mediaeval Studies* 50 (1988): 279–310.

68. Nifo *De intellectu* 1.3.26, fol. 35va–b. On the problem of the connection between Siger and Albert, see Albert Zimmermann, "Albertus Magnus und der lateinische Averroismus," in *Albertus Magnus: Doctor Universalis 1280/1980*, ed. G. Meyer and A. Zimmermann (Mainz: Matthias Grünewald, 1980), pp. 465–493.

is that when Nifo attempts to explain how in fact the intellect is one for Averroës and yet can be called many souls, he refers the reader to the very passages in the *Destructio* that were the occasion for his narrating Pico's account of how Plato could maintain there is only one soul.[69] Plato, Averroës, Siger, and the comparison that Pico borrowed from Albert thus continued to be interconnected for Nifo at the time that he finished and published his *De intellectu*. He clearly took very seriously Pico's explication of Plato and also Siger's interpretation of Averroës in order to reconcile various philosophers. Nonetheless, Nifo rejected both that explication of Plato and also Siger's interpretation of Averroës.

Obviously Pico's own understanding of Siger merits more detailed attention for the light that it will throw both on Pico's own thought and on Nifo's own interpretation of Siger and Averroës. Much remains to be done to establish in a more definitive manner the impact of medieval philosophy on what we call "Renaissance Aristotelianism."[70]

Duke University

---

69. Nifo *De intellectu* 1.3.26, fol. 35va–b. See Nifo *Expositio Destructio destructionum* 1 doubt 8, fol. 9rb, and 1 doubt 23, fol. 23rb. Nifo also refers here back to his earlier discussion of Averroës in *De intellectu* 1.1.14, fol. 21va–b, where he also cites his *Expositio Destructio destructionum* 1 doubts 23–24.

70. After the completion of this study, the recent monograph by Fernand Roulier, *Jean Pic de la Mirandole (1463–1494), humaniste, philosophe, et théologien*, Bibliothèque Franco Simone 17 (Geneva: Slatkine, 1989), came to my attention. Roulier does allude to Pico's stay at Padua and his connection to Vernia and Nifo. He also refers to Pico's conversation with Nifo regarding Plato (see especially p. 369, n. 69; pp. 407 and 409). Unfortunately, he seems unaware of changes in Vernia's and Nifo's positions and ignores most recent scholarship in English dealing with Padua, Vernia, and Nifo. I should like to note that different versions of this paper were read to the University Seminar on the Renaissance, Columbia University, on 6 March 1984, and to a meeting of the Society for Medieval and Renaissance Philosophy at San Diego on 28 March 1992. It is my intention to return to Nifo on Pico, Siger, and Simplicius on another occasion. I must express once again my gratitude to the Duke University Research Council for grants for travel and microfilming that made this study possible.

64764

DATE DUE			
DE 1 4 '99			

B
56
.M4
v.2

64764

Medieval philosophy and
theology.

HIEBERT LIBRARY
Fresno Pacific College - M.B. Seminary
Fresno, CA 93702

DEMCO